Agile Project Management with Azure DevOps

Concepts, Templates, and Metrics

Joachim Rossberg

Apress®

Agile Project Management with Azure DevOps: Concepts, Templates, and Metrics

Joachim Rossberg
Kungsbacka, Sweden

ISBN-13 (pbk): 978-1-4842-4482-1   ISBN-13 (electronic): 978-1-4842-4483-8
https://doi.org/10.1007/978-1-4842-4483-8

Managing Director, Apress Media LLC: Welmoed Spahr
Acquisitions Editor: Joan Murray
Development Editor: Laura Berendson
Coordinating Editor: Jill Balzano

Cover image designed by Freepik (www.freepik.com)

Distributed to the book trade worldwide by Springer Science+Business Media New York, 233 Spring Street, 6th Floor, New York, NY 10013. Phone 1-800-SPRINGER, fax (201) 348-4505, e-mail orders-ny@springer-sbm.com, or visit www.springeronline.com. Apress Media, LLC is a California LLC and the sole member (owner) is Springer Science + Business Media Finance Inc (SSBM Finance Inc). SSBM Finance Inc is a **Delaware** corporation.

For information on translations, please e-mail rights@apress.com, or visit http://www.apress.com/rights-permissions.

Apress titles may be purchased in bulk for academic, corporate, or promotional use. eBook versions and licenses are also available for most titles. For more information, reference our Print and eBook Bulk Sales web page at http://www.apress.com/bulk-sales.

Any source code or other supplementary material referenced by the author in this book is available to readers on GitHub via the book's product page, located at www.apress.com/9781484244821. For more detailed information, please visit http://www.apress.com/source-code.

Printed on acid-free paper

To my kids, Amelie and Eddie.
Love you forever.

Table of Contents

About the Author

Joachim Rossberg is an expert in Agile project management, SAFe, DevOps processes, and Azure DevOps/TFS, working for Solidify in Sweden. An IT consultant for more than two decades, primarily in the role of product owner, Agile coach and trainer, and project manager, he has extensive experience as a system developer and designer and holds certifications in PSM I & II, SAFe SPC, PSPO I, PSD I, CSPO, and PAL I. He is the author of seven books.

About the Technical Reviewer

Gregor Suttie lives near Glasgow, Scotland, and has been in the IT industry for 20-plus years. He started with Visual Basic 6 and Com +, along with Visual Interdev and the original Active Server Pages. After that period in his career, he moved on to .Net and has been developing with it since its original release. More recently, he has been concentrating on learning Azure, which he had never used until the end of 2018.

During the last quarter of 2018, Gregor sat for eight Azure beta exams and received most of his results by January 2019. He is a certified Azure developer and is one transition exam away from being a certified Azure architect. He is still waiting for the results of his Azure DevOps beta exam.

Gregor has a passion for learning, and you can access his blog at `http://gregorsuttie.com` and on twitter at @gregor_suttie. He is enthusiastic about Azure and DevOps, and he has been using them daily at work and has learning more about Azure DevOps since its release. Every week he discovers something new. When the opportunity arose to be a technical reviewer for a book about Azure DevOps, he jumped at the chance!

The book covers a few different areas, but its guts cover Azure Boards and how to go about using this feature successfully. Gregor hopes you enjoy reading the book as much as he did reviewing it.

Introduction

Throughout the years, many things have happened with Team Foundation Server (TFS) and the Visual Studio Team System. The product has gone through several names and is now called Azure DevOps and Azure DevOps Server. It's kind of hard to keep track of them all.

This book is written with Agile leaders in mind, such as product owners, Scrum masters, Agile project/product managers, and the like. Members of Agile teams can benefit a lot as well.

In this book, I write about how we can use the features and functionality of Azure DevOps, and customize our work process. I cover Kanban board customizations in both Azure DevOps and Azure DevOps Server/TFS.

In Chapter 1, we start with a brief introduction to a concept called *application life cycle management*, which, to this day, I still think describes the areas of DevOps well. After that, we look at DevOps (Chapter 2) and then at Agile concepts (Chapter 3) such as Scrum, Kanban, SAFe, and more. In Chapters 4 and 5, I talk about the underlying logic of Azure DevOps. You will see what work items are and how we can customize them to fit our way of working. Chapter 6 covers Agile practices in Azure DevOps. We examine things like test-driven development, the Scaled Agile Framework, (SAFe) framework, and how we can use Azure DevOps to implement SAFe and more. Before we look at a fictional project implementation in Chapter 8, Chapter 7 takes you through some Agile metrics that are good to monitor.

CHAPTER 1

Introduction to Application Life Cycle Management

What do you think about when you hear the term *application life cycle management* (ALM)? During a seminar tour in 2005 in Sweden, presenting on Microsoft's Visual Studio Team System, we asked people what ALM was and whether they cared about it. To our surprise, many people equated ALM with Operations and Maintenance. This is still often the case when we visit companies, although today more people are aware of the term.

Was that your answer as well? Does ALM include more than just Operations? Yes, it does. ALM is the thread that ties together the development life cycle. It involves all the steps necessary to coordinate development life cycle activities. Operations are just one part of the ALM process. Other elements range from requirements gathering to more technical things such as the build-and-deploy process.

These days we do not talk as much about ALM as a concept as we used to. These days we talk more about DevOps. But, let's start by talking some ALM in this chapter to lay a foundation for DevOps and Azure DevOps, as Microsoft calls it.

© Joachim Rossberg 2019
J. Rossberg, *Agile Project Management with Azure DevOps*,
https://doi.org/10.1007/978-1-4842-4483-8_1

Microsoft renamed Visual Studio Team Services (VSTS) to Azure DevOps at the end of 2018. As of this writing, Microsoft's Team Foundation Server (TFS) is in version 2018. In the near future, the TFS name will be changed to Azure DevOps Server.

Aspects of the ALM Process

All software development includes various steps performed by people playing specific roles. There are many different roles, or disciplines, in the ALM process, and some of them are defined in this section. (The process could include more roles, but we focus on the primary ones.)

Look at Figure 1-1, which illustrates ALM and some of its aspects. You can see the flow from the birth of an application, when the business need first arises, to when the business need no longer exists and the application dies. Once the thought of a new application (or system) is born, many organizations do some portfolio rationalization. This means you discuss whether an existing system can handle the need or whether a new system has to be developed. If a new system must be built, you enter the *software development life cycle* (SDLC) and develop the system, test it, and deploy it into operation. This is the point at which you do a handover so that Operations personnel can maintain and refine the system. Once in production, the system (hopefully) delivers the intended business value until retirement. While in operation, the system usually is updated or undergoes bug fixes; at such times, *change requests* (CRs) are written. For each CR, you go through the same process again.

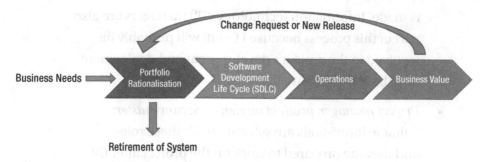

Figure 1-1. *The application life cycle management process*

It's essential to understand that all business software development is a team effort. The company personnel who play specific roles collaborate on projects to deliver business value to the organization. If you don't have this collaboration, the value of the system will most likely be considerably less than it could be. One step up from the project level, at the program level, it's also important to have collaboration between all roles involved in the ALM process so that you perform this process in the most optimal way.

The roles in the ALM process include, but aren't limited to, the following:

- *Stakeholders*: Stakeholders are usually the people who either pay for the project or have decision-making rights about what to build. We like to also include end users in this group, so not only management has a stake in a project.

- *Business manager*: Somebody has to decide that a development activity is going to start. After initial analysis of the business needs, a business manager decides to initiate a project to develop an application or system that delivers the expected business value. A business manager, for instance, must be involved in the approval process for a new suggested project, including portfolio rationalization, before a decision to go ahead

3

is made. Information technology (IT) managers are also part of this process because IT staff will probably be involved in the project's development and deployment into the infrastructure.

- *Project manager, product owner, or Scrum master*: Suitable individuals are selected to fill these roles, and they are prepared to work on the project after the decision to go ahead is made. Ideally, these people continue leading the project all the way through, so that you have continuity in project management.

- *Project management office (PMO) decision makers*: These individuals are also involved in planning because a new project may change or expand the company's portfolio.

- *Business analyst*: After requirements collection starts, the business analyst has much to do. Usually, initial requirements are gathered when the business need arises, but the real work often begins after portfolio rationalization. A business analyst is responsible for analyzing the business needs and requirements of the stakeholders to help identify business problems and propose solutions. Within the system's development life cycle, the business analyst typically performs a collaborative function between the business side of an enterprise and the providers of services to the enterprise.

- *Architect*: The architect draws an initial picture of the solution. In brief the architect draws the blueprint of the system, and the system designers or engineers use this blueprint. The blueprint includes the level of freedom necessary in the system: scalability, hardware replacement, new user interfaces, and so on. The architect must consider all these issues.

- *User experience (UX) design team*: UX design should be a core deliverable, not something you leave to the developers to handle. Unfortunately, this design often overlooked; it should be given more consideration. It's important to have close collaboration between the UX team (which could be just one person) and the development team. The best solution is to have a UX expert on the development team throughout the project, but sometimes that isn't possible. The UX design is important in making sure users can perceive the value of the system. You can write the best business logic in the world, but if the UX is designed poorly, users probably won't think the system is any good.

- *Database administrators (DBAs)*: Almost every business system or application uses a database in some way. DBAs can make your databases run like lightning, with good uptime, so it's essential to use their expertise in any project involving a database. Be nice to them; they can give you lots of tips about how to make a smarter system. Alas, for DBAs, developers handle this work more and more frequently. This means developers are expected to have vertical knowledge and not just focus on coding.

- *Developers*: "Developers, developers, developers!" as Microsoft Chief Executive Officer (CEO) Steve Ballmer shouted in a famous video. And who can blame him? These are the people who work their magic to realize the system by using the architecture blueprint drawn from the requirements. Moreover, developers modify or extend the code when CRs come in.

- *Testers*: I'd rather not see testing as a separate activity. Don't get me wrong: It's a role, but testing is something you should consider from the first time you write down a requirement and should continue doing during the whole process. Testers and test managers help to secure quality, but modern development practices include testing by developers as well. For instance, in test-driven development (TDD), developers write tests that can be automated and run at build time or as part of checking in to version control.

- *Operations and maintenance staff*: When an application or system is finished, it's handed over to operations. The Operations staff takes care of it until it retires, often with the help of the original developers, who come in to do bug fixes and new upgrades. Don't forget to involve these people early in the process, at the point when the initial architecture is considered, and keep them involved with the project until everything is done. They can provide great input about what can and can't be done within the company infrastructure. So, Operations is just one part—although an important one—of ALM. In Chapter 3, this book talks about DevOps, which is a practice that ties developers and Operations personnel more closely.

All project efforts are done collaboratively. No role can act separately from the others if you're to succeed with any project. It's essential for everybody involved to have a collaborative mind-set and to have the business value as their primary focus at every phase of the project.

If you're part of an Agile development process, such as a Scrum project, you might have only three roles: product owner, Scrum master, and team members. This doesn't mean the roles just described don't apply though! They're all essential in most projects; it's just that, in an Agile project, you may not be labeled a developer or an architect. Rather, you're a team member, and you and your comembers share responsibility for the work you're doing. We go deeper into the Agile world later in Chapter 4.

Four Ways of Looking at ALM

ALM is the glue that ties together the roles just discussed and the activities they perform. Let's consider four ways of looking at ALM (Figure 1-2). We've chosen these four because we've seen this separation in many of the organizations with which we've worked or individuals to whom we've spoken:

1. *SDLC view*: The SDLC view is perhaps the most common way of looking at ALM, because development has "owned" management of the application life cycle for a long time. This could be an effect of the gap between the business side and the IT side in most organizations, and IT has taken the lead.

2. *Service management or operations view*: Operations has also been (in our experience) unfortunately separated from IT development. This has resulted in Operations having its own view of ALM and the problems that can occur in this area.

7

3. *Application portfolio management (APM) view*: Again, perhaps because of the gap between business and IT, we've seen many organizations with a portfolio ALM strategy in which IT development is only one small part. From a business viewpoint, the focus has been on how to handle the portfolio, not on the entire ALM process.

4. *Unified view*: Fortunately, some organizations focus on the entire ALM process by including all three of the preceding views. This is the only way to take control of, and optimize, ALM. For a chief information officer (CIO), it's essential to have this view all the time; otherwise, things can get out of hand easily.

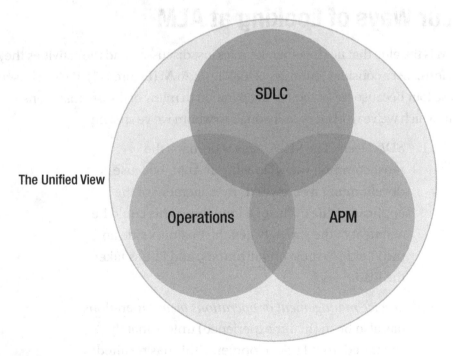

Figure 1-2. *The four ways of looking at ALM*

Let's look at these four views in more detail, starting with the SDLC view.

The SDLC View

Let's consider ALM from an SDLC perspective first. In Figure 1-3, you can
see the different phases of a typical development project and the roles
most frequently involved. Keep in mind that this is a simplified view for the
sake of this discussion. We've also tried to fit in the different roles from the
ALM process presented earlier.

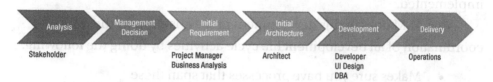

Figure 1-3. *A simplified view of a typical development project*

First, somebody comes up with an idea based on an analysis of
business needs: "Hey, wouldn't it be great if we had a system that could
help us do [whatever the idea is]?" It can also be the other way around: The
idea comes first, and the business value is evaluated based on the idea.

An analysis or feasibility study is performed, costs are estimated, and
(hopefully) a decision is made by IT and business management to start
an IT project. A project manager (PM) is selected to be responsible for
the project and begins gathering requirements with the help of business
analysts, PMO decision makers, and users or others affected. The PM also
starts planning the project in as much detail as possible at this moment.

When that is done, the architect begins looking at how to realize
the new system, and the initial design is chosen. The initial design is
evaluated and updated based on what happens during the project and
how requirements change throughout the project. Development beings,
including work performed by developers, user interface (UI) designers, and
DBAs (and anyone else not mentioned here but important for the project).

Testing is, at least for us, something done all along the way—from requirements specification to delivered code—so it doesn't get a separate box in Figure 1-3. We include acceptance testing by end users or stakeholders in the Development box. After the system has gone through acceptance testing, it's delivered to Operations for use in the organization. Of course, the process doesn't end there. This cycle is generally repeated over and over as new versions are rolled out and bug fixes are implemented.

What ALM does in this development process is support the coordination of all development life cycle activities by doing the following:

- Makes sure you have processes that span these activities.

- Manages the relationships between development project artifacts used or produced by these activities (in other words, provides traceability). These artifacts include UI mockups done during requirements gathering, source code, executable code, build scripts, test plans, and so on.

- Reports on progress of the development effort as a whole so you have transparency for everyone regarding project advancement.

As you can see, ALM doesn't support a specific activity. Its purpose is to keep all activities in sync. It does this so you can focus on delivering systems that meet the needs and requirements of the business. By having an ALM process that helps you synchronize your development activities, you can determine more easily whether an activity is underperforming and thus take corrective actions.

The Service Management or Operations View

From a Service Management or Operations view, you can look at ALM as a process that focuses on the activities that are involved with the development, operation, support, and optimization of an application so that it meets the service level that has been defined for it.

When you see ALM from this perspective, it focuses on the life of an application or system in a production environment. If, in the SDLC view, the development life cycle starts with the decision to go ahead with a project, here it starts with deployment into the production environment. Once deployed, the application is controlled by the Operations crew. Bug fixes and CRs are handled by them, and they also pat it on its back to make it feel good and run smoothly.

This is a healthy way of looking at ALM in our opinion: Development and Operations are two pieces of ALM, cooperating to manage the entire ALM process. You should consider both pieces from the beginning when planning a development project; you can't have one without the other.

The APM View

In the APM view of ALM, you see the application as a product managed as part of a portfolio of products. APM is a subset of project portfolio management (PPM).[1] Figure 1-4 illustrates this process.

This view comes from the Project Management Institute (PMI). Managing resources and the projects on which they work is very important for any organization. In Figure 1-4, you can see that the product life cycle starts with a business plan—the product is an application or system that

---

[1]The Project Management Institute (PMI) is the world's leading not-for-profit professional membership association for the project, program, and portfolio management profession. Read more at www.pmi.org.

is one part of the business plan. An idea for an application is turned into a project and is carried out through the project phases until it's turned over to Operations as a finished product.

When business requirements change or a new release (an upgrade, in Figure 1-4) is required for some other reason, the project life cycle starts again, and a new release is handed over to Operations. After a while (maybe years), the system or application is discarded (this is called *divestment*, which is the opposite of investment). This view doesn't speak specifically about the operations part or the development part of the process but should instead be seen in the light of APM.

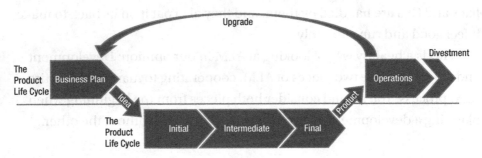

Figure 1-4. The APM view of ALM

The Unified View

Finally, there is a unified view of ALM. In this case, an effort is made to align the previous views with the business. Here you do as the CIO would do: You focus on business needs, not on separate views. You do this to improve the capacity and agility of a project from beginning to end. Figure 1-5 shows an overview of the unified ALM view of a business.

You probably recognize this figure from Figure 1-1. We want to stress that with the unified view, you need to consider all aspects—from the birth to the death of an application or a system—hence the curved arrow that indicates continuous examination of an application or system and how it benefits the business

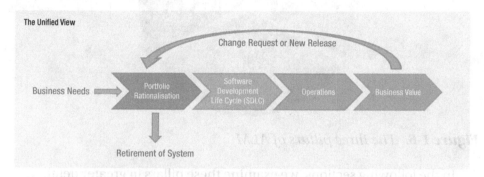

Figure 1-5. *The unified view takes into consideration all three previously mentioned views*

Three Pillars of Traditional ALM

Let's now look at some important pillars of ALM that are independent of the view you might have (Figure 1-6). These pillars were first introduced by Forrester Research.[2]

---

[2]Dave West, "The Time Is Right For ALM 2.0+," Forrester Research, www.forrester.com/The+Time+Is+Right+For+ALM+20/fulltext/-/E-RES56832?objectid=RES56832, October 19, 2010.

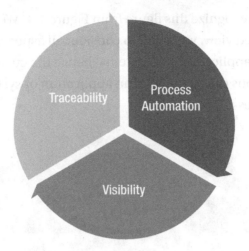

Figure 1-6. *The three pillars of ALM*

In the following sections, we examine these pillars in greater detail, starting with traceability.

Traceability

Some customers we've seen have stopped doing upgrades on systems running in production because their companies had poor or no traceability in their systems. For these customers, it was far too expensive to do upgrades because of the unexpected effects even a small change could have. The companies had no way of knowing which original requirements were implemented where in the applications. The effect was that a small change in one part of the code might affect another part, which would come as a surprise because poor traceability meant they had no way of seeing the code connection in advance. One customer claimed (as we've heard in discussions with many other customers) that traceability can be a major cost driver in any enterprise if not done correctly.

There must be a way to trace requirements all the way to delivered code—through architect models, design models, build scripts, unit tests, test cases, and so on—not only to make it easier to go back into the system when implementing bug fixes, but also to demonstrate that the system has delivered the things the business wants.

You also need traceability to achieve internal as well as external compliance with rules and regulations. If you develop applications for the medical industry, for example, you must comply with Food and Drug Administration (FDA) regulations. You also need traceability when CRs come in so you know where you updated the system and in which version you performed the update.

Automation of High-Level Processes

The next pillar of ALM is automation of high-level processes. All organizations have processes. For example, approval processes control handoffs between the analysis and design or build steps, or between deployment and testing. Much of this is done manually in many projects, and ALM stresses the importance of automating these tasks for a more effective and less time-consuming process. Having an automated process also decreases the error rate compared to handling the process manually.

Visibility into the Progress of Development Efforts

The third and last pillar of ALM is providing visibility into the progress of development efforts. Many managers and stakeholders have limited visibility into the progress of development projects. The visibility they have often comes from steering group meetings, during which the PM reviews the current situation. Some would argue that this limitation is good; but, if you want an effective process, you must ensure visibility.

Other interest groups, such as project members, also have limited visibility of the entire project despite being part of the project. This is often a result of the fact that reporting is difficult and can involve a lot of manual work. Daily status reports take too much time and effort to produce, especially when you have information in many repositories.

15

A Brief History of ALM Tools and Concepts

You can resolve the three pillars of ALM manually if you want to, without using tools or automation. (ALM isn't a new process description, even though Microsoft, IBM, Hewlett-Packard (HP), Atlassian, and the other big software houses are pushing ALM to drive sales of their respective ALM solutions.) You can, for instance, continue to use Excel spreadsheets or, like one of our most dedicated Agile colleagues, use sticky notes and a pad of paper to track requirements through use cases/scenarios, test cases, code, build, and so on, to delivered code. It works, but this process takes a lot of time and requires much manual effort. With constant pressure to keep costs down, you need to make the tracking of requirements more effective.

Of course, project members can simplify the process by keeping reporting to the bare minimum. With a good tool or set of tools, you can cut time (and thus costs) and effort, and still get the required traceability you want in your projects. The same goes for reporting and other activities. Tools can, in our opinion, help you be more effective and also help you automate much of the ALM process into the tools.

Having the process built directly into your tools helps prevent the people involved from missing important steps by simplifying things. For instance, the Agile friend we mentioned could definitely gain much from this, and he is looking into Microsoft's TFS to determine how that set of tools can help him and his teams be more productive. Process automation and the use of tools to support and simplify daily jobs are great, because they can keep you from making unnecessary mistakes.

Serena Software Inc. is one supplier of ALM tools, and the company has interesting insight into ALM and related concepts. According to Serena Software, there are eight ALM concepts[3]:

---

[3]Kelly A. Shaw, "Application Lifecycle Management for the Enterprise," Serena Software Inc., www.serena.com/docs/repository/company/serena_alm_2.0_for_t.pdf, April 2007.

1. *Modeling*: Software modeling

2. *Issue management*: Keeping track of incoming issues during both development and operations activities

3. *Design*: Designing the system or application

4. *Construction*: Developing the system or application

5. *Production monitoring*: The work of the operations staff

6. *Build*: Building the executable code

7. *Test*: Testing the software

8. *Release management*: Planning application releases

To synchronize these concepts, according to Serena Software, you need tools that span them and that help you automate and simplify the following activities. If you look closely, you can see that these activities compare to ALM 2.0+, which we examine shortly:

- Reporting

- Traceability

- Policies

- Procedures

- Processes

- Collaboration

Imagine the Herculean task of keeping all these things in order manually. It's impossible, if you want to get things right and keep an eye on the project's status. Projects today seem to be going better because the number of failed projects is decreasing. Much of this progress is, according to Michael Azoff at the Butler Group,[4] the result of "major changes in software development: open source software projects; the Agile development movement; and advances in tooling, notably Application Lifecycle Management (ALM) tools." Some of these results have also been confirmed by later research, such as that by Scott W. Ambler at Ambysoft.[5] Now you understand why finding tools and development processes to help you with ALM is important.

There is increasing awareness of the ALM process among enterprises, and we see this among our customers. ALM is much more important now than it was only five years ago.

ALM 1.0

Forrester Research has introduced some very useful concepts for ALM,[6] including different versions of ALM and ALM tools. This section looks at how Forrester defined ALM 1.0, then continues to the latest version: ALM 2.0+.

As software has become more and more complex, role specialization has increased in IT organizations. This has led to functional silos in different areas (roles), such as project management, business analysis, architecture, development, database administration, testing, and so on. As you may recall from the beginning of this chapter, you can see this in the ALM circle. Having these silos in a company isn't a problem, but having them without any positive interaction between them is an issue.

---

[4]Michael Azoff, "Application Lifecycle Management Making a Difference," February 2007, Enterprise Networks and Services, OpinionWire.

[5]Scott W. Ambler, "2011 IT Project Success Rates Survey Results," www.ambysoft.com/surveys/success2011.html.

[6]West, "The Time Is Right For ALM 2.0+."

There is always a problem when you build impenetrable walls around you. ALM vendors have driven this wall construction, because most of their tools have, historically, been developed for particular silos. For example, if you look at build-management tools, they have supported the build silo (naturally), but have little or no interaction with test and validation tools (which is strange because the first thing that usually happens in a test cycle is the build). This occurs despite the fact that interaction among roles can generate obvious synergies with great potential. You need to synchronize the ALM process to make the role-centric processes part of the overall process. This might sound obvious, but it hasn't happened until recently.

Instead of having complete integration among the roles or disciplines mentioned at the start of this chapter, and the tools they use, there has been point-to-point integration. For example, a development tool is integrated slightly with a testing tool (or, probably, the other way around). Each tool uses its own data repository, so traceability and reporting are hard to handle in such an environment (Figure 1-7).

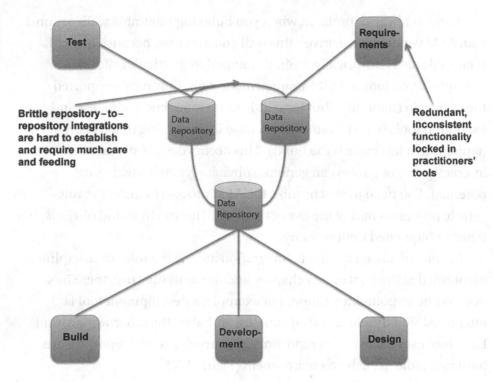

Figure 1-7. ALM 1.0

This point-to-point integration makes the ALM process fragile and expensive. However, this isn't just a characteristic of ALM 1.0; it's true for all integrations. Imagine that one tool is updated or replaced. The integration may break, and then new solutions have to be found to get it working again. This scenario can be a reality if, for example, old functions in the updated or replaced tool are obsolete and the new tool doesn't support backward compatibility. What would happen if Microsoft Word (to take an easy example) suddenly stopped supporting older Word files? There would be more or less a riot among users until the situation was fixed. This can be hard to solve even with integration between two tools. What if you have a more complex situation, including several tools? We've seen projects that use six or seven tools during development, which creates a fragile solution when new versions are released.

Tools have also been centered on one discipline. In real life, a project member working as a developer, for instance, often also acts as an architect or a tester. Because the people in each of these disciplines have their own tool (or set of tools), the project member must use several tools and switch among them. It could also be that the task system is separated from the rest of the tools, so to start working on a task, a developer must first retrieve the task from the task system—perhaps they must print it out or copy and paste it—then open the requirements system to check the requirement, then look at the architecture in that system, and finally open the development tool to begin working. Hopefully, the testing tools are integrated into the development tool; otherwise, yet another tool must be used. All this switching costs valuable time that could be better put into solving the task.

Having multiple tools for each project member is obviously costly as well, because everyone needs licenses for the tools they use. Even with open-source tools that may be free of charge, you have maintenance costs, adaptions of the tools, developer costs, and so on. Maintenance can be very expensive, so you shouldn't forget this even when the tools are free. Such a scenario can be very costly and very complex. It's probably also fragile.

As an example, take two coworkers at a large medical company in Gothenburg. They use a mix of tools in their everyday work. We asked them to estimate how much time they needed to switch among tools and transfer information from one tool to another. They estimated they spend half an hour to an hour each day syncing their work. Usually, they're on the lower end of that scale, but in the long run, all the switching takes a lot of time and money. Our friends also experience problems whenever they need to upgrade any of the systems they use.

One other problem with traditional ALM tools that's worth mentioning is that vendors often add features—for example, adapting a test tool to support issue and defect management. In the issue management system, some features may have been added to support testing. Because neither tool has enough features to support both disciplines, users are confused and don't know which tool to use. In the end, most purchase both, just to be safe, and end up with the integration issues described earlier.

ALM 2.0

Let's look at what the emerging tools and practices (including processes and methodologies) in ALM 2.0 try to do for you. ALM is a platform for the coordination and management of development activities, not a collection of life cycle tools with locked-in and limited ALM features. Figure 1-8 and Table 1-1 summarize these efforts.

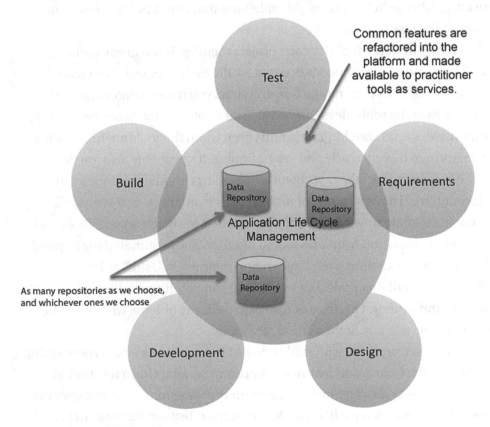

Figure 1-8. *ALM 2.0*

Table 1-1. *Characteristics of ALM 2.0*

Characteristic	Benefit
Practitioner tools assembled from plug-ins	Customers pay only for the features they need.
	Practitioners find the features they need more quickly.
Common services available across practitioner tools	Easier for vendors to deploy enhancements to shared features.
	Ensures correspondence of activities across practitioner tools.
Repository neutral	No need to migrate old assets.
	Better support for cross-platform development.
Use of open integration standards	Easier for customers and partners to build deeper integrations with third-party tools.
Microprocesses and macroprocesses governed by an externalized workflow	Processes are "versionable" assets.
	Processes can share common components.

One of the first things you can see is a focus on plug-ins. This means, from one tool, you can add the features you need to perform the tasks you want, without using several tools! If you've used Visual Studio, you've seen that it's straightforward to add new plug-ins to the development environment. Support for the Windows Communication Foundation (WCF) and Windows Presentation Services, for example, was available as plug-ins long before support for them was added as part of Visual Studio 2008.

Having the plug-in option and making it easy for third-party vendors to write plug-ins for the tool greatly eases the integration problems discussed earlier. You can almost compare this to a smorgasbord, where you choose the things you want. So far, this has mostly been adopted by development tool vendors such as IBM and Microsoft, but more plug-ins are coming. IBM has its Rational suite of products, and Microsoft has TFS.

Another thing that eases development efforts is that vendors in ALM 2.0 focus more on identifying features common to multiple tools and integrating them into the ALM platform, including the following:

- Collaboration

- Workflow

- Security

- Reporting and analysis

Another goal of ALM 2.0 is that the tools should be repository neutral. There shouldn't be a single repository, but many, so you aren't required to use the storage solution the vendor proposes. IBM, for example, has declared that its forthcoming ALM solution will integrate with a wide variety of repositories, such as Concurrent Versions System (CVS) and Subversion, just to mention two. This approach removes the obstacle of gathering and synchronizing data, giving you easier access to progress reports and so on. Microsoft uses an extensive set of web services and plug-ins to solve the same issue. It has one storage center (SQL Server); but, by exposing functionality through the use of web services, Microsoft has made it fairly easy to connect to other tools as well.

An open and extensible ALM solution lets companies integrate their own choice of repository into the ALM tool. Both Microsoft and IBM have solutions—data warehouse adapters—that enable existing repositories to be tied into the ALM system. A large organization that has invested in tools and repositories probably doesn't want to change everything for a new ALM system; hence, it's essential to have this option. Any way you choose to solve the problem will work, giving you the possibility of having a well-connected and synchronized ALM platform.

Furthermore, ALM 2.0 focuses on being built on an open integration standard. As you know, Microsoft exposes TFS functionality through web services. This isn't documented publicly and isn't supported by Microsoft, however, so you need to do some research and go through some trial and error to get it working. This way, you can support new tools as long as they also use an open standard, and third-party vendors have the option of writing cool and productive tools.

Process support built in to the ALM platform is another important feature. By this, we mean having automated support for the ALM process built right into the tools. You can, for instance, have the development process (RUP, Scrum, XP, and so on) automated in the tool, reminding you of each step in the process so you don't miss creating and maintaining any deliverables or checkpoints.

In the case of TFS, this support includes having the document structure, including templates for all documents, available on the project web site as soon as a new TFS project is created. You can also imagine a tool with built-in capabilities that help you with requirements gathering and specification—for instance, letting you add requirements and specs to the tool and have them transformed into tasks that are assigned to the correct role without you having to do this manually.

An organization isn't likely to scrap a way of working just because the new ALM tool says it can't import that specific process. A lot of money has often been invested in developing a process, and an organization won't want to spend the same amount again learning a new one. With ALM 2.0, it's possible to store the ALM process in a readable format such as XML.

The benefits include the fact that the process can be easily modified, version controlled, and reported on. The ALM platform can then import the process and execute the application development process descriptions in it. Microsoft, for example, uses XML to store the development process in TFS. The process XML file describes the entire ALM process, and many different process files can coexist. This means you can choose the process template on which want to base your project when creating a new project.

It's also important for an enterprise to have control over its project portfolio to allocate and control resources more effectively. So far, none of the ALM vendors have integrated this support into the ALM platform. There may be good reasons for this, though. For instance, although portfolio management may require data from ALM, the reverse probably isn't the case. The good thing is that having a standards-based platform makes integration with PPM tools much easier.

ALM 2.0+

So far, not all ALM 2.0 features have been implemented by most of the major ALM tool vendors. There are various reasons for this. One is that it isn't easy for any company to move to a single integrated suite, no matter how promising the benefits may appear. Making such a switch means changing the way you work in your development processes and maybe even throughout your company. Companies have invested in tools and practices, and spending time and money on a new platform may require considerably more investment.

For Microsoft-focused development organizations, the switch might not be as difficult, however—at least not for the developers. They already use Visual Studio, SharePoint, and many other applications in their daily life, and the switch isn't that great. But Microsoft isn't the only platform out there, and competitors like IBM, Serena, and HP still have some work to do to convince the market.

In addition, repository-neutral standards and services haven't evolved over time. Microsoft, for instance, still relies on SQL Server as a repository and hasn't built in much support for other databases or services. The same goes for most competition to TFS.

Note Virtually all vendors use ALM tools to lock in customers to as many of their products as possible—especially *expensive*, major strategic products like relational database management systems (RDBMSs). After all, these companies live mostly on license sales.

The growth of Agile development and project management in recent years has also changed the way ALM must support development teams and organizations. There has been a clear change from requirements specs to backlog-driven work, and the tools you use need to support this.

It becomes critical for ALM tools to support Agile practices such as build-and-test automation. TDD is being used with increasing frequency, and more and more developers require their tools to support this way of working. If the tools don't do this, they're of little use to an Agile organization. Microsoft has taken the Agile way of working to heart in the development of TFS, and this book will show you all you need to know about TFS's support for Agile practices.

There has also been a move from traditional project management toward an Agile view in which the product owner and Scrum master require support from the tools. Backlog refinement (the art of refining requirements in the Agile world), Agile estimation and planning, and reporting—important to these roles—need to be integrated to the overall ALM solution.

The connection between Operations and Maintenance also becomes more and more important. ALM tools should integrate with the tools used by these parts of the organization.

In the report "The Time Is Right for ALM 2.0+," Forrester Research presented the ALM 2.0+ concept, illustrated in Figure 1-9 [7]. This report extended traditional ALM with what Forrester called ALM 2.0+. Traditional ALM covers traceability, reporting, and process automation, as you've seen. Forrester envisions the future of ALM also including collaboration and work planning.

---

[7] West, "The Time Is Right For ALM 2.0+."

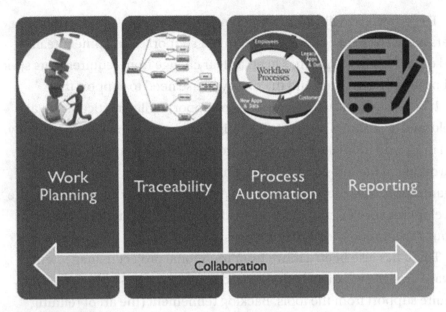

Figure 1-9. *Future ALM, according to Forrester Research*

These concepts are essential and are discussed in detail in this book. A chapter is dedicated to each one except for traceability; traceability and visibility are combined into one chapter because they are closely related. The book's focus is on ALM 2.0+, but it includes some other older concepts as well. We've already looked at the first three cornerstones, but let's briefly examine the two new ones introduced in ALM 2.0+:

1. *Work planning*: For this concept, Forrester includes planning functions, such as defining tasks and allocating them to resources. These planning functions shouldn't replace the strategic planning functions that enterprise architecture and portfolio management tools provide. Instead, they help you execute and provide feedback on those strategic plans. Integration of planning into ALM 2.0+ helps you follow up on projects so you can obtain estimates and effort statistics, which are essential to all projects.

2. *Collaboration*: As mentioned, collaboration
    is essential. ALM 2.0+ tools must support the
    distributed development environment that exists in
    organizations. The tools must help team members
    work effectively—sharing, collaborating, and
    interacting as if they were collocated. The tools
    should also do this without adding complexity to the
    work environment.

We take a closer look at these topics farther down the road. But before
we do that, we examine a new topic on the horizon: DevOps. DevOps is
important because it has the potential to solve many ALM problems.

DevOps

In the past couple years, the concept of DevOps has emerged. In our
view, DevOps is close to, or even the same as, the unified view of ALM
presented earlier in the chapter. One big difference compared to a
more traditional approach is that DevOps brings development and
operations staff closer—not just in thought, but also physically. Because
they're all part of the DevOps team, there is no handoff from one part
to the other. Team members work together to deliver business value
through continuous development and operations. Figure 1-10 shows
how Microsoft looks at DevOps (https://azure.microsoft.com/en-us/
overview/devops/).

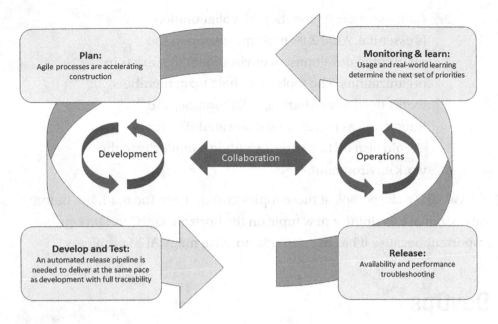

Figure 1-10. *DevOps according to Microsoft*

DevOps isn't a method on its own; instead, it uses known Agile methods and processes like Kanban and Scrum, which are popular in many IT organizations. Basically, these are project management methods based on Agile concepts and are used for development (mostly Scrum) and operations (mostly Kanban). The key concepts are continuous development, continuous integration, and continuous deployment. What is important is working with small changes instead of large releases (which minimizes risk), getting rid of manual steps by automating processes, and having development and test environments that are as close as possible to the production environment.

The purpose of DevOps is to optimize the time from the development of an application until it's running stably in the production environment. The quicker you can get from idea to production, the quicker you can respond to changes in, and influences from, the market, which is crucial to have a successful business.

Azure DevOps Introduction

In 2018, Microsoft introduced the concept of Azure DevOps, which includes a new suite of tools or services. This new concept was previously known Visual Studio Team Services, or VSTS. Azure DevOps Services is a cloud service for collaborating on application development (https://docs.microsoft.com/en-us/azure/devops/user-guide/what-is-azure-devops-services?view=vsts). It provides an integrated set of features that you access through your web browser or integrated development environment (IDE) client, including the following:

- Git repositories for source control of code

- Build-and-release services to support continuous integration and delivery of apps

- Agile tools to support planning and tracking work, code defects, and issues using Kanban and Scrum processes

- A variety of tools to test your apps, including manual/exploratory testing, load testing, and continuous testing

- Highly customizable dashboards for sharing progress and trends

- Built-in wiki for sharing information with your team

The Azure DevOps ecosystem also provides support for adding extensions, integrating with other popular services (such as Campfire, Slack, Trello, UserVoice, and more), and developing your own custom extensions.

Azure DevOps is available as a set of services that we can chose to use parts or all of it. This means we can tailor it to our specific needs. Each Azure DevOps service is open and extensible. They work great for any type of application regardless of the framework, platform, or cloud. You can use them together for a full DevOps solution or with other services. Here is an overview of the services available:

31

- *Azure Boards*: Powerful work tracking with Kanban boards, backlogs, team dashboards, and custom reporting. This is where this book has its biggest focus.

- *Azure Pipelines*: Continuous integration/ continuous delivery (CI/CD) that works with any language, platform, and cloud. Connect to GitHub or any Git repository and deploy continuously.

- *Azure Artifacts*: Maven, npm, and NuGet package feeds from public and private sources

- *Azure Repos*: Unlimited cloud-hosted private Git repos for your project; collaborative pull requests, advanced file management, and more

- *Azure Test Plans*: All-in-one planned and exploratory testing solution

With Azure DevOps comes a brand new graphic user interface (GUI) that has been in preview since late 2018 (Figure 1-11). All settings and navigation now take place in the navigation bar on the left. From there, you can access every aspect of your Azure DevOps project.

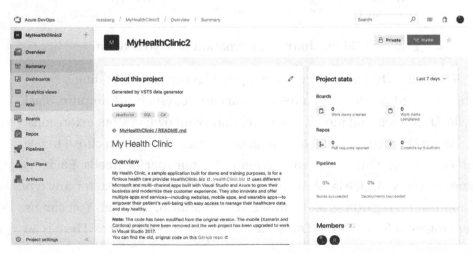

Figure 1-11. *The new GUI of Azure DevOps*

Clicking Boards, for instance, expands the menu on the left and show more options for viewing boards and backlogs (Figure 1-12).

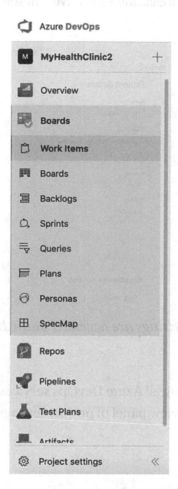

Figure 1-12. *The new GUI of Azure DevOps can be expanded to show more options for the Azure DevOps services—in this case, for Azure Boards*

The project settings are now available in the lower left corner, as shown in Figure 1-13. This is the place for configuring teams, security, notifications, iterations, areas, and so on. We will see these features throughout this book.

Figure 1-13. *Project settings are accessed at the bottom of the navigation bar*

If you will not be using all Azure DevOps services, you can turn them off (or on) from the overview panel of project settings (Figure 1-14).

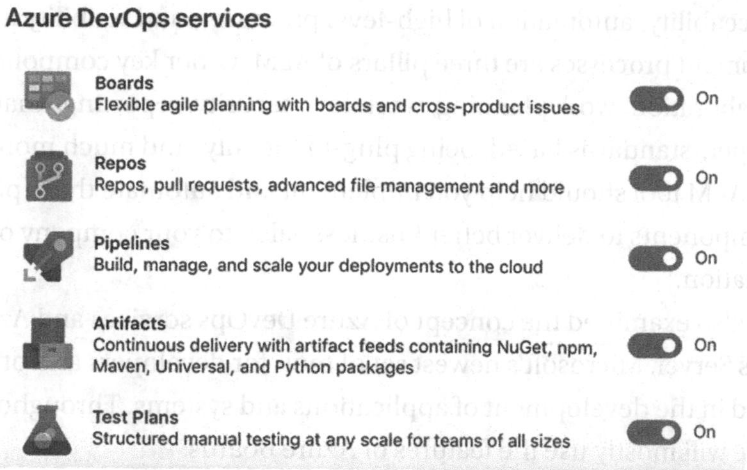

Azure DevOps services

Boards
Flexible agile planning with boards and cross-product issues   On

Repos
Repos, pull requests, advanced file management and more   On

Pipelines
Build, manage, and scale your deployments to the cloud   On

Artifacts
Continuous delivery with artifact feeds containing NuGet, npm,
Maven, Universal, and Python packages   On

Test Plans
Structured manual testing at any scale for teams of all sizes   On

Figure 1-14. *Turning on Azure DevOps services from project settings*

As stated earlier in this chapter, TFS server will be renamed to Azure DevOps Server. It will still be an on-prem installation and it will be exciting to see the direction it takes.

Summary

This chapter presented an overview of what ALM aims for and what it takes for the ALM platform to support a healthy ALM process. You've seen that ALM is the coordination and synchronization of all development life cycle activities. There are four ways of looking at it:

1. SDLC view

2. Service management or operations view

3. APM view

4. Unified view

Traceability, automation of high-level processes, and visibility into development processes are three pillars of ALM. Other key components are collaboration, work planning, workflow, security, reporting, analytics, being open-standards based, being plug-in friendly, and much more. A good ALM tool should help you implement and automate these pillars and components to deliver better business value to your company or organization.

We also examined the concept of Azure DevOps services and Azure DevOps Server, Microsoft's newest set of tools for developers and others involved in the development of applications and systems. Throughout this book we will mostly use the features of Azure Boards.

CHAPTER 2

An Overview of Azure DevOps

In this chapter, we examine a tool that makes it clear why DevOps is an important process for organizations engaged in IT development. A good implementation of ALM helps an organization deliver better business value to fulfill its business needs. Automating tasks by using tools such as Visual Studio 2017, Azure DevOps, and TFS 2018 (soon to be renamed Azure DevOps Server) supports this process.

We will take a look at how Azure DevOps can be used to fulfill the three main pillars of ALM and the issues addressed by ALM, which were covered in Chapter 1. We start with an overview of ALM and of Azure DevOps, then move on to the specifics of using Azure DevOps for ALM.

ALM Overview

As you may recall from Chapter 1, there are three main pillars of an ALM process:

1. *Traceability of relationships between artifacts*: The lack of traceability can be a major cost driver in any enterprise. There must be a way to trace requirements all the way to delivered code and back again—through architect models, design models, build scripts, unit tests, test cases, and

© Joachim Rossberg 2019

J. Rossberg, *Agile Project Management with Azure DevOps*,
https://doi.org/10.1007/978-1-4842-4483-8_2

so on. Practices such as TDD and configuration management can help, and they can be automated and supported by Azure DevOps.

2. *Automation of high-level processes*: There are approval processes to control handoffs between analysis and design. There are other handoffs among build, deployment, testing, and so on. Much of this is done manually in many projects, and ALM stresses the importance of automating these tasks for a more effective and less time-consuming process.

3. *Visibility into the progress of development efforts*: Many managers and stakeholders have limited visibility into the progress of development projects. Their visibility often comes from steering group meetings during which the PM goes over the current situation. Other interest groups such as project members may also have limited visibility of the whole project even though they are part of it. This often occurs because reporting is hard to do and can involve a lot of manual work. Daily status reports may, quite simply, take too much time and effort to produce—for example, especially when we have information in many repositories.

Other important topics that ALM addresses are as follows:

- *Improving collaboration*: Collaboration is needed among teams, team members, stakeholders, and users, just to mention a few relationships. When development is spread around the world in different locations, collaboration can be hard to manage without the help of a proper tool.

- *Closing the gap between IT and business*: The big gap between IT and the business side of an organization is a serious problem for organizations, preventing us from delivering the greatest business value that can be achieved from our projects.

- *Using one tool*: The complexity of using several tools for solving project issues as a team member can be tough, and costly as well. Switching between tools can be a cost driver. Using one tool that enables us to add plug-ins and use more features directly in our ordinary GUI, instead of switching between applications, is preferable. So, if you have several roles in a project, you can still use one tool to get the job done.

- *Enhancing role switching*: ALM also addresses the potential to use one tool when switching among different roles in a project. In many cases, project members play several roles in the same project. A developer, for instance, might also work with tests or databases. If that person can use the same GUI for all tasks, there will be minimal overhead for switching among these roles.

Azure DevOps Overview

TFS and Azure DevOps have come a long way toward fulfilling the ALM vision, but it does not cover everything. As mentioned, VSTS has now been renamed Azure DevOps; TFS 2018 will be renamed Azure DevOps Server in the near future. The features of the former VSTS are now separate services in Azure DevOps (Table 2-1):

Table 2-1. *Comparison between VSTS Features and Azure DevOps Services*

VSTS feature name	Azure DevOps service name	Description
Build & Release	Azure Pipelines	CI/CD that works with any language, platform, and cloud
Code	Azure Repos	Cloud-hosted private Git and Team Foundation Version Control (TFVC) repos for your project.
Work	Azure Boards	Work tracking with Kanban boards, backlogs, team dashboards, and custom reporting
Test	Azure Test Plans	All-in-one planned and exploratory testing solution
Packages (extension)	Azure Artifacts	Maven, npm, and NuGet package feeds from public and private sources

Azure DevOps is an open and extensible product that lets us adjust its features to our needs and add the things it might lack at this point to support our specific needs. It is also important to know that Microsoft is spending a lot of time, energy, and money on developing this product further. This is not a tool set that will go away quickly (although one never knows); it is one of the most important tool sets in the Microsoft ecosystem.

Azure DevOps is now available in two versions: TFS and the cloud-based Azure DevOps. In this book, we mostly use Azure DevOps for illustrations.

Team Foundation Server

You can see that the heart of DevOps in the Azure DevOps/TFS world is TFS or, if you use the cloud-based version, Azure DevOps (Figure 2-1).

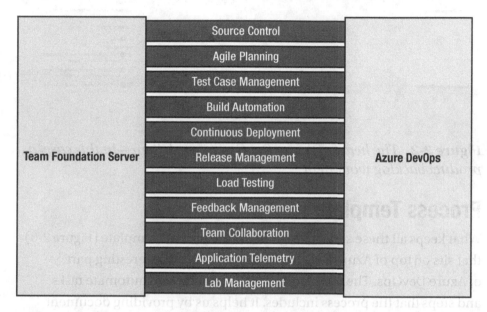

Figure 2-1. *An overview of TFS and Azure DevOps*

TFS and Azure DevOps expose different functions and services for developers, PMs, and others such as version control, reporting, build, and work item tracking. Not shown in Figure 2-1. is the fact that TFS uses Microsoft SQL Server as its data repository.

Note   Work items (Figure 2-2) are used to manage different types of information in TFS and Azure DevOps. There are work items for requirements, bugs, general tasks, and so on. To put it simply, a work item is a piece of work that must be completed for a project. The work item tracking system is one of the core parts of Azure DevOps for DevOps process implementation.

Figure 2-2. The heart of Azure DevOps: a work item—in this case, a product backlog work item

Process Template

What keeps all these services together is the process template (Figure 2-3) that sits on top of Azure DevOps/TFS. This is a very interesting part of Azure DevOps. The template helps us visualize and automate tasks and steps that the process includes. It helps us by providing document templates for requirements specs, test cases, scenarios, handoffs, and other artifacts we should produce.

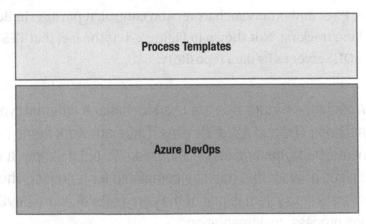

Figure 2-3. The process template customizes Azure DevOps behavior

Most companies use some kind of process for their development or ALM. Although some companies don't think they have a process, they do. The process might not be written down, but the company still has ways of doing things that, in reality, is the process—for instance, naming conventions, where to store builds, how to handle CRs, and so on.

In many cases, we have seen companies with lots of money invested in their processes. They have sent staff to training, provided large process manuals, and so on. However, they have had problems getting project members to *use* the processes in their daily work. The excuses are many: The process is hard to understand, remembering all the process steps is difficult, the process is not automated or included in the tools, and many others.

The end result has been that PMs use their own variant of the process, causing confusion during the project's lifetime. This also causes severe problems, because handoffs between the development team and the operations team are often difficult. A typical bad scenario can occur when a system has to wait for deployment because the infrastructure isn't in place for the new system. Operations was not involved (or perhaps not even informed) during the project and suddenly they are expected to run the system on hardware they don't have.

With Azure DevOps, you can implement your development process as a template that is mandatory for all new projects. When you create a new project, you also create a new instance of the process template. You don't have to stop at the development project level either. You can implement most parts of your DevOps cycle in the template as well, enabling you to take advantage of Azure DevOps all along the way. The template helps you visualize and automate tasks and steps that the process includes. It helps you by providing document templates for requirements specs, test cases, scenarios, handoffs, and other artifacts you produce.

The template also provides information about which reports you have available for each new project—reports that you can use to retrieve information about the status of your projects and many other things. The template also contains information about one of the most important core parts of Azure DevOps: the work items. These items can be adjusted as needed so you can make sure they contain the information the organization must have. This information could be status information for a bug, for instance, such as Active, Resolved, or Closed.

This template is so flexible you can develop and implement your own process, you can choose to use any of the three that Microsoft supplies, you can use a third-party template, or you can choose to customize the Microsoft templates to your own liking. You also have several process templates in Azure DevOps, so you can use different templates for different projects. Because Azure DevOps really is not used to its full potential without the process templates, it cannot be stressed enough that you should consider which templates you want to use and the information you want them to include.

Visual Studio 2017 Editions

Most developers use Visual Studio to access the features of Azure DevOps. At the time of writing this book, Visual Studio 2017 is the current version, but 2019 is just around the corner. There are several editions of 2017 available:

- *Visual Studio Community*: Full-featured IDE for building Web, Windows Desktop, and cross-platform iOS, Android, and Windows apps. This edition is free for open-source projects, academic research, training, education, and small professional teams.

- *Visual Studio Professional*: Professional developer tools and services for individual developers or small teams. This edition includes powerful features to improve a team's productivity, such as CodeLens. Improve team collaboration with Agile project planning tools, team rooms, charts, and more

- *Visual Studio Enterprise*: Enterprise-grade solution with advanced capabilities for teams working on projects of any size or complexity, including advanced testing and DevOps. Build quality applications at scale with advanced features such as load testing, automated and manual testing, and new IntelliTest capabilities. Manage complexity and resolve issues quickly with features such as Code Map and IntelliTrace.

- *Visual Studio for Mac*: Developer productivity of the Windows version to a Mac. The experience has been developed to optimize the workflow for the Mac developer.

- *Visual Studio Test Professional*: a tool for testers. Tools are also included in the Ultimate edition, but it lacks the development tools included in the other editions.

- *Team Explorer Everywhere* (TEE): access to Azure DevOps for developers on other platforms, such as Eclipse on the Mac. This is the perfect add-on for teams with development on multiple platforms such as .NET and Java.

Azure DevOps

All projects in Azure DevOps have their own web sites available. They are created when the project itself is created. By using this portal, you can access most of the functionality in Azure DevOps. The project portal lets you access the parts of Azure DevOps available from inside Visual Studio, from an easy-to-use interface, especially for nontechnical project members. Figure 2-4 shows what Azure DevOps could look like.

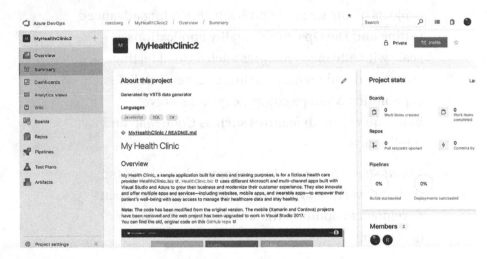

Figure 2-4. *The project start page on Azure DevOps*

Many of our customers use a team project portal primarily to provide access to reports and work items for nontechnical people not used to the Visual Studio interface. When we want to give an external user (such as a customer or remote stakeholder) access to work item creation and editing, or another more advanced task, we usually use the web interface.

Microsoft Office

Microsoft Office can be used by PMs, product owners, or Scrum masters, for example, who want to use tools familiar to them, such as Microsoft

Project and Microsoft Office Excel, during a project. The integration is very nice and valuable to these roles.

IDE Integration

When it comes to add-ins, one thing we should mention in particular is Team Explorer. This tool can be used as an add-in to Visual Studio, and it gives access to Azure DevOps directly from within Visual Studio. From there, you can open reports, add new work items, and run queries against the Azure DevOps database.

Azure DevOps is a flexible tool, as we have mentioned. It is also very extensible, because all functionality can be accessed via web services. This is a very nice feature that enables you to build your own support for Azure DevOps in other applications as well. Many third-party vendors have done this, and a wide array of add-ins and tools are available. Our favorite came from Teamprise, a company that has built add-ins to Eclipse so that you can use Azure DevOps features in your Java development environment as well. Teamprise was purchased by Microsoft, and its suite of client applications has been available as TEE since Azure DevOps 2010. Briefly, it offers the same IDE integration into both Eclipse and Visual Studio, which allows you to work as one team, regardless of whether you use Eclipse or Visual Studio.

Traceability

Having traceability in your DevOps processes is key to the successful delivery and maintenance of your applications and systems. I once visited a company that stopped making changes to its systems just because no one ever knew where a change (or bug fix) might have its impact. You don't have to deal with such a situation.

Azure DevOps features can help you with traceability so you can avoid such problems:

- Work item tracking

- TDD/unit testing

- Azure Pipelines

- Check-in policies

- Version control system

Let's look at some of the specifics involved with these features, starting with how the work item tracking system implements traceability.

The Azure DevOps Work Item Tracking System

Sometimes you might have tons of Post-its on your monitors and desk, which each note containing at least one task you are supposed to address. Most likely, you would want to track these tasks using a tool that can help you, but often this just isn't possible. It could be that some tasks are connected with one project and others with another. You may have tried recording them in an Excel spreadsheet and saving it to the computer. But, you may soon realize that the spreadsheet is located on your laptop, your customer's computer, your desktop, another customer computer, and so on. And, you have no idea which spreadsheet is the current version.

The same thing often occurs with projects. PMs have their to-do lists for a project, and they all have their own way of keeping them updated. Let's say a PM uses Excel to keep track of the tasks—the status of tasks, to whom they are assigned, and so on. How can PMs keep the team updated with the latest to-do list? If PMs choose to e-mail it, chances are that some team members won't save the new version to disk or will miss it in their endless stream of incoming e-mail. Soon there are various versions floating around, and things are generally a mess.

Work Items

With Azure DevOps, there is a task tracking system at your service. We take a closer look at work items in Chapter 4, so we'll keep our discussion brief here. The core of this system is represented by the tasks themselves, which as we said earlier are called *work items*. A work item can be pretty much what we want it to be. It can be a bug, a requirement of some sort, a general to-do item, and so on. Each work item has a unique ID that helps you keep track of the places it is referenced (Figure 2-5). The ID lets you follow a work item—say, a requirement—from its creation to its implementation as a piece of executable software (component).

Work items provide a great way for you to simplify task management in a project while at the same time enable traceability. No more is there confusion regarding which version of the task list is current; no more is manual labor required to gather status reports on work progress used only at steering group meetings. Now you have a solution that lets you collaborate more easily with your teams, and enables all members and stakeholders to view status reports whenever they want. You can also collaborate more easily with people outside the project group by adding work items via the web client.

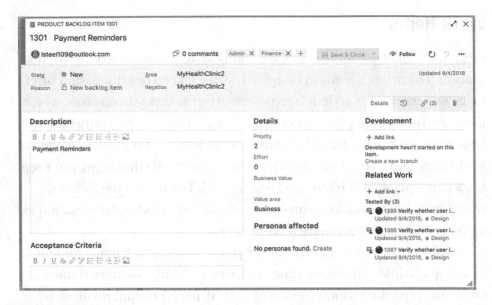

Figure 2-5. *Each work item has a unique ID—in this case, 1301*

Azure DevOps is so flexible in this regard that it lets us tailor the work items as we want them to be. The work item tracking system is one of the core components of Azure DevOps. This system enables you to create work items, or units of work, and can be used to enable traceability. You can use the work items included with Azure DevOps from the beginning, you can choose to adjust them to your needs, or you can even create your own work item types. Each work item instance has a unique ID that you can attach to the things you do in Azure DevOps. This enables you to follow one work item—let's say, a requirement, for example—from its creation to its implementation as a piece of executable software (component). You can also associate one work item with others and build a hierarchy of work items.

The work items can contain information in different fields that define the data to be stored in the work item. This means that each field has a name and a data type.

All work items can have different information attached to them. You can have information about to whom the work item is assigned and the status of the work at the moment (for example, a bug could be open, closed, under investigation, resolved, and so on). The State field can be modified so that each work item type has its own state mechanism. This is logical because a bug probably goes through states differently from those that a general task goes through. You can also attach documents to the work item and link one work item to other work items. You can even create a hierarchy of work items if you want. Let's say you implement a requirement as a work item and that this requirement contains many smaller tasks. Then, you can have the requirement itself at the top and nest the other requirements below that so you know which work items belong to which requirement.

When a bug is discovered, for instance, you can quickly follow the original requirement by its work item ID, and see in which places in the code you might have to make some fixes. You can also visualize the associated work items so that you can evaluate whether other parts of the code need to be changed as a result of the bug fix.

Azure DevOps saves information about the work item on the data tier, which helps you follow the change history of the work item. You can see who created it, who resolved it, who closed it, and so on. The information in the databases can be used for display on reports, which allows you to tailor them depending on your needs. One report could show the status of all bugs, for instance. Stakeholders can see how many open bugs exist, how many are resolved, and much, much more. It is completely up to you how you choose to use the work items.

If you implement a requirement as a work item, you can use the work item ID to track this requirement through source code to the final build of the executable system. By requiring all developers to add one or more work item IDs to the check-in using a check-in policy, you can enable this traceability.

Configuration Management Using Azure DevOps

In any (development) organization, there needs to be version control of the systems in production. If you don't have that, the overall DevOps process suffers, because you suddenly lose traceability. This makes it harder to implement changes and bug fixes, because you won't know which versions you need to update.

Without the help of a proper tool, you will soon get lost in the variety of applications you have. Azure DevOps can help you with version control in many ways. After a brief description of software configuration management, I cover some of the most important concepts that have great support in Azure DevOps and Visual Studio tools:

- Version control

- Azure Pipelines

In software engineering, software configuration management (SCM) is the task of tracking and controlling changes in the software. Configuration management practices include revision control and the establishment of baselines, and are very important. There are several goals of SCM, including the following:

- *Configuration identification*: Ensuring you know the code with which you are working

- *Configuration control*: Controlling the release of a product and its changes (version control)

- *Build management*: Managing the process and tools used for builds

- *Defect tracking*: Making sure every defect has traceability back to the source

If these issues are not covered by your DevOps process, you could very soon find yourself in a troublesome situation. It is crucial for the development teams to have full control over those versions of the applications that exist, those that are in production, and where they are in production. This topic is closely related to portfolio management teams. In general, a big company has one or more persons devoted to keeping track of SCM.

Version Control and Release Management in Azure DevOps

Using the version control system in Azure DevOps, you can manage and control multiple revisions of the same information in your projects. This information can be source code, documents, work items, and other important information that you want to submit to version control. When you want to work on an item under source control, you check it out to your local computer so you can start working on it. When work is done and tested, you check in your changes so the version on the server is updated.

The version control features of Azure DevOps are powerful. Microsoft supports Git and the native Visual Studio version control. They are fully integrated into the GUI, which is something that ALM prescribes as well. If you want, you can access some of the features from a project portal as well. Many people want to use the command line for their work, and Azure DevOps enables them to use the command line for working with version control as well.

However, if you do want to use Visual Studio to access the Azure DevOps version control system, you can do that. The extensibility of Azure DevOps makes this possible. One example of this is the TEE suite of client applications that can access Azure DevOps, including the version control system. TEE lets you access Azure DevOps from Eclipse on Mac OS X and also through command lines. In this way, you can integrate different development platforms more easily in an Azure DevOps project. You will still use the Azure DevOps repository and have the ability to get reports and other information directly from Azure DevOps.

Build Management Using Azure Pipelines

A build is basically the process of taking the source code and all other items necessary in an application and building it into executable software. Azure Pipelines is a cloud service that you can use to build and test your code automatically and make it available to other users. It works with just about any language or project type. Pipelines combines both CI and CD to test a build your code constantly and consistently, and ship it to any target.

CI is all about automating tests and builds for your project. It helps to catch bugs or problems early during the development cycle, which makes them easier and faster to fix. Items known as *artifacts* are produced from CI systems and used by the CD release pipelines to drive automatic deployments.

CD is all about deploying and testing code automatically in multiple stages to help drive quality. CI systems produce the deployable artifacts, including infrastructure and apps, then automated release pipelines consume these artifacts to release new versions and fixes to the target of your choice.

There are plenty of reasons to use Azure Pipelines for your CI/CD solution:

- It works with any language or platform.

- It deploys. to different types of targets at the same time.

- It is the best integration experience for deploying to Azure.

- You can build on Windows, Linux, or Mac machines.

- It provides great integration for GitHub.

- It's a great offer for open-source projects.

Automation of High-Level Processes

Without one or more templates, Azure DevOps is not used to its full potential, as mentioned earlier. You can still use its version control system and some other tools, but the real value comes from using Azure DevOps to automate your DevOps process. With the process template, your entire DevOps process is defined.

The template defines the following:

- *Work item types*: These refer to those work item types that are necessary and the information they should have attached to them. You can also define the workflow for a work item. For a bug, you might have different states through which the item flows, such as active, resolved, closed, and so on.

- *Project phases*: By using areas and iterations, you can define the initial project phase setup of your projects. If you use RUP, you can define the process phases in that model or you can create the first sprints of a Scrum project. Areas and iterations are flexible, and you can create your own way of working through these concepts.

- *Document structure and templates*: The number of documents that should be produced during a project differs depending on your process model. In the process template, you define the document structure you need and the templates you should use. For instance, you can add templates for requirement specifications or acceptance testing.

- *Reports and queries*: In the process template, you can
  specify which reports and work item queries you need
  to have as defaults in your projects. You probably want
  reports and queries that show the progress of your
  project, such as the status of bugs or work remaining.
  You can create your own reports by using Power BI,
  SQL Server Reporting Services (TFS 2018) or Excel, and
  then add them to all projects by adjusting the process
  template.

- *Security*: The template also adds information about
  which users or user groups have access to which
  information. You can connect Azure DevOps groups to
  your Active Directory accounts, for instance.

The process template is the overall process for our ALM
implementation. Many of our customers create different templates for
different kinds of projects. They also create templates for Operations, so
that when a development project is finished and deployed, the operations
staff can use the template to run the system until the system dies. A few
customers have started creating a template for Information Technology
Infrastructure Library (ITIL), for instance, and we are looking forward to
seeing the result of that work.

It is important to remember that you can adjust the process to your
needs. You should consider changing the default templates or even
replacing them, rather than adjusting your own way of working to the
templates that come with Azure DevOps out of the box. Microsoft enables
this flexibility by letting you access the process templates easily to adjust
them or to add new templates.

Visibility

Information about project status is important to all participants of a project—and we don't mean team members only, but stakeholders and decision makers as well. As project managers, we have spent too much time chasing down information to answer questions about the status of projects, how much work remains, and what the latest bug status is.

Azure DevOps provides three primary ways of enabling visibility:

1. *Widgets and dashboards*: Customizable, highly configurable dashboards provide us and our teams with the flexibility to share information, monitor progress and trends, and improve our workflow.

2. *Queries*: Queries are used to ask questions of the work item tracking service. Some questions might be: How many bug work items do we have? How many and which are dedicated to me? How many bugs are there? And so on. You can create new queries when necessary.

3. *Power BI*: The integration of the analytics service with Power BI makes getting the data into Power BI easy, so you can focus on creating Power BI reports.

By using these components, it is easier to gather the information you need for your status reports for a steering group meeting or project meeting. You won't have to look around in several places and in several applications for this information anymore; instead, you can use the automated reports and queries from inside Azure DevOps.

Project owners, PMs, and Scrum masters certainly benefit from Azure DevOps. Because Azure DevOps has all data in the same repository, you can retrieve the correct information more easily when you want it. The flexibility of the SQL Server database that stores all information is great.

You can work with the data warehouse information just as you would with any other database.

By using the Azure DevOps web (Figure 2-6), you can publish information (in the form of custom-built controls that users cannot change at this time) so that everybody who has privileges can see it. This is an easy way to make sure that information is available all the time. Just this little, relatively nontechnical improvement offloads work from the PMs, freeing some of the PM's or product owner's time for better things.

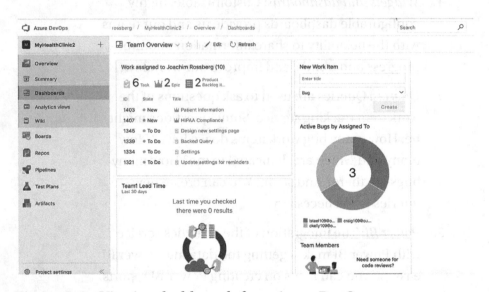

Figure 2-6. *Viewing dashboards from Azure DevOps*

Collaboration

As you know, Azure DevOps comes with Team Explorer, which is an add-in to Visual Studio. With this tool, developers can access every aspect of an Azure DevOps project. They can view reports and queries, for instance, as well as access the documents in the project. Developers can access the version control system as well as build systems, tests, and so on.

Team Explorer is full featured, but it is still a tool for people used to working in Visual Studio. For us, that is no problem; but, for most PMs and stakeholders, the GUI is confusing. They want to have a tool that's easy to use to access relevant information.

Each project created with Azure DevOps has a project portal created as well. This portal gives you access to reports, documents, project process guidance, and other project-related information through a web interface, which enables people who are not used to the Visual Studio interface to retrieve the information they need easily.

There is also a wiki (Figure 2-7) that can be used for each Azure DevOps project. It is a collaboration area where team members can share information.

Figure 2-7.   *The Azure DevOps wiki*

Collaboration does not only mean giving access to information, although this is as important as any other means of collaboration. Collaboration also means you should be able to work together to fulfill one or more goals. One other way to enable this is that every work item can have a discussion thread Figure 2-8). In the thread, you can add comments, ask questions, and so on, in a discussion regarding this particular work item with your coworkers and stakeholders.

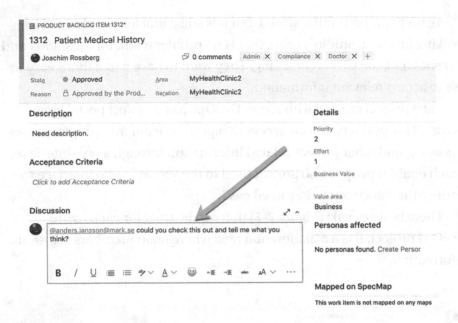

Figure 2-8. *Sample discussion thread in a work item*

Work Items for Collaboration

You can use the work item features of Azure DevOps to enable your
process workflows. Let's say a PM, or someone responsible for inputting
requirements as work items into Azure DevOps, creates a new work item
of the Scenario type. This scenario should probably be assigned to a
developer to implement. The PM can use the work item system to assign
(Figure 2-9) the scenario to a specific developer—in this case, Joachim.
Joachim continues to work on the scenario until it is ready for testing. He
then assigns the work item to a tester, who performs the testing. When the
testing is done, the work item is closed. If a bug is found, either the tester or
anyone finding the bug can use the work item tracking system to see who
developed the scenario implementation and reassign it to that developer—
in this case, Joachim again. Azure DevOps keeps track of who has worked
on a work item so you don't have to keep track of this manually.

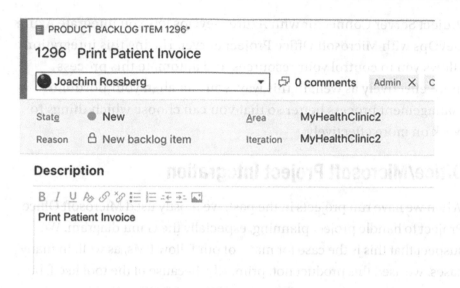

Figure 2-9. Assigning work items to a specific person

The Gap between IT and Business

Closing the gap between IT and business is obviously a very tough problem to solve. Azure DevOps won't get us all the way; that's for sure. We don't think any tool ever will, because so much depends on the people in the organization, which is an important consideration. But, tools can help us bridge the gap, so you should consider carefully how you can use them for this. Organizations need to improve on their ALM process and way of working to start addressing this issue. Once a new way of working is in place, Azure DevOps can support much of their efforts using, for instance, the process template to implement this new way of working.

The gap between IT and business is often a question of work process. It requires considering many things, and when we have a solution—or start working toward a solution—we must evaluate which parts of this work process we can automate and use tools for solving. One thing worth mentioning here is that the use of the Azure DevOps

Project Server Connector with Azure DevOps lets you integrate Azure DevOps with Microsoft Office Project Server. Having this integration allows you to control your resources and automate this process more effectively as well. In this way, you can align your portfolio management process better so that you can choose which things to work on more effectively.

Office/Microsoft Project Integration

When we have run projects in the past, we mostly used Microsoft Office Project to handle project planning, especially the Gantt diagram. We suspect that this is the case for many of our fellow PMs, as well. In many cases, we used this product not, primarily, because of the tool itself, but because so many of our customers use Microsoft Office that it becomes natural for them to use Project. Project has its strengths and weaknesses, as all tools do, and we cannot say we don't like it, but we have never become friends with it. Sometimes it does things we don't expect, and even though we know this is because we are not very familiar with its features, we still blame the product from time to time (which is unfair, but that's life sometimes).

Excel and Project are two tools that most companies use on both the business and the IT sides of the company. By being able to use these tools, business people can be a part of the ALM process more easily, because they can use a tool with which they are already used to working. A nice feature here is that the communication between Office and Azure DevOps is two-way. This means an update in Azure DevOps is reflected in Office, and the other way around. This allows for a dynamic way of working with Azure DevOps information.

Use of One Tool/Role Based

A good ALM tool should enable you to use add-ins that provide new features inside one interface. If a developer needs testing features, you should be able to integrate them into the development tool. The developer should not have to switch tools to do testing tasks. This is also what Visual Studio offers. There is no context switching because team members can use the same GUI no matter what role they are performing at the moment. Azure DevOps is also extensible and lets you create your own add-ins as well as purchase third-party add-ins that are accessible from inside Azure DevOps.

Extensibility

When the built-in features of Azure DevOps are not enough, you can use the extensibility features to expand and enhance it. Azure DevOps is often seen as a closed black box that Microsoft ships, when it's more like an enterprise resource planning (ERP) system for DevOps. Any DevOps environment must be customized for an organization's processes, existing applications, and services.

Many of our customers have been a bit reluctant to customize TFS. They have instead tried to squeeze their way of working into the templates Microsoft provides. We think this is the wrong way to do it. Our suggestion is that you start the other way around. Start by asking yourself how your organization wants to work. This process involves all parts of the organization, from the business side to Operations. Try to find agreement on how to work in the DevOps process. By doing so, you will see that this also is a good start for collaboration within the company. With Azure DevOps you can customize your process (more easily than with TFS), so you should not avoid customizations.

For instance, consider the work items and the information in them. If the fields and information in the templates are not enough, you can extend or edit them. Azure DevOps lets you do this by changing the process template. You can choose to add the information you need, and it is stored in the Azure DevOps databases, so you can have access to it from within your reports and queries. Don't forget to change the reports or queries, as well; otherwise, you will not see your information.

Some of our customers have changed the workflow of a work item by adding more states to it when the ones supplied have not been enough. Often, we have used TFS Power Tools to do this for TFS (and still do for TFS 2018), but Azure DevOps provides an easy way to do this through the web interface.

When you have an initial idea of how you want to conduct the DevOps process, start looking into what Azure DevOps gives you out of the box. Use what can be used, change other things, and build your own solution when needed.

One great strength of Azure DevOps is its extensibility and flexibility. You can adjust the whole tool to fit most parts of your DevOps process. If you want to, you can develop your own add-ins by giving support to roles not included from the start. We strongly encourage you to use these extensibility features; but, in the end, it is your choice.

Extensibility is a great way to integrate existing systems and potentially migrate some of them into Azure DevOps to reduce the tool set in the organization.

Difference between TFS and Azure DevOps

Azure DevOps is cloud based. This is also the version of TFS for which Microsoft deploys all new features first. Every three weeks, Microsoft aims to update Azure DevOps. These updates are then packaged to a

TFS update that is released approximately every three months. Table 2-2 presents an overview of the difference in features between Azure DevOps and TFS. Keep in mind that the information in the table changes as time goes by. VSTS is updated every three weeks with new functionality, and the difference between the two will probably be overbridged.

Table 2-2. *Comparison between TFS and Azure DevOps*

Feature	TFS	Azure DevOps
Work items, version control, and build	✓	✓
Agile product/project management	✓	✓
Test case management	✓	✓
Heterogeneous development (Eclipse, Git)	✓	✓
Ease of installation and setup	Good	Better
Collaborate with anyone, from anywhere	Good	Better
Data stay inside your network	✓	✗
Process template and work item customization	✓	Good
Data warehouse and reporting	✓	✗
CodeLens support	✓	✓
Cloud load testing	✗	✓
Application insights	✗	✓
Always running the latest version of Azure DevOps	✗	✓

Summary

In our opinion, Azure DevOps can help you implement a good, automated, and robust DevOps process. There are features for all aspects of ALM. When used correctly, these features help improve the DevOps process, which result in better business value and more successful projects.

The three pillars of ALM—traceability, process automation, and visibility—are important to all organizations. Azure DevOps is a great foundation on which to build DevOps solutions. Azure DevOps has work item tracking for traceability, process template implementation in the tool itself for process automation, and reports and queries for visibility. Through a project portal, accessible via the Internet, you can improve collaboration among all parties that have an interest in your projects.

Azure DevOps is role based in the sense that it supports different development roles. It has support for architects, developers, DBAs, testers, and more. They are not given separate tools; all are accessible from a unified GUI. You can also add custom add-ins to the GUI and do not have to use several tools to get the job done.

Product owners and PMs have the ability to use tools with which they are already familiar. Many use Excel or Project for project planning, and there is integration between these tools and Azure DevOps. You can sync information easily between tools.

The extensibility of Azure DevOps makes it fairly easy to write your own code that integrates Azure DevOps with other applications. This is an incredible strength of the tool, and something for which we should give Microsoft credit.

So, all in all, Azure DevOps is a great foundation on which to build your ALM and DevOps process.

CHAPTER 3

Introduction to Scrum and Agile Concepts

Our experience is that there has been a great deal of improvement in projects during the past decade. To be more specific, we've seen the Agile movement make an impact on how projects deliver business value.

The focus of this book, when it comes to processes and frameworks, is on Agile methods such as Scrum and XP. The reason is simply that Agile fits nicely with the concept of ALM.

This chapter looks at how you can use Scrum as an Agile project management model to deliver software. We cover the Scrum process in depth, including how you can use Scrum and Agile practices, such as Agile estimation and planning, in combination with an ALM tool. This chapter gives you insight into why Agile and ALM are a good match.

This chapter also shows you some other Agile processes that are popular. Scrum is a great framework, but for some projects or some organizations, you may need another process to help you run your projects.

The Scrum Framework

Next we examine one of our favorite development models: Scrum. With all the attention Scrum has been getting in recent years, you may be misled into believing it's a fairly new model. The truth is that the Scrum approach,

© Joachim Rossberg 2019
J. Rossberg, *Agile Project Management with Azure DevOps*,
https://doi.org/10.1007/978-1-4842-4483-8_3

although not called Scrum at the time, was first presented as "the rugby approach" in 1986. In the January-February 1986 issue of the *Harvard Business Review*, Hirotaka Takeuchi and Ikujiro Nonaka described this approach for the first time.[1] In their article, they argued that small cross-functional teams produced the best results from a historical viewpoint.

It wasn't until 1990, however, that the rugby approach was referred to as *Scrum*. In 1990, Peter DeGrace and Leslie Hulet Stahl[2] highlighted this term from Takeuchi and Nonaka's original article. The term comes from rugby originally (Figure 3-1), and means the quick, safe, and fair restart of a rugby game after a minor infringement or stoppage.[3] www.planetrugby.com is the source of the following quotation:

Figure 3-1. *A real scrum*

---

[1]Hirotaka Takeuchi and Ikujiro Nonaka, "The New New Product Development Game," *Harvard Business Review*, www.sao.corvallis.or.us/drupal/files/ The%20New%20New%20Product%20Development%20Game.pdf, January/February 1986.

[2]Peter DeGrace and Leslie Hulet Stahl, "Wicked Problems, Righteous Solutions," http://www.gbv.de/dms/ilmenau/toc/608728446.PDF.

[3]www.planetrugby.com, 1990.

A scrum is formed in the field when eight players from each team, bound together in three rows for each team, close up with their opponents so that the heads of the front rows are interlocked. This creates a tunnel into which a scrum-half throws in the ball so that front-row players can compete for possession by hooking the ball with either of their feet.

Keep this definition in mind as we describe the development version of Scrum.

Ken Schwaber started using Scrum at his company in the early 1990s, but to be fair, Jeff Sutherland was the first to call it *Scrum*.[4] Schwaber and Sutherland teamed up and presented this approach publicly in 1996 at Object-Oriented Programming, Systems, Languages, and Applications (OOPSLA) in Austin, Texas. They collaborated to use their experience and industry best practices to refine the model until it achieved its current look. Schwaber described the model in *Agile Software Development with Scrum* in 2001.[5]

Let's continue by looking at empirical process control and see what that means in software development.

Empirical Process Control

What is this model, or framework, all about? First, let's define two ways to solve problems. We touched on the issues with projects in Chapter 1. When you have an issue that is similar time after time (like road construction, for example, or implementing a standard system), you pretty much know what to expect from the various tasks at hand. You can

---

[4]Jeff Sutherland, "Agile Development: Lessons Learned from the First Scrum," www.scrumalliance.org/resources/35, 2004.

[5]Ken Schwaber and Mike Beedle, *Agile Software Development with Scrum* (Prentice Hall, 2001).

then easily use a process—the Waterfall model, perhaps—that produces acceptable-quality output over and over again.[6] This approach is called *defined process control.*

When it comes to a more complex problem, however, such as building a software system, as you saw earlier, traditional models don't work. You must use something called *empirical process control*, according to Schwaber.[7] Empirical process control has three legs to stand on:

1. Transparency

2. Inspection

3. Adaptation

"Transparency means that the aspects of the process that affect the outcome must be visible to those controlling the process."[8] This means, to be able to approve the outcome, you must agree on the criteria for the outcome. Two people can't say they're "done" with a task unless they both agree on what the criteria are for "done."

The next leg is inspection. The process must be inspected as frequently as necessary to find unacceptable variances in it. Because any inspection may lead to a need to make changes to the process itself, you also need to revise the inspections to fit the new process. To accomplish this, you need skilled inspectors who know what they're inspecting.

The last leg is adaptation. An inspection may lead to a change in the process; this is one example of an adaptation. Another is that you must adapt the material being processed as a result of an inspection. All adaptations must be made as quickly as possible to minimize deviation later.

---

[6]Ken Schwaber, *The Enterprise and Scrum* (Microsoft Press, 2007).
[7]Ibid.
[8]Ibid.

Schwaber uses the example of code review when he discusses empirical process control:

> *The code is reviewed against coding standards and industry best practices. Everyone involved in the review fully and mutually understands these standards and best practices. The code review occurs whenever someone feels that a section of code is complete. The most experienced developers review the code, and their comments and suggestions lead to the developer adjusting his or her code.*[9]

Simple, isn't it? We could not have said it better ourselves.

Complexity in Projects

What makes a software development process so complex? We discussed this a bit previously, but let's dive deeper here. In theory, building a software system may seem pretty straightforward. You write code that instructs the CPU to control the computer. How hard can it be? Alas, it isn't that simple, we're afraid. The people writing the code are complex machines in themselves. They have different backgrounds, IQs, EQs, views, attitudes, and so on. Their personal lives also add to their complexity.

The requirements may also be complex and tend to change over time. According to Schwaber, a large percentage of the requirements gathered at the beginning of a software project changes during the project—and 60% of the features you build are rarely or never used in the end. Many times in our projects, several people at the customer site are responsible for the requirements. Often, they have diverging agendas as to why and what to build. And just as often, the stakeholders have a hard time expressing what they really want. Only when they see a first prototype of the system do they fully begin to see the possibilities of the software, and only then can they begin to understand what they want.

---

[9]Ibid.

Rarely is it the case that just one computer is involved in a system either. In general, there is interaction among several machines. You may have a web farm for your GUI, a cluster for your application tier, a back-end SQL Server, some external web services, and often a legacy system, all of which need to integrate to solve the needs of the new system.

When complex things interact—as people, requirements, and technology do in a software project—the level of complexity increases greatly. So, it's safe to say we don't have simple software problems anymore. They're all complex. Schwaber realizes this as well. Figure 3-2 shows his complexity assessment graph.

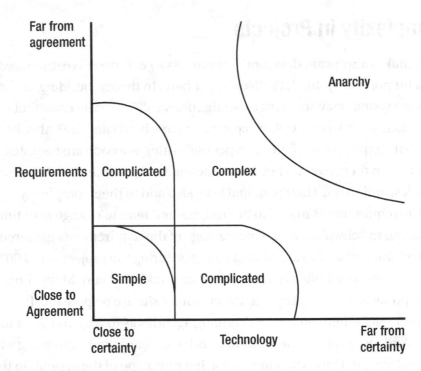

Figure 3-2. *Schwaber's complexity graph*

The projects in the anarchy area are chaotic and unworkable. To get them to their finish lines, you probably need to resolve serious issues before you even start the projects.

What Scrum tries to do is address this inherent complexity by implementing inspection, adaptation, and visibility, as you saw in the section "Empirical Process Control." Scrum does so by having simple practices and rules.

What Scrum Is

Scrum is a powerful, iterative, and incremental process. Many are fooled by its perceived simplicity, but it takes time to master. Figure 3-3 shows the skeleton of the Scrum model, to which we attached the rules and practices. In Scrum, you do development in time-boxed intervals called *iterations*. An iteration is usually between two and four weeks. Each iteration consists of daily inspections. Such an inspection—or daily Scrum, as it's called—is performed by the team once every day at a preset time.

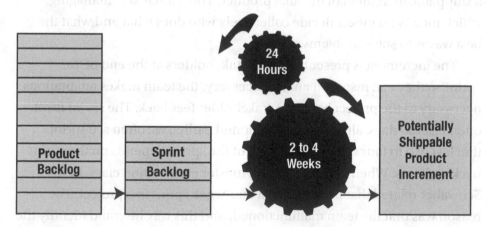

Figure 3-3. *The Scrum skeleton*

During these inspections, team members evaluate each other's work and the activities performed since the last inspection. If necessary, adjustments (*adaptations*) are found and implemented as quickly as possible. The iterations also conclude with inspections, when more adaptations can be made. This cycle repeats until it's no longer funded.

All the requirements that are known at the beginning of the project are gathered in the product backlog, which is one of the artifacts of Scrum. We come back to this shortly. The project team reviews the backlog and selects which requirements should be included in the first iteration—or *sprint*, as it's called in Scrum. These selected requirements are added to the sprint backlog, where they're broken down into more detailed items (*tasks*). Many teams visualize their work in a sprint using a scrum board, which can be electronic or it can be a whiteboard with sticky notes. The board shows the tasks that have been determined for each backlog item and where in the development process each task is currently located (development, test, and so on).

The team then makes its best effort to turn the sprint backlog into a shippable increment of the final product. The team is self-managing, which means members decide collectively who does what and what the best way is to solve problems.

The increment is presented to the stakeholders at the end of the sprint so they can inspect it and, if necessary, the team makes adaptations necessary to the project based on stakeholder feedback. The sprint most often lasts 30 days, although, as mentioned earlier, we often see sprints that last two to four weeks. The length of the sprint depends on the sprint backlog items. When I took his Scrum master certification class, Ken Schwaber related that he once had a one-week sprint in a project. The reason was that the team malfunctioned, and this way he could identify the reason for this more easily and adjust the process so the project ran more smoothly.

The stakeholders' adaptations and feedback are put into the product backlog and prioritized again. The team then starts the process over and selects the backlog items they think they can finish during the next sprint. These items are put into the sprint backlog for the next sprint and are broken down into more manageable items. And so it continues, until the stakeholders think they have received the business value they want, and then funding stops.

If you look again at the three legs of empirical process control, you can see that Scrum covers them nicely. Transparency is implemented by letting the team and stakeholders agree on the expected outcome of the project and of each iteration. Inspection occurs daily and also at the end of each sprint. Adaptations are the direct result of these inspections and are a necessary thing in Scrum.

Roles and Responsibilities in Scrum

There are only three core roles in the Scrum framework—a fact that has surprised many people over the years, especially those used to a more traditional process. The roles are as follows:

1. The product owner

2. The Scrum master

3. The development team

These people are, ideally, collocated to deliver potentially releasable product increments every sprint, but this can be hard to accomplish in a global organization (we'll come back to this topic later). Together, these three roles form the Scrum team.

Product owners represent the business side of the organization. This role is very important to any team in an organization. Without clear and strong product owners, teams will probably soon run into problems.

Product owners are the voice of the customer, and they make sure the team adds value to the organization throughout the project (or product development). One of the most important responsibilities of product owners is to manage the backlog and make sure the backlog reflects the needs of the company. To do this, product owners need to work closely with the project/product stakeholders. They also need to work closely with the development team and the Scrum master.

Product owners have several responsibilities, which are presented in Table 3-1.

Table 3-1. *Product Owner Responsibilities*

Responsibilities	Meaning in practice
Maximize the value of the product and the work of the development team.	Express product backlog items clearly.
Manage the product backlog.	Order the items in the product backlog to achieve goals and missions effectively
Be the business interface for high-level requirements.	Optimize the value of the work performed by the development team.
Own and communicate the product vision.	Ensure the product backlog is visible, transparent, and clear to all, and make sure it shows what the Scrum team will work on next.
Define the product road map.	Ensure the development team understands items in the product backlog to the level needed.

The Scrum master role is different from a traditional PM. Many people think the Scrum master is some kind of technical lead for the team, but this is not the case. The *Scrum Guide* (`www.scrumguides.org`) describes the Scrum master as a servant leader to the development team, the product owner, and the surrounding organization. This means the Scrum master works as a coach for the whole Scrum team, encouraging team members to perform better and better. The responsibilities for the Scrum master are shown in Table 3-2.

Table 3-2. *Scrum Master Responsibilities*

Responsibilities	Meaning in practice
Ensure Scrum is understood and enacted.	Ensure the Scrum team adheres to Scrum theory, practices, and rules.
	Lead and couch the organization in its Scrum adoption.
	Plan Scrum implementations within the organization.
Help those outside the Scrum team understand which of their interactions with the Scrum team are helpful and which aren't.	Help everyone change their interactions to maximize the value created by the Scrum team.
Remove impediments.	Protect the team by finding the resources to remove impediments so the team can work at a sustainable pace.

The responsibilities of the development team are described in Table 3-3. Team members are on the development team because they have a certain skill. If you are a member of this team, you are a developer. This simple arrangement removes any team hierarchy.

The team is jointly responsible for fulfilling the forecasted work of the sprint. Although one name be written beside a task, all team members are responsible for completing that task. The goal of this team structure is to foster collaboration.

The development team is a self-organizing team, responsible for planning and executing what is on the sprint backlog. But, being self-organizing may be hard, so the Scrum master might help the team achieve this.

Table 3-3. Development Team Responsibilities

Responsibilities	Meaning in practice
Do the work to complete the tasks by the end of each sprint.	Organize and manage the tasks assigned.

Development team members may have specialized skills and areas of expertise, but accountability for completing a product backlog task belongs to the entire development team. No one, not even the Scrum master, tells the development team how to turn the product backlog into increments of potentially releasable functionality.

Deliverables in Scrum

Now let's take a look at the deliverables described in the Scrum guide.

The Product backlog

The product backlog is an ordered list of all requirements on the product. They could be business requirements or technical requirements. Nonfunctional requirements, such as response times, regulatory requirements, and so on, are often part of the "definition of done" the team maintains for its work, but they could also be included in the product backlog.

The product owner is responsible for maintaining the backlog but does so in close collaboration with other stakeholders and business representatives as well as with the development team. The product owner needs to prioritize the backlog so it reflects the needs of the organization.

You can think of the product backlog as a living document that follows the product for as long as the product lives. Items, or product backlog items (PBIs) are often estimated using story points or some other relative estimation technique, which is discussed later.

Sprint Backlog

The sprint backlog is the development team's forecast of what it will deliver during the sprint. It is also the plan for how the team will do the work to accomplish the increment at the end of the sprint.

The sprint backlog consists of tasks broken down from PBIs during sprint planning. In many cases, these tasks are estimated with remaining work—a number that many teams update each day. In this way, they can track progress with a burndown chart (Figure 3-4) that allows good transparency on the progress of the work during the sprint, making it easy to see whether the team will reach the forecast.

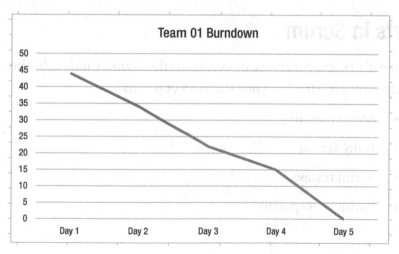

Figure 3-4. *A burndown chart*

This backlog is also a living document, but it is the development team that owns and updates the sprint backlog. Because it is a self-organizing team, team members can add and remove tasks as they wish as long as they follow the PBIs selected during sprint planning.

Product Increment

The increment is the sum of all backlog items completed during a sprint and includes what has been delivered so far in the project. At the end of a sprint, the new increment must be done, which means it must be in useable condition and meet the Scrum team's definition of "done."

Sprint Goal

The sprint goal is created at sprint planning and is the target for the sprint. It is a vision that guides the team to why they built the increment in the sprint.

Although the team and the product owner collaborate on this goal, it is important that product owners explain their vision for the coming three to four sprints.

Events in Scrum

There are also some meetings, or events, as the *Scrum Guide* calls them, that helps you keep track of your status as you work:

- Sprint planning

- Daily Scrum

- Sprint review

- Sprint retrospective

Sprint planning

The purpose of the sprint planning meeting is to decide the following:

- What can be delivered in the increment resulting from the upcoming sprint?

- How will the work needed to deliver the increment be achieved?

This is the first meeting that occurs in a sprint, and the entire Scrum team is present. The meeting has a time box of eight hours for a calendar-month sprint. For a shorter sprint, this time is usually shorter. The *Scrum Guide* is not more specific than this, but a good rule is that the time box is four hours for a two-week sprint, six hours for a three-week sprint, and so on.

During the sprint planning meeting, any changes to the product backlog since last refinement meeting are discussed so that the team has a good product backlog from which to work. The capacity (or the number of hours available for the team to work during the sprint) of the team—for the entire team and for the individual competences in the team—is reviewed. After this is determined, the team starts to break down the PBIs, starting from the top.

The team does this by figuring out which tasks are needed for each PBI. The tasks could be designing, writing code, writing tests, performing tests, and so on. Then, these tasks are estimated with the remaining hours to build a good burndown chart during the sprint.

Daily Scrum

The daily Scrum meeting is a meeting (see Figure 3-5) that, in the best of worlds, takes place every 24 hours (working days), at the same place, and at the same time. The reasoning behind this is that this approach reduces complexity. We don't have to think about where the meeting is or when it is; it's where and when it always is. When team members are spread out

81

in different locations and time zones, this is harder to accomplish, but you can overcome these obstacles by using tools such as Azure DevOps and Microsoft Teams.

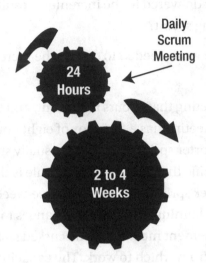

Figure 3-5. *The daily Scrum event in Scrum*

During the meeting, individual members of the development team answer three questions:

1. What did you complete yesterday that contributed to the team meeting its sprint goal? This is a status report to the other team members.

2. What do you plan to complete today to contribute to the team meeting its sprint goal? This is the plan for the next 24 hours.

3. Do you see any impediments that could prevent you or the team from meeting its sprint goal? This is a way to identify any risks that could prevent the team from meeting its goal.

This is the suggested way of doing this meeting according to the *Scrum Guide*, but it is not set in stone. It is an efficient way for the team to get quick feedback and see if it needs to change anything in the short term.

Sprint Review

When the sprint comes to an end, it is time for the development team to show what it delivered and to get feedback on it from the product owner and stakeholders. This is done during a sprint review, which is another time boxed-meeting: three hours for a calendar-month sprint.

To this meeting, the Scrum team should invite persons that can give valuable feedback on the work delivered so far. To get this feedback, the team demonstrates real code (if software is the deliverable) to the audience and then discusses any feedback received. The feedback is then input to either the product backlog or to the retrospective following the review.

Sprint retrospective

During the sprint retrospective, the team reflects on the past sprint, and identifies and agrees on continuous process improvement actions.

Some guidelines valuable to sprint retrospectives include the following:

- Two main questions are asked during the sprint retrospective: What went well during the sprint? What could be improved during the next sprint?

- The recommended duration is one and a half hours for a two-week sprint (and is proportional for other sprint durations).

- This event is facilitated by the Scrum master.

There are many ways a retrospective can be performed. It is important not to let this meeting become boring. It is an important meeting, and the Scrum master needs to infuse inspiration into the meeting.

Backlog Refinement

The last event is the backlog refinement (previously known as *backlog grooming*). Backlog refinement is an ongoing process of reviewing PBIs and checking that they are prioritized appropriately and prepared in a way that makes them clear and executable for teams after they enter sprints via sprint planning.

Larger PBIs may be broken into multiple smaller ones; acceptance criteria may be clarified; and dependencies, investigation, and preparatory work may be identified and agreed as technical spikes (similar to a small proof of concept). Count on spending up to 10% of the available capacity on refinement.

Definition of Done

The definition of done is very important, but it also tends to be forgotten. In many projects, at the end of (or during) a sprint or the project, we've seen arguments between the delivering development organization and the person ordering the project about whether a task has been completed. Perhaps testing was not done the way the client assumed it would be, or the software doesn't comply with certain regulations. The following conversation is typical:

> [Product owner, Sofia, stops by the office of developer Mike to check on how things are going.]
>
> S: Hi! How's the cool new feature you're working on coming along?
>
> M: It's going great. I'm done with it right now and will start the next feature soon.
>
> S: Great! Then I can show it to our customer, who's coming here after lunch. He'll be very excited!

M: No, no. Hold on. I am not "done" done with it. I still need to fix some test cases, do some refactoring, get it into the build process, and so on. I thought you were wondering if I had gotten somewhere with it.

For the most part, such discussions can be avoided if people sit down together at the beginning and write and sign a definition of done.

There are other reasons for having a definition of done as well. For the team to estimate a user story, the team members need to know when they're done with it; otherwise, it's very hard to complete the estimate. For a specific user story (requirement), you know it's done when you've fulfilled its acceptance criteria. But where do all those general things such as style guides, code analysis, build automation, test automation, regulatory compliance, governance, nonfunctional requirements, and so on, fit in? They affect the estimate of a user story as well.

Here is where the definition of done comes into play. The definition of done tells you what requirements, in addition to the user story's acceptance criteria, you need to fulfill to be done with the story. You include the general requirements in the definition of done because they affect all user stories in the end.

The definition of done is your primary quality document. If you don't accomplish what is in it, you don't deliver quality. It's essential that the product owner and the team agree on the definition of done. The definition of done is part of the agreement between the team and the product owner.

There shouldn't be an argument over this concept during the project. If the product owner thinks it's too costly to use pair programming or TDD, have the product owner sign the definition of done, which specifies that these things have been removed. If, at the end of a sprint, the product owner complains about the number of bugs, you can present the document and say the product owner removed essential parts of the testing process, so bugs will be present.

A good starting point for a definition of done could be something like the following:

- *Environments are prepared for release*: First check that no unintegrated *work in progress* (WIP) has been left in any development or staging environment. Next, check that the continuous integration framework is verified and working, including regression tests and automated code reviews. The build engine ought to be configured to schedule a build on check-in. It may also trigger hourly or nightly builds. Also, check that all of the test data used to validate the features in the release have been validated.

- *Handover to support is complete*: All design models and specifications, including user stories and tests, must be accepted by support personnel who will maintain the increment henceforth. They must also be satisfied that they are in control of the supporting environment. (Note: This may be elided in a DevOps context or when a development team follows the product through to support.)

- *Review is ready*: Part of the work in a sprint includes preparing for the review. Sprint metrics should be available, including burndown or burnup charts. Any user stories that have not been completed need to be reestimated and returned to the product backlog.

- *Code is complete*: Any and all to-do annotations are resolved, and the source code is commented to the satisfaction of the development team. Source code is refactored to make it understandable, maintainable, and better able to support future changes. (Note that the red-green-refactor pattern found in TDD is helpful here.)

Unit test cases are complete: Unit test cases are designed for all features in development and allow requirements to be traced to the code implementation, such as by clear, feature-relevant naming conventions. The degree of code coverage is established and meets or exceeds the standard required. The unit test cases are executed and the increment is proved to work as expected.

Peer reviews are complete: Source code is checked into the configuration management system with appropriate peer-reviewed comments added. The source code is merged with the main branch, and automatic deployment into elevated environments is verified. (Note: If pair programming is used, a separate peer review session might not be required.)

- *Testing is complete*: Functional testing is done, including both automated testing and manual exploratory testing. A test report is generated. All outstanding defects (or incidents such as build issues) are elicited and resolved or accepted by the team as not being contraindicative to release. Regression testing is completed and the functionality provided in previous iterations is shown to work. Performance, security, and user acceptance testing is done, and the product works on all required platforms.

Sometimes it is also good to have a definition of "ready," which states the requirements a team has on the requirement itself before accepting it into a sprint. One example could look like the following:

- Story is clearly defined so that all team members can understand what needs to be done.

- Story includes clear business value for product owner to prioritize.

- Story includes acceptance criteria.

- Story includes any required enabling specs, wire frames, storyboards, and so on.

- Story is estimated and sized to complete easily within one sprint.

- Story is free from external dependencies so the team can start working on it.

Let's continue by looking at how you can manage requirements and estimations with an Agile mind-set.

Agile Requirements and Estimation

Agile requirements and estimation is a huge but important topic. This section covers some of the most important topics, but there are a lot of ways you can manage requirements and estimates. If you want to master this subject, there are several training courses you can take and books to read. A good starting point is to visit www.scrum.org or www.scrumalliance.com and see what they currently suggest.

Most of the Agile planning and estimation tips and tricks in this chapter come from the Agile community but aren't specific to Scrum. Scrum really doesn't tell you how to do specific things such as planning, estimation, and so on. Scrum is the process framework or process method you use for running your Agile projects. However, Scrum works very well with the concepts we look at next.

Requirements

In Agile projects, you usually represent requirements in something called *user stories.* These can be looked at as fluffy requirements—a bit like use cases. You write user stories like this:

> As a <type of user>, I want <some functionality> so I may have <some business value>.

An example is as follows:

> As a manager, I want my consultants to be able to submit expense reports through the Internet so that I can be more efficient in processing expense reports.

Figure 3-6 shows how Microsoft has implemented a user story into the work item type PBI in Microsoft TFS. The terminology is a little different from the previous description, but it works.

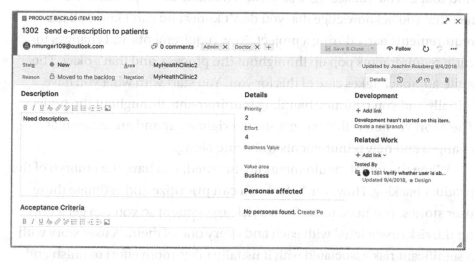

Figure 3-6. *A user story implementation in the Scrum template Microsoft provides with TFS*

User stories capture requirements at a high level and aren't tangled up with detailed functions or implementation details. The details and nonfunctional requirements are instead captured as acceptance criteria for the user story. Based on these acceptance criteria, you can develop acceptance tests at the same time you write the requirements. The definition of done is also important here because it describes other critical requirements that all user stories need to fulfill before they're considered done.

So, how can you begin gathering requirements before you start a project? Product owners should use any method they think is suitable. We often use story-writing workshops, during which key stakeholders, end users, business analysts, experienced developers, and others participate to brainstorm user stories. During such a workshop, you focus on the big picture and don't dive into details. These big-picture user stories are often called *epics* because they're large and not broken down yet.

But don't you need to find all requirements at the beginning? No. And that is what makes Agile so great. The Agile concept builds on the fact that you acknowledge that you don't know and can't know all the requirements early during a project. New requirements and changes to early requirements pop up throughout the process, and that's okay. The Agile approach takes care of this for you. You start with what you have initially and you continue handling requirements throughout the project. The short version is that you get started right away and are aware that changes and new requirements will come along.

When the initial requirements are finished, you have the embryo of the product backlog. However, before you can prioritize and estimate these user stories, you need to perform a risk assessment so you can get a grip on the risks associated with each and every one of them. A user story with a significant risk associated with it usually takes more effort to finish and should probably be done early during development.

Estimation

To know how much effort is involved with a user story, you need to estimate it. The sum of all initial estimates gives you a (very) rough estimate of how much time the entire project may take. But, because you know things usually change over time, you don't consider this estimate written in stone.

You have what you need to estimate: You know the requirements, you have a definition of done, and you have acceptance criteria. In the Agile world, it's recommended that you estimate time using a measure called *story points*. Story points aren't an exact size—instead, they're relative.

Here is an easy example we use when running Agile training. Take four animals—let's say a cat, a pig, a zebra, and an elephant. Without being a zoologist, most people can say that the pig is three times the size of the cat, the zebra is twice the size of a pig, and the elephant is maybe four times the size of the zebra. If you have a couple of people sit down and discuss these animal sizes, you can pretty soon come up with an agreement about their relative sizes.

The same goes for user stories. Most developers can agree pretty quickly about the relative size of user stories. User story A is twice as big as user story B, and so on. You don't need to be very experienced with the details of each user story to reach this agreement. Novice developers usually end up with the same estimates as experienced ones. Keep in mind that you aren't talking exact time yet, only relative size.

The most common scale for expressing story points is a modified Fibonacci scale. This scale follows the sequence 1, 2, 3, 5, 8, 13, 20, 40, 100.

Often, teams use a technique called *planning poker* when doing estimates. Each player has a deck of cards containing the numbers from the modified Fibonacci scale. Here is how planning poker goes:

1. The product owner/Scrum master reads the first user story.

2.   The team members briefly consider the user story and select a card each, without showing it to the others.

3.   The team members show their cards at the same time.

4.   If the result varies much, the people with the highest and lowest cards explain their reasoning.

5.   After a short discussion, the team plays again.

6.   When consensus is reached (or the team members are only one step apart), you're finished.

7.   If the team still disagrees, you pick the highest value.

But what about time? How do you get down to time? You need to know several things to estimate time. The first is *team capacity*. Consider the following when calculating team capacity:

- How long is the sprint?

- How many working days are available in the sprint?

- How many days does each team member work during the sprint? Consider planned vacation or other days off, planned meetings, and so on.

- Deduct the time for sprint planning, review, and retrospective meetings.

The result is the capacity before drag (*drag* is waste time or unknown activities). You should measure drag in each sprint, but during initial planning it's hard to know how much to include. The longer the project, the more accurate the drag. If you don't know from experience what the drag is, 25 percent is a good landmark; included in this is the 10% backlog refinement.

Now you have the available number of hours in the sprint, and you can connect points and time. You need to know the *team velocity*, which is the number of story points the team can handle in a sprint. Initially, this is impossible to know. The easiest way to figure it out is to conduct a sprint planning meeting and create a theoretical team velocity. At this meeting, the team breaks down a user story into manageable tasks—and this is where time becomes interesting. During this meeting, the team estimates tasks in hours so it can plan the sprint and decide how many user stories it can take on. The team usually does this as follows:

1. Estimate the first user story in detail.

2. Break down what the team needs to do to deliver the story.

3. Estimate hours for each activity, then summarize.

4. Deduct the summary from the available time the team has in the sprint.

5. Is there still time left? If so, take a new user story and repeat the process until no time is left.

6. Summarize the number of story points from the stories included in the sprint.

Now you have a theoretical velocity.

At this point, you can make a rough time plan for the entire (at this point) project. This is good input for the product owner to use in discussions with stakeholders, and also for return on investment (ROI) calculations. The sprint planning process continues throughout the project, and the theoretical velocity can soon be replaced with one based on experience.

Backlog

When the initial user stories are in place and estimated with story points, the product owner can begin prioritizing the backlog. In Scrum, this is called *ordering the backlog.* Based on business needs, the product owner makes sure the order of the backlog reflects what the business wants. In Figure 3-7, you can see a backlog in Azure DevOps. Usually, we do a rough estimate for each backlog item and then velocity planning. After that, we can see which backlog items should be completed during which sprint.

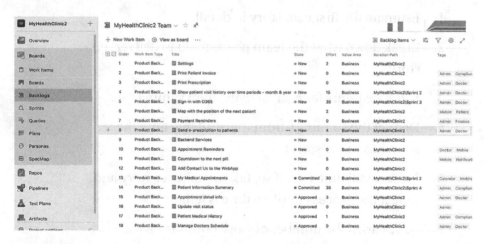

Figure 3-7. *A sample backlog in Azure DevOps*

The product owner needs to keep the backlog in good shape throughout the project. This means it needs to be ordered. It also needs fine granularity at the top (perhaps three or four sprints down the list) and rougher granularity farther down. Keeping the backlog in your ALM tool set gives you the benefit of visibility and traceability. In the best of all worlds, you can link backlog items to code, check-ins, builds, and so on, giving you good traceability.

The product owner can also start to look at release planning at this point. It's important to get an overview of coming releases, especially if you have a larger project. Release planning can be done on the epics (the larger user stories). A good approach is to look for themes among the user stories. What could be useful to release at the same time? If you find such features, you can make a theme from them and plan the theme for a certain release. When this is done, you can also do a very rough time estimate on the releases—and suddenly you also have a rough time plan for the entire project.

Now you have as much information that you could possibly ask for this early in a project. The next step is the sprint planning meeting, when the team members (as you saw earlier) select the backlog items they feel they can commit to during the sprint.

During the Sprint

During the sprint, you use several important meetings to inspect and adapt your process. We already covered the sprint planning meeting, which takes place at the start of each sprint, but there are other meetings as well, and all important to the Agile team.

Daily Standup

The daily standup is a meeting that takes place every day during a sprint. It is primarily a developer team meeting and is used to provide status updates to the team members. As the name suggests, this is a standup meeting, which comes from the practice of having attendees stand at a meeting because the discomfort of standing for long periods helps keep the meeting short.

The daily standups are kept short, at around 15 minutes, so participants can infer this isn't a working meeting.

As mentioned earlier, all participants should answer these three questions:

1. What did you complete yesterday that contributed to the team meeting its sprint goal?

2. What do you plan to complete today to contribute to the team meeting its sprint goal?

3. Do you see any impediments that could prevent you or the team from meeting its sprint goal?

Although it may not be practical to limit all discussion to these three questions, the goal is to stick to them as closely as possible. If further discussions are needed, they should be scheduled for after the meeting. For instance, when team members ask for short clarifications and brief statements, they should try to remember that they should talk about those more after the meeting.

One of the important features of the daily standup is that it's intended to be a communication meeting for team members and not a status update for management or other stakeholders. However, it can be valuable for product owners to participate in the meeting so they can identify any issues they need to address. This may remove the need for other status meetings afterward.

The meeting is usually held at the same time and place every workday. All team members are encouraged to attend, but meetings aren't postponed if some team members aren't present.

This practice also promotes closer working relationships with its frequency, need for follow-up conversations, and short duration, which in turn results in a greater rate of knowledge transfer—a much more active result than a typical status meeting.

Kanban

We'd like to present another method that is usually mentioned with Agile frameworks. *Kanban* is very popular in many organizations and is used by one of our customers today. Although our preferred project management method is Scrum for development projects, we realize that Scrum isn't perfect in every situation. Scrum can be scary in the sense that it requires major changes in the way people work in their organizations. It can be hard to implement Scrum fully because humans seem to have an inherent resistance to change. And if you don't have management with you, it's even harder to implement. Wouldn't it be great if you could find a process that was agile, but made it possible for you to make changes gradually?

Operations can also be difficult to perform using Scrum. Think about this situation for a moment. Let's assume you have three-week sprints for your operations team. One week into a sprint, you suddenly realize there is a bug in the system that affects production. This bug needs to be fixed right away, so you write a backlog item and present it to the product owner. You need to bring it to the next sprint planning meeting, which will be held in two weeks. Then, it will take three weeks for the bug to be fixed, because you have three-week sprints. In the worst case, you'll have to wait five weeks before the fix is available for deployment.

Of course, this is a rare situation. There are obviously ways to handle this better using Scrum. You could, for instance, always have a PBI of 10% of your available time set aside for bug fixes, and put this PBI at the top of your sprint backlog, allowing you to work on bugs as they're discovered. But, we still don't think Scrum is optimal for operations work. This is why we started to look at Kanban.

The name *Kanban* comes from the Japanese word for *sign board*. Kanban goes back to the early days of the Toyota production system. Between 1940 and 1950, Taiichi Ohno developed kanbans to control production between processes and to implement just-in-time manufacturing at Toyota manufacturing plants in Japan. The *Kanban method* was developed by David J. Anderson and is an approach to an incremental, evolutionary process as well as systems change for organizations.[10] By using a work-in-progress limited pull system as the core mechanism, it exposes system operation (or process) problems. In such a pull system, tasks that are to be performed are pulled into the workflow, similar to when you pull a PBI into the sprint backlog. But, you can only pull a task into the workflow when there is free capacity to handle the task. It also stimulates collaboration to improve the system continuously.

The Kanban method has three basic principles[11]:

1. Start with what you do now.

2. Agree to pursue incremental, evolutionary change.

3. Respect the current process, roles, responsibilities, and titles.

Let's take a closer look at these.

---

[10]David J. Anderson, *Agile Management for Software Engineering: Applying the Theory of Constraints for Business Results* (Prentice Hall, 2003), and *Kanban: Successful Evolutionary Change for your Technology Business* (Blue Hole Press, 2010).

[11]Taiichi Ohno and Norman Bodek, *Toyota Production System: Beyond Large-Scale Production* (Productivity Press, 1988).

Start with What You Do Now

The Kanban method doesn't prescribe a specific set of roles or process steps. There is no such thing as the Kanban software development process or the Kanban project management method. The Kanban method starts with the roles and processes you have and stimulates continuous, incremental, and evolutionary changes to your system. This is the thing we like the best about Kanban. It allows you to continue using what you've invested in; the biggest difference is that you can implement big improvements to the existing process without worrying employees.

Agree to Pursue Incremental, Evolutionary Change

The organization (or team) must agree that continuous, incremental, and evolutionary change is the way to make system improvements and make them stick. Sweeping changes may seem more effective, but more often than not they fail because of resistance and fear in the organization. The Kanban method encourages continuous, small, incremental, and evolutionary changes to your current system.

Respect the Current Process, Roles, Responsibilities, and Titles

It's likely that the organization currently has some elements that work acceptably and are worth preserving. You must seek to drive out fear to facilitate future change. By agreeing to respect current roles, responsibilities, and job titles, you eliminate initial fears. This enables you to gain broader support for your Kanban initiative. Presenting Kanban—rather than an alternative, more sweeping approach that could lead to changes in titles, roles, and responsibilities, and perhaps the wholesale removal of certain positions—may help individuals realize the benefits of this approach.

The Five Core Properties

David Anderson, in his book *Kanban*, identified five core properties that are part of each successful implementation of the Kanban method:

1. Visualize the workflow.

2. Limit WIP.

3. Manage flow.

4. Make process policies explicit.

5. Improve collaboratively (using models and the scientific method).

Let's look at these and see what they mean.

Visualize the Workflow

The knowledge work of today hides its workflow in information systems. to understand how work works, so to speak, it's important to visualize the flow of work. The right changes are harder to perform if you don't understand the workflow. One common way to visualize workflow is by using a wall with cards and columns, called a *Kanban board*. The columns on the card wall represent the different states or steps in the workflow, and the cards are the feature, story, task, and/or result of the workflow, usually referred to as *work items*.

What is great is that you use the steps of your existing workflow. You don't need to enforce a new way of working that changes the current approach dramatically. You basically place the Kanban process on top of what you have, then visualize this flow. This often feels more comfortable to coworkers and makes them more positive about the small changes you're imposing on them.

Figure 3-8 shows a Kanban board used to visualize flow. But wait! Some might of you might say: Isn't this just like the Scrum board shown in Figure 3-9? Yes, but there is one significant difference if you compare the figures closely. Above each Kanban board column is a number that identifies the WIP limit. This takes us to the next core property: limit WIP.

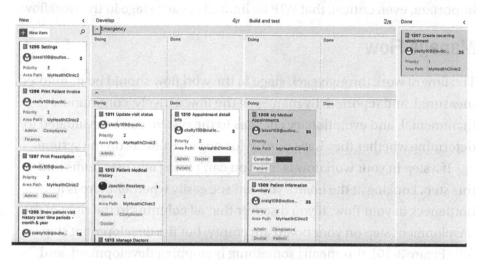

Figure 3-8.   A Kanban board in Azure DevOps

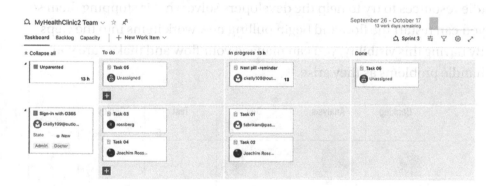

Figure 3-9.   A Scrum board

Limit WIP

The WIP limit is important and tells you how many work items you can have in each step (column on the Kanban board). When the limit is reached, you can't pull any new items into this step until a work item leaves the step. Limiting WIP implies that a pull system is implemented on parts or all of the workflow. The pull system acts as one of the main stimuli for continuous, incremental, and evolutionary changes to your system. It's important, even critical, that WIP be limited at each stage in the workflow.

Manage Flow

The flow of work through each stage in the workflow should be monitored, measured, and reported. By managing the flow actively, continuous, incremental, and evolutionary changes to the system can be evaluated to determine whether they have positive or negative effects on the system.

If a step in your workflow is full, you can't bring any new items into this step. Looking at the board, you can see easily whether there is a bottleneck in your flow. If you discover that all columns to the right of the development step on your board are empty, but the development step is full (Figure 3-10), this means something is stopping development, and people working on development can't finalize their work. You should use idle resources to try to help the developers solve what is stopping them so you can restart the flow and begin pulling new work items into the steps. By having this visibility, you can manage your flow and make sure you handle problems as they arise.

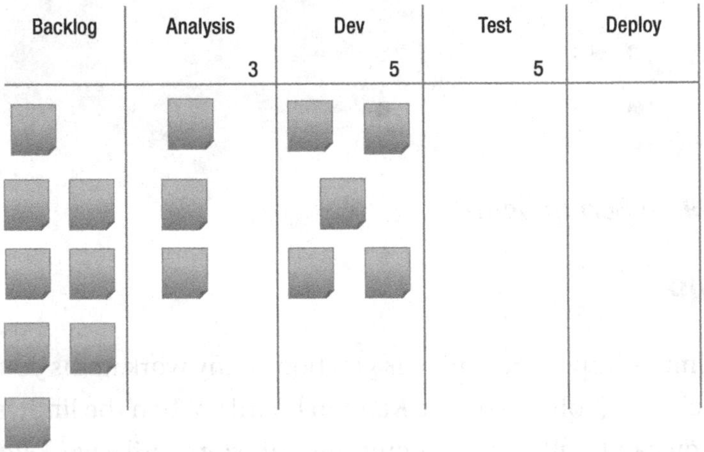

Backlog	Analysis	Dev	Test	Deploy
	3	5	5	

Figure 3-10. *A bottleneck in the workflow is discovered*

102

Make Process Policies Explicit

It's often hard to improve, or even start a discussion of improving, a process until the mechanism of the process is made explicit. Without an explicit understanding of how things work and how work is actually done, any discussion of problems often seems subjective or emotional. To get a more rational, empirical, and objective discussion of issues, explicit understanding is important. This will most likely lead to consensus on improvement suggestions.

Improve Collaboratively

Kanban encourages small, continuous, incremental, and evolutionary changes that stick. David Anderson also discovered this was very effective. Resistance to change, as we've mentioned, is easier to overcome if the steps are small and each step has a great payback. Teams that have a shared understanding of theories about work, workflow, process, and risk are more likely to be able to build a common understanding of a problem and thereby suggest improvement actions that can be agreed on by consensus. The Kanban method proposes a scientific approach to be used to implement continuous, incremental, and evolutionary changes, but the Kanban method doesn't prescribe a specific scientific method to use.

Common Models Used to Understand Work in Kanban

Some common models are often used with Kanban to understand how work actually works. We don't go into these in detail here, but we include them for reference:

- The theory of constraints (the study of bottlenecks)

- The system of profound knowledge (a study of variation and how it affects processes)

- The lean economic model [based on the concepts of "waste" (or muda, muri, and mura)]

eXtreme Programming

eXtreme Programming (XP) is a deliberate and disciplined approach to software development. XP, like Scrum, was a direct outcome of the Agile Manifesto and incorporates many of its values. Aspects of these models were in the minds of their founders for a long time though and were used in many projects. XP stresses customer satisfaction—an important part of the Agile Manifesto. The methodology is designed to deliver the software the customer needs, when it's needed. XP focuses on responding to changing customer requirements, even late in the life cycle, so that customer satisfaction (business value) is ensured.

XP also emphasizes teamwork. Managers, customers, and developers are all part of a team dedicated to delivering high-quality software. XP implements a simple and effective way to handle teamwork.

There are four ways XP improves software teamwork:

1. *Communication*: It's essential that XP programmers communicate with their customers and fellow programmers.

2. *Simplicity*: The design should be simple and clean.

3. *Feedback*: Feedback is supplied by testing the software from the first day of development. Testing is done by writing the unit tests before writing the code. This is called *TDD*, and it is becoming a frequently used practice in many projects, not only Agile ones. Later, we describe how TFS implements TDD.

4. *Courage*: The software should be delivered to customers as early as possible, and a goal is to implement changes as suggested. XP stresses that developers should be able to respond courageously to changing requirements and technology based on this foundation.

RUP has use cases and XP has *user stories*. These serve the same purpose as use cases, but they aren't the same. They're used to create time estimates for the project and also replace bulky requirements documentation. The stakeholders (managers, end users, project sponsors, and so on) are responsible for writing the user stories, which should be about things the system needs to do for them. Stakeholders write stories because they're the ones who know what functionality they need and desire; developers rarely have this kind of information. Each user story consists of about three sentences of text written by the stakeholder in the stakeholder's own terminology, without any of the technical software jargon that a developer may use.

Another important issue is that XP stresses the importance of delivering working software in increments so the customer can give feedback as early as possible. By expecting that this will happen, developers are ready to implement changes.

The last topic we want to highlight with XP is *pair programming*. All code to be included in a production release is created by two people working together at a single computer. This approach increases software quality without impacting time to delivery. Although we've never had the benefit of trying this ourselves, coworkers with whom we've spoken who have used pair programming are confident that it adds as much functionality as two developers working separately. The difference is that quality is much greater. Laurie Williams of the University of Utah in Salt Lake City has shown that pair programmers are 15% slower than two independent individual programmers, but "error-free" code increases from 70% to 85%.[12] In our opinion, this more than makes up for the decrease in speed.

We can make a reference to my old job as an assistant air-traffic controller here. Many are the times I sat in the tower when airplane traffic was so heavy that I needed help to keep track of every airplane. We're aware that this isn't the same thing, but the fact remains that two pairs of eyes see more than one pair—and this is what makes pair programming so attractive.

To learn more about XP, we encourage you to visit `www.extremeprogramming.org/`.

Scaling Agile

What happens if you have more team members than can fit on a Scrum team (seven plus/minus two people)? What if 90 people are involved in the project? Can Scrum scale to handle this? According to Mike Cohn, in an article on the Scrum Alliance web site,[13] you can use a process called *Scrum of Scrums*.

The Scrum-of-Scrums meeting is an important technique in scaling Scrum to large-team projects. These meetings allow clusters of teams to discuss their work, focusing especially on areas of overlap and integration. Imagine a perfectly balanced project comprising seven teams each with seven team members. Each of the seven teams would conduct (simultaneously or sequentially) its own daily Scrum meeting. Each team

---

[12]Laurie Williams and Robert Kessler, *Pair Programming Illuminated* (Addison-Wesley, 2003).

[13]Mike Cohn, "Advice on Conducting the Scrum of Scrums Meeting," `www.scrumalliance.org/articles/46-advice-on-conducting-the-scrum-of-scrums-meeting`, May 7, 2007.

would then designate one person to attend a Scrum-of-Scrums meeting. The decision of who to send should belong to the team. Usually the person chosen is a technical contributor on the team—a programmer, tester, DBA, designer, and so on—rather than a product owner or Scrum master.

By using this technique, you can scale Scrum infinitely, at least in theory.

But there are other ways to scale Scrum, and Agile as well. We take a look at three of them here:

1. Scrum of Scrums

2. Scaled Agile Framework (SAFe)

3. Scaled Professional Scrum (SPS)

Scrum of Scrums

The simplest and easiest way of scaling Scrum is by holding a Scrum-of-Scrums meeting. This way of syncing among teams is good when we have five to eight teams that need to sync.

The Scrum teams (A, B, C, D, E, and F in Figure 3-11) each have their ordinary Scrum meetings. Each day at the daily Scrum they select one or two persons to attend the next-day Scrum-of-Scrums meeting together with the other teams' representatives. Some teams send their Scrum master whereas others may send a developer. It is up to the team to decide who attends.

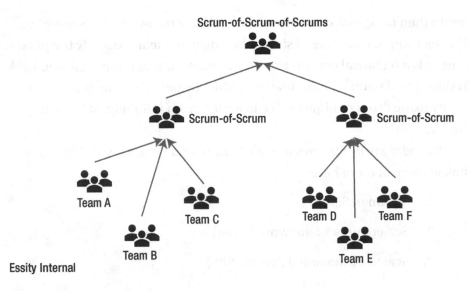

Essity Internal

Figure 3-11. *Scrum of Scrums*

The Scrum-of-Scrums meeting is like any of the other daily Scrums during which representatives talk about what their teams have done since the last meeting, what they are going to do to before the next meeting, and whether they have impediments that may affect their progress.

A recommended way of running the meeting is to focus on the following questions (Mike Cohn, `https://www.mountaingoatsoftware.com/articles/advice-on-conducting-the-scrum-of-scrums-meeting`):

- What has your team done since we last met?

- What will your team do before we meet again?

- Is anything slowing your team down or getting in its way?

- Are you about to put something in another team's way?

The reason for asking the last question is that it can be very helpful when we need to coordinate many teams.

Impediments are resolved with focus on the challenges of coordination among the teams. Solutions may include agreeing to interfaces among teams, negotiating responsibility boundaries, and so on.

The participants of the Scrum of Scrums tracks items via a backlog of its own, and each item contributes to improving among-team coordination. The Scrum of Scrums, however, very seldom manage that backlog like the team's backlog with sprint planning. The reasoning is that the participants first and foremost are members of their own team and the focus is on that team.

SAFe

SAFe started out as a book by Dean Leffingwell in 2007. In 2011, it was named the Scaled Agile Framework (SAFe) and the organization Scaled Agile was founded. This is the organization that works on refining the framework. Right now, SAFe is in version 4.6.

SAFe is freely available on the company's web site, so anybody can access the framework. There are numerous training sessions offered by SAFe partners and consultants, and it is strongly recommended that you attend such training before implementing SAFe. The Agile leaders in the implementation are the first that should be trained so that the implementation is as successful as possible.

When a team setup reaches more than 40 to 50 people, it might be worthwhile to look into SAFe because a Scrum-of-Scrums might not be effective any longer.

SAFe is available in four flavors at this point, and they all depend on how an organization is set up and the needs it has. There is no way to cover the entire framework here, so we look at these four versions as an overview in this chapter.

Essential SAFe

The starting point for all SAFe implementations is the Essential SAFe setup (Figure 3-12). Agile teams work in what is called an *Agile release train* (ART) that consists of 125 to 150 persons and delivers value with a certain cadence.

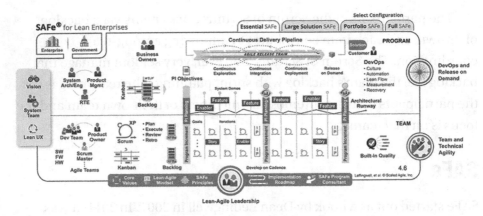

Figure 3-12. *Essential SAFe*

The ART leaves the station at certain intervals. A common setup is to have an ART leave the station every five sprints. The length of the sprints is two to three weeks, so a train leaves every 10 to 15 weeks (Figure 3-13).

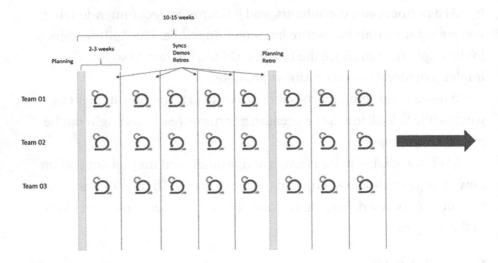

Figure 3-13. *Cadence*

A train starts with a two-day session called *program iteration planning*, or PI planning for short. It takes place during the last iteration of the previous ART. This is a big-room planning in which all members of all teams on the ART are present as well as business owners, product managers, and system architects/engineers. This meeting is the heart of SAFe and is necessary to run SAFe.

PI planning delivers many business benefits according to the SAFe documentation:

- Establishes face-to-face communication across all team members and stakeholders.

- Builds the social network on which the ART depends.

- Aligns development to business goals with the business context, vision, and team and program PI objectives.

- Identifies dependencies and fosters cross-team and cross-ART collaboration.

- Provides the opportunity for "just the right amount" of architecture and Lean user experience guidance.

- Matches demand to capacity, thus eliminating excess WIP.

- Enables fast decision making.

A successful PI planning event delivers two primary outputs:

1. *Committed PI objectives*: A set of objectives created by each team with the business value assigned by the business owners

2. *Program board*: A board that highlights new-feature delivery dates, feature dependencies among teams and with other ARTs, and relevant milestones

When the train leaves the station, the first iteration of the ART starts. The teams work according to Scrum and have the same iteration length. They can also use Kanban if they want.

Every team has one product owner, one Scrum master, and three to nine developers. This is the same setup found in the *Scrum Guide*.

The final iteration is called the *innovation and planning iteration*, which acts as an estimating buffer for meeting PI objectives and provides dedicated time for innovation, continuing education, PI planning, and inspect and adapt events. The goal of this iteration is to have some time devoted to innovation and not simply focus on deliver. During this iteration, the entire ART demos the combined solution and gets feedback on that.

The release train engineer (RTE) is the person who runs the train. Look on this role as an Agile PM. The RTE works in close collaboration with the system engineer/architect and the product management team.

There is a backlog, called the *program backlog*, for the whole ART managed by the product managers. The program backlog is the holding area for upcoming features, which are intended to address user needs and deliver business benefits for a single ART. It also contains the enabler features necessary to build the architectural runway (the technical infrastructure necessary for building features).

If we have bigger needs than Essential SAFe, we can scale up to the Large-Solution SAFe.

Large-Solution SAFe

The Large-Solution SAFe (Figure 3-14) contains the roles, artifacts, and processes needed to build large and complex solutions. This version of SAFe includes a stronger focus on capturing requirements in something called the *solution intent*, which is the intent you have for your solution, what you will accomplish in the longer term. With Large-Solution SAFe, you also work on coordinating multiple ARTs and even suppliers. You might also have needs that ensure compliance with regulations and standards.

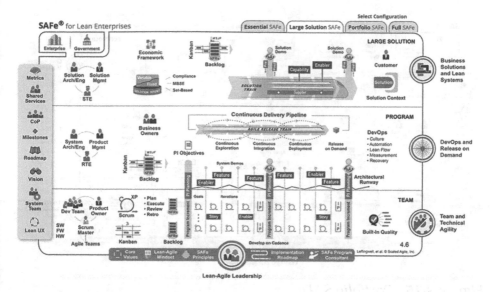

Figure 3-14. *Large-Solution SAFe*

So, a Large-Solution SAFe is an ART (called a *solution train*) that runs more than one ART within itself. There is basically no upper limit on how many trains you can run in this configuration. Each individual ART is run as it is in Essential SAFe. What differs is that the setup is extended with a solution train engineer, solution architect/engineer, and solution management. Solution management works with a solution backlog the same way product management does for a program.

Portfolio SAFe

So far, we have assumed that we only work with one value stream in our organization. The level above this includes several value streams and is called *Portfolio SAFe* (Figure 3-15). Each of these value streams can include one or more solution trains. Here you start working with strategy and investment funding, which are defined for the value streams and their solutions. At this level, you also provide Agile portfolio operations and Lean governance for the people and resources needed to deliver the solutions.

113

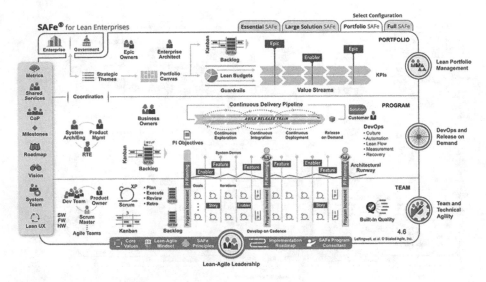

Figure 3-15. *Portfolio SAFe*

At this level you try to align your organization's strategy to your portfolio execution by organizing the Lean–Agile enterprise around the flow of value through the value streams. Delivering the basic budgeting and necessary governance mechanisms, it ensures that investment in solutions provides the ROI the organization needs to meet its strategic objectives. With a large enterprise, there may be multiple SAFe portfolios, and the need for running full SAFe might arise.

Full SAFe

Full SAFe (Figure 3-16) is the largest SAFe implementation available. In the largest enterprises, multiple instances of various SAFe configurations may be required and Full SAFe might be necessary. Full SAFe supports organizations that build and maintain large, integrated solutions that require hundreds of people or more, and includes all levels of SAFe: team, program, large solution, and portfolio.

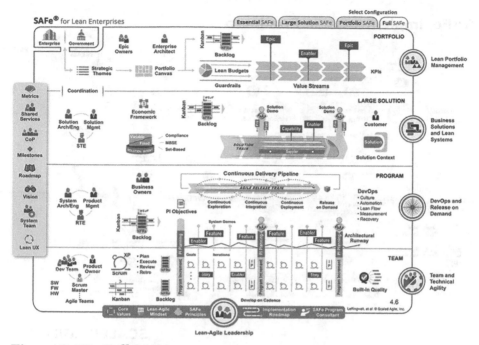

Figure 3-16. *Full SAFe*

Working with Portfolio SAFe and Full SAFe might require some major changes to the enterprise. You will most likely need to change your way of budgeting, for instance, because these two setups fund value streams instead of projects. But even for the other two SAFe setups, you can benefit from another way of funding programs and solutions. The goal here is that personnel in each value stream can make the decisions necessary without having a stricter and more time-consuming escalation process when a change is needed. You want to achieve a more decentralized decision-making process.

SAFe Implementation Road Map

Scaled Agile has tried to make it easier to implement SAFe by providing an implementation road map (Figure 3-17).

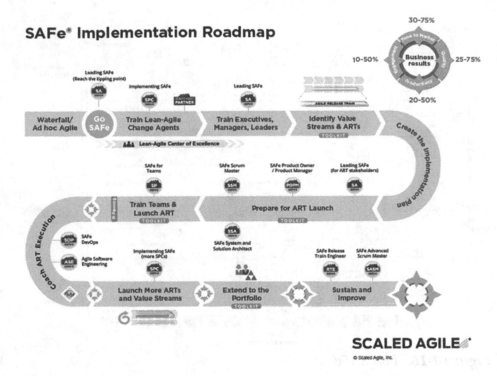

Figure 3-17. *SAFe Implementation Roadmap*

It starts with a tipping point (Go SAFe in Figure 3-17) that usually comes from one of two things:

1. *The need to make an obvious change*: Making a change can sometimes be obvious. It could be that you have a burning platform, as SAFe calls it—meaning, you somehow realize that your way of working is not adequate any more. You have problems with delivering business value, for instance, and need to change.

2. *The need to make a change for future betterment*: If you do not have a burning platform, sometimes proactive leaders will drive change so that you can be in a better spot in the future. Lean-Agile leaders

must exhibit what Toyota calls "a constant sense of
danger"—a never-ending sense of potential crisis
that fuels continuous improvement. This might not
be the most obvious reason to drive change, and
leaders in this case must promote that maintaining
the status quo is simply not a way forward.

With the implementation road map we get step-by-step guidance to
drive a change regardless of the reason that kicked it off.

SAFe is one way to scale Scrum. Now let's take a look at another way to
do this. It originates from Ken Schwaber and Scrum.org.

NEXUS–SPS

In SPS, a Nexus (nexusguide.org) is an exoskeleton that rests on top of
multiple Scrum teams when they are combined to create an integrated
increment. Nexus is consistent with Scrum, and its parts will be familiar
to those who have worked on Scrum projects. The difference is that more
attention is paid to dependencies and interoperation among Scrum teams
delivering one "done" integrated increment at least every sprint.

The result can be an effective development group of up to around 90
people. Scrum.org recommends three to nine Scrum teams with three
to nine developers. This includes the Nexus integration team. For larger
initiatives, the Nexus becomes a unit of scale. This is called *Nexus+*, a
unification of more than one Nexus.

As displayed in Figure 3-18, Nexus consists of the following:

- *Roles*: A new role, the Nexus integration team, exists
  to coordinate, coach, and supervise the application of
  Nexus and the operation of Scrum so the best outcomes
  are derived. The Nexus integration Team consists of
  the product owner, a Scrum master, and three to nine
  developers.

- *Artifacts*: All Scrum teams use the same, single product backlog. As the PBIs are refined and made ready, indicators of which team will do the work inside a sprint are made visual. A new artifact, the Nexus sprint backlog, exists to raise this transparency during the sprint. All Scrum teams maintain their individual sprint backlogs.

- *Events*: Events are appended to, placed around, or replace (in the case of the sprint review) regular Scrum events to augment them. As modified, they serve both the overall effort of all Scrum teams in the Nexus, and each individual team. Backlog refinement has become a proper event as well. This is an important practice for single teams, but at scale it becomes mandatory.

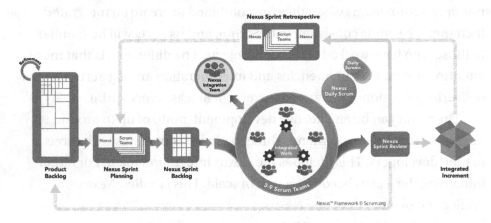

Figure 3-18. *The Nexus framework (*`nexusguide.org`*)*

All work in a Nexus may be done by all members of the Scrum teams as cross-functional members of the Nexus. Based on dependencies, the teams may select the most appropriate members to do specific work.

- *Refine the product backlog*: The product backlog needs to be decomposed so that dependencies are identified and removed or minimized. PBIs are refined into thinly sliced pieces of functionality, and the team likely to do the work is identified as early as possible.

- *Nexus sprint planning*: Appropriate representatives from each Scrum team meet to discuss and review the refined product backlog. They select PBIs for each team. Each Scrum team then plans its own sprint, interacting with other teams as appropriate. The outcome is a set of sprint goals that align with the overarching Nexus goal, each Scrum team's sprint backlog, and a single Nexus sprint backlog. The Nexus sprint backlog makes the Scrum team's selected PBIs, and any dependencies, transparent.

- *Development work*: All teams develop software, frequently integrating their work into a common environment that can be tested to ensure the integration is done.

- *Nexus daily Scrum*: Appropriate representatives from each Scrum development team meet daily to indicate whether any integration issues exist. If identified, this information is transferred back to each Scrum development team's daily Scrum. Scrum development teams then use their daily Scrum to create a plan for the day, being sure to address the integration issues raised during the Nexus daily Scrum.

- *Nexus sprint review*: All teams meet with the appropriate stakeholders to review the integrated increment. Stakeholder feedback may result in adjustments to the product backlog.

- *Nexus sprint retrospective*: Appropriate representatives from each Scrum team meet to identify shared challenges. Then, each Scrum team holds individual sprint retrospectives. Appropriate representatives from each team meet again to discuss any actions needed based on shared challenges to provide bottom-up intelligence.

Let's now take a look at Large-Scale Scrum (LeSS)

Large-Scale Scrum

LeSS is a framework based on standard Scrum. There are two variants of the LeSS framework:

1. LeSS: Up to eight teams (of eight people each)

2. LeSS Huge: Up to a few thousand people on one product

LeSS (Figure 3-19) is a scaled-up version of standard Scrum and it contains many of the practices and ideas of Scrum for one team. We can also see similarities to how Nexus is designed. In LeSS, you'll find the following:

- A single product backlog (because it's for a product, not a team)

- One definition of done for all teams

- One potentially shippable product increment at the end of each sprint

- One product owner

- Many complete, cross-functional teams (with no single-specialist teams)

- One sprint

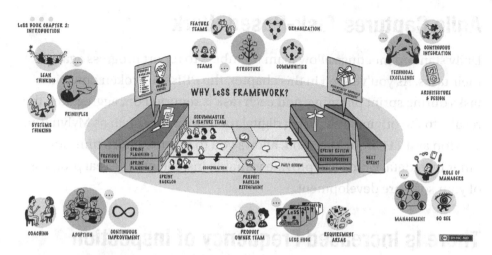

Figure 3-19.   *The LeSS framework*

In LeSS, all teams are in a common sprint to deliver a common shippable product, every sprint.

We can see that SAFe, Nexus, and LeSS take different approaches to scaling Agile. I would say that, so far, SAFe is the framework I see the most.

How Agile Maps to ALM

According to Forrester Research, Agile adoption has brought about significant support for ALM practices.[14] The Agile way of working using frequent inspection and adaption coupled with an increased delivery cadence has made teams more disciplined in their way of working. When Agile was introduced, many people thought the opposite would be true, but reality has proved them wrong.

What parts of Agile map to the ALM process? Let's look at what Forrester says.

---

[14]Dave West, "The Time Is Right For ALM 2.0+," Forrester Research, www.forrester.com/The+Time+Is+Right+For+ALM+20/fulltext/-/E-RES56832?objectid=RES56832, October 19, 2010.

Agile Captures Task-Based Work

Daily standup meetings allow team members to report progress against their tasks. As you've seen in this chapter, the PBIs are broken down into tasks during sprint planning, and each task is reported on, aggregating the results to the original PBI. Using digital tooling for this, such as Mylyn from Tasktop and TFS from Microsoft, allows you to capture effort, time, and other metadata, which can provide valuable insight into the real progress of your software development.

There Is Increased Frequency of Inspection

The iterative approach to development improves the frequency of inspection. During each sprint, you have project inspection at each daily standup. At the end of a sprint, during the sprint retrospective, you define what you've done well and what needs to be improved. This facilitates the feedback loop and, together with better visibility for reporting and traceability, has far-reaching implications for ALM.

Many Tools Collect Much Information

Many Agile teams use tools that help them collect, build, and integration information in their continuous integration flow. This improves visibility into the build process as well as traceability, because the tools often allow the team to see which requirements, work items, and tests each build included.

Continuous integration is a software development practice where members of a team integrate their work frequently, usually each person integrates at least daily - leading to multiple integrations per day. Each integration is verified by an automated build (including test) to detect integration errors as quickly as possible. Many teams find that this approach leads to significantly reduced integration problems and allows a team to develop cohesive software more rapidly.[15]

Test Artifacts Are Important

Agile teams often use TDD and increase the importance of test artifacts. Business analysts and quality assurance practices are converging, which is something that Agile methods encourage. Agile's emphasis on the definition of *done* and frequent inspection increase the desire to link work items with test plans and cases. The result is that Agile teams create simpler requirements but see greater integration with test assets.

Agile Teams Plan Frequently

Agile teams plan more frequently than traditional teams. Planning takes place when creating work items, during sprint planning, during daily standups, during backlog refinement, and so on.

As a result, Agile teams have more information about their projects, such as estimates, actual results, and predictions. This enables ALM to move center stage, because planning activities are an important management component of an ALM application.

Summary

This chapter gave you an introduction to Agile concepts. It focused on Scrum and Kanban because they are so commonly used. You looked at the details of Scrum so you can understand why the Agile approach maps so well to the ALM process.

You also examined ways to scale Scrum and Agile to become more effective in larger projects or larger organizations. In addition, you learned that agile techniques can help you with visibility, traceability, and collaboration.

---

[15]Martin Fowler, "Continuous Integration," http://martinfowler.com/articles/continuousIntegration.html, May 1, 2006.

CHAPTER 4

Work Items and Process Templates

ALM Revisited

Having traceability in your ALM processes is key to the successful delivery and maintenance of your applications and systems. In Chapter 1, you saw that traceability is one of the three cornerstones of a successful ALM solution:

1. *Traceability of relationships between artifacts*: Traceability can be a major cost driver in any enterprise if not done correctly. There must be a way of tracing the requirements all the way to delivered code—through architect models, design models, build scripts, unit tests, test cases, and so on. Practices such as TDD and configuration management can help, and these can be automated and supported by Azure DevOps.

2. *Automation of high-level processes*: There are approval processes to control handoffs between analysis and design. There are other handoffs between build, deployment, testing, and so on. Much of this is done manually in many projects, and ALM stresses the

© Joachim Rossberg 2019
J. Rossberg, *Agile Project Management with Azure DevOps*,
https://doi.org/10.1007/978-1-4842-4483-8_4

importance of automating these tasks for a more effective and less time-consuming process.

3. *Visibility into the progress of development efforts*: Many managers and stakeholders have limited visibility into the progress of development projects. Their visibility often comes from steering group meetings during which the PM goes over the current situation. Other interest groups such as project members may also have limited visibility of the whole project even though they are part of it. This often occurs because reporting is hard to do and can involve a lot of manual work. Daily status reports can, quite simply, take too much time and effort to produce, especially when there is information in many repositories.

Let's now look in more detail how work items in Azure DevOps will help you accomplish traceability in your projects and organizations.

Traceability

Unfortunately, we have seen companies that have stopped making changes to their systems just because no one ever knew where a change (or bug fix) might have its impact. This is not a situation any organization wants to be in, yet it is quite common.

At the Swedish Road Administration some years ago, a new version of our system suddenly made old bug fixes disappear. The operators at the Traffic Management Center found themselves with no working phones because of an upgrade. This had the potential to make an accident worse than it already was, because the operators communicate with the rescue team and the police using phones. Having communications suddenly stop working can actually be a matter of life or death.

126

The vendor of that piece of software did not have control over its different software versions and did not have a good testing strategy. If the vendor had used automated tests, for instance, it would have discovered broken tests for the bug fix when the fix itself was not included in the next release. By checking which work items were associated with the failed tests, the vendor would have been able to see which of them contained the problem. This would have indicated why they created the test in the first place, so they could have fixed the problem more easily. This traceability would greatly improve their code.

And if they had used a good configuration management process, they would also have had the capability to trace all versions where the bug fix needed to be inserted, so they wouldn't forget to include it in future releases.

Work item tracking in Azure DevOps can help you with traceability so you can avoid such problems. Let's now see how the work item tracking system implements traceability.

The Azure DevOps Work Item Tracking System

Sometimes it seems like we can have tons of Post-its on our monitors and desks—each one containing at least one task we are supposed to do. Often, it just isn't possible to track them with a tool. It could be that some tasks are connected with one project, and others with another. You could try writing them all down in an Excel spreadsheet and saving that to your computer, but soon you might find that the spreadsheet is located on your laptop, a customer's computer, your desktop computer, on another customer computer, and so on. And you have no idea which one is the current version. This can be a real problem when you find you have no clue as to which version you should trust.

The same thing is often visible in projects. PMs have their to-do lists for a project, and they all have their own way of keeping them updated. Let's say a PM uses Excel to keep track of the tasks—the status of tasks, to whom they are assigned, and so on. How can the PM keep the team updated with the latest to-do list? If the PM chooses to e-mail it, chances are that some won't save the new version to disk or will just miss it in the endless stream of e-mails coming into their mailbox. Soon there are various versions floating around, and things are generally a mess.

One way to solve this could be to use a project web site running on Microsoft Office SharePoint Server or some other tool like that. This could help, although you could still be in trouble if people forget to save changes or check in the document after they have updated it.

Another problem may occur if, for example, an Excel sheet is updated by a tester who discovers a bug and changes the status of one entry in the task list to indicate that a developer should look at the task again and solve the bug. How can you alert the developer that the bug exists? You would want this action to take place automatically, right? That would be hard if you used only an Excel spreadsheet. The same thing occurs the other way around. When a developer has fixed a bug, you want the tester to be alerted that the problem has been resolved, so the tester can then check whether the bug issue can be closed.

What about requirements traceability? If the only place you keep track of the connection between requirements and the code is in a document, how do you know that the document is really updated? Can you trust that information?

Even if you purchase a separate tool to help you keep track of tasks, it is still be a separate tool for all categories of team members. There are tools for bug tracking, requirements management, test management, and so on—the list can go on for a while. Chances are that someone will forget to update the tool because it takes too long to open or is too difficult to work in or any other excuse for not doing the update. This could cost the project lots of money and time.

Work Items

In Azure DevOps there is a task tracking system at your service. The core of this system is represented by the tasks themselves, called *work items*. A work item can be pretty much whatever you want it to be. It can be a bug, a requirement of some sort, a general to-do item, and so on. Each work item represents an object that is stored in the Azure DevOps database. All work items have a unique ID that helps you keep track of the places it is referenced (Figure 4-1).

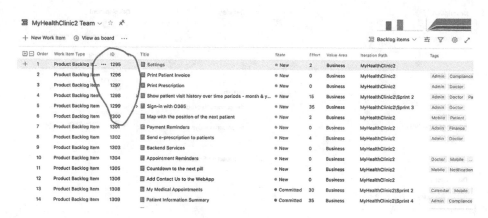

Figure 4-1. *Each work item has a unique ID*

The ID lets you follow one work item, let's say a requirement, from its creation to its implementation as a piece of executable software (component). Work item IDs are unique across all work item types in all team projects in a project collection. The work item type determines the work item fields available for tracking information, defaults defined for each field, and rules and constraints positioned on these fields and other objects that specify the work item workflow. Every change made to a work item field is stored in the work item log, which maintains a historical record of changes.

You can create and modify work items by using Team Explorer, Azure DevOps, Office Excel, or Office Project. When creating or modifying individual work items, you can work in the work item form by using Team Explorer or the Web GUI (Figure 4-2). You can make bulk updates to many work items at a time by using Azure DevOps, Office Excel, or Office Project.

Figure 4-2. *Creating a work item using Azure DevOps*

Work items provide a great way for you to simplify task management during a project while at the same time enabling traceability. No more confusion as to which version of the task list is the current one. No more manual labor for gathering status reports on work progress that are used only at steering group meetings. Now you have a solution that lets you collaborate more easily with your teams and enables all members and stakeholders to view status reports whenever they want. You can also collaborate more easily with people outside the project group by adding work items via the Web.

Azure DevOps is so flexible that it lets you tailor the work items. By installing TFS Power Tools, you get an additional menu option called Process Editor, under Tools in Visual Studio (Figure 4-3), that simplifies editing the work items and the whole process as well (for TFS 2018 on-prem). In Process Editor, you can modify your work items in the project so they contain new information. Later in this chapter, you'll see more on how you can change your process template, including the work items. If you make a change to the current project (by modifying a work item, for example), it may affect all new work items you create, not the existing ones. You only get the change in your current project as well. All new projects created with the same process template do not have these changes unless you modify the process template on the TFS server.

When it comes to the Azure DevOps cloud version, you modify the process in a different way through the web interface. We come back to this later in the chapter.

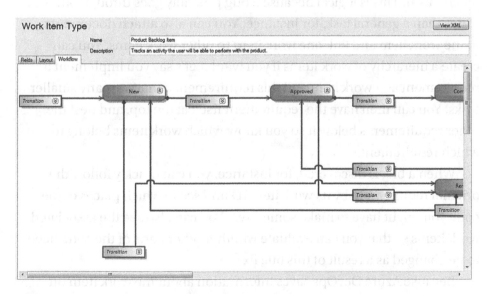

Figure 4-3. *Modifying a work item using Process Editor*

The work items can contain information in different fields that define the data to be stored in the work item. This means that each field has a name and a data type. Data types supported in fields are the primitive data types such as string, integer, and double, as well some complex types such as DateTime, PlainText, HTML, and others. System fields are one example of a field (or more correct, a label for a group of fields) that must be present in every work item type, and represent the minimal recommended subset of fields that any custom work item template should contain. Having such a common subset allows reusing basic Work Item Query Language (WIQL) queries or reports from predefined templates for your custom templates.

All work items can have different information attached to them. You can have information about to whom the work item is assigned and the status of the work at the moment (for example, a bug could be open, closed, under investigation, resolved, and so on). The State field can be modified (Figure 4-3) so that each work item type has its own state mechanism. This is logical because a bug probably goes through other states than a general task, for instance. You can also attach documents to the work item and link one work item to other work items. You can create a hierarchy of work items if you want. Let's say you implement a requirement as a work item and this requirement contains many smaller tasks. You can then have the requirement itself at the top, and nest the other requirements below it so you know which work items belong to which requirement.

When a bug is discovered, for instance, you can quickly follow the original requirement by its work item ID and see in which places of the code you might have to make some fixes. You can also see the associated work items so that you can evaluate whether other parts of the code need to be changed as a result of this bug fix.

Because Azure DevOps saves information about the work item on the data tier, you can see the history of the work item. You can see who created it, who resolved it, who closed it, and so on. The information in the databases can be used for display on reports, allowing you to tailor them depending on your needs. One report could show the status of all bugs, for instance. Stakeholders can see how many open bugs exist, how many are resolved, and much, much more. It is completely up to you how you choose to use the work items.

For those of you familiar with and used to working with pivot tables, you can use Excel as well to drill down into the information in the Azure DevOps TFS server data warehouse. There are people who think it is better to use Excel to connect directly to these tables and who use very detailed information in their reports. If you want to do this from Azure DevOps in the cloud, you need to use Power BI and create your queries there instead.

The Work Item Form

The work items are defined in the project template in Azure DevOps. The template and the work item types are defined in a set of XML files stored on the Azure DevOps server. The XML files for your work items define the information the work item includes on its form in Azure DevOps (Figure 4-4).

Figure 4-4. *The bug form in Microsoft Scrum*

As you can see in Figure 4-4, the Bug work item type in Microsoft Scrum includes fields for many aspects of the bug. You can assign the bug to a specific person, set state (status), set severity, and much more. You can also add a description of the problem and attach files such as screenshots of the bug. There are other options as well, but they are not covered in this book.

The fields on the work item form can have properties set for them. You can let a field be read-only, required, automatically populated, and so on. Because you can also change the information included on this form by editing the XML, you can make sure it contains the information you want.

We have heard some customers say they have had problems using the process templates that Microsoft provides because the information required to fill in the forms is not the information they want to track or record. Instead of changing the work item types, they have tried to adapt to the work items. Don't make this mistake! If you need other information besides what is included in the templates, or if you need the information in another way, change the template. That's the whole point of having an open and flexible solution such as Azure DevOps. You can adjust the tool to fit your needs. I have, for instance, seen the Bug work item that Microsoft uses, and it looks nothing like what is included in any of the templates you get with Azure DevOps. Instead, Microsoft encourages you to adjust the tool to your needs. This includes adjusting the work items.

Work Item Traceability

Let's look at an example of how you can use work items to increase traceability. You start with a requirement in the form of a user story:

> As a manager, I want to search expense reports so I
> can get an overview of expenses easily.

You enter this user story into Azure DevOps and Azure DevOps assigns an ID to it (Figure 4-5). This ID follows the work item throughout its life.

Figure 4-5. *Traceability starts with a work item in Azure DevOps*

In Figure 4-6, you can see that you can associate the work item with test cases, tasks, and other work items. This means you get traceability from a requirement to test cases, to storyboards, and to other work items.

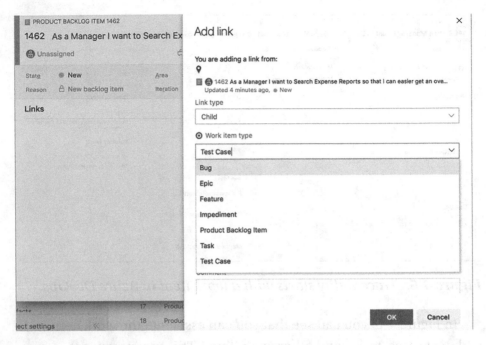

Figure 4-6. *Linking work items to features, test cases, and tasks (other work items) enables you to achieve traceability*

You can also do this the other way around. When creating bug work items, test cases, or work items, you can link them to a new work item (Figure 4-7) or to another, existing, work item. This is a huge benefit over keeping this information in our head or on an Excel spreadsheet.

×

Add link

You are adding a link from:

♀ ⚱ ⑧ **1461 New Bug**
Updated 10 minutes ago, ● New

Link type

Parent	⌄

⊙ Work items to link

Enter ID or search for work items

⊙   🗐 ⑧ **1462 As a Manager I want to Search Expense Repor...**
      Updated 7 minutes ago, ● New

Comment

OK	Cancel

Figure 4-7. Linking work items to new or existing work items

You can also define check-in rules for your developers, which forces them to associate a check-in/"changeset" with a work item (Figure 4-8). There shouldn't be a need for a check-in unless the code change is associated with a work item. You should never do any code changes unless they are required to solve an issue, and this issue should always be documented as a work item.

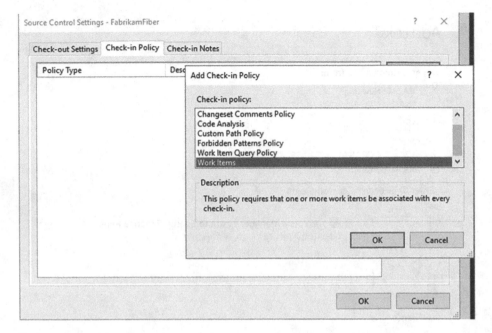

Figure 4-8. *Linking a work item to a check-in can be required by a check-in policy*

A changeset in Azure DevOps is a logical container into which Azure DevOps bundles everything related to a single check-in operation. A changeset consists of the following:

- Source file and folder revisions (adds, renames, edits, deletes, moves)

- Related work items (bugs and so on)

- System metadata (owner, date/time, and so on)

- Check-in notes and comments

By associating a build with a changeset, you create traceability from the original requirement (user story, in this case) to the built executable. This traceability can help you avoid problems such as the ones described at the beginning of this chapter.

By using the reporting functionality of Azure DevOps, you can see quickly what a work item is associated with and hence know that if you change some part of the code (like with a bug fix), this change affects a specific work item. Knowing this, you can see that some test cases will be affected by the change and that you need to run those tests again to determine whether the change broke anything. You can also get warnings from Azure DevOps that a check-in affects certain test cases.

Figure 4-9 shows what traceability can look like. When you examine this figure, you should be able to understand easily the importance of traceability and the help you have from good traceability implementation. You can also see that this way of working leaves you in a much better spot if you, somewhere down the road of a production system, need to implement changes. You can then follow the trace to determine which parts of the code are affected by a change and which test cases might need to be changed.

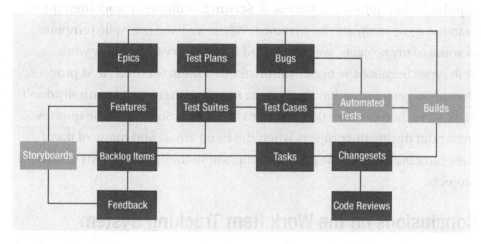

Figure 4-9. *Work item traceability*

Work Item Queries

Using Team Explorer, you can query work item databases (Figure 4-10) by using WIQL, which has a SQL-like construct. From Team Explorer or Azure DevOps, you can create new queries or modify existing ones.

Figure 4-10. *Work item queries in Azure DevOps*

Depending on the process template you use, the work item queries supplied differ quite a bit. Microsoft Scrum has different work item queries than the Agile template, for instance. When we used the Agile template in some of my projects, we have found it necessary to add new work item types because the organization needed them for their ALM process. Queries to get information about these new work item types naturally don't exist, so we had to make these queries ourselves. Some of these queries were built during the projects when the need arose, and many of them were later included in the process template so they are now part of all new projects.

Conclusions on the Work Item Tracking System

The work item tracking system is one of the core components of Azure DevOps. This system allows you to create work items and enable traceability. You can use the work items included with Azure DevOps from the beginning, you can adjust them to your needs, or you can even create your own work item types. Each work item has a unique ID (as you saw earlier in Figure 4-1) that you can attach to the things you do in Azure DevOps. This enables you to follow one work item—let's say a requirement, for example—from its creation to its implementation as a piece of executable software. You can also associate one work item with others and build a hierarchy of work items.

When a bug is discovered, you can quickly follow the original requirement by its work item ID and see in which places of the code you might have to make some fixes. You can also see the associated work items, so you can evaluate whether other parts of the code need to be changed as a result of this bug fix.

If you implement a requirement as a work item, you can use the work item ID to track the requirement through source code to the final build of the executable system. By requiring all developers to add one or more work item IDs to the check-in using a check-in policy, you enable this traceability.

Our suggestion is that you look closely at the work item types supplied by Microsoft. Then you can decide which of these you can use for yourself and which you might adjust to suit your organization's needs. If none of the ones supplied can be used, you can create your own work item types. Use this opportunity! Don't adjust your way of working to the Microsoft templates. Adjust Azure DevOps to your needs instead.

The Process in Azure DevOps

When you create a new team project in Azure DevOps or TFS, you must choose a process for the project. The process was formerly known as the *process template*, but the name has changed. The process is a collection of files that defines the features, rules, behaviors, and work items associated with a specific process. Both Azure DevOps and VSTS have the same processes available, but there are some differences between the two.

The process defines the work item tracking system as well as other subsystems you can access from the web portal for an on-premises TFS or through Azure DevOps.

There are three processes you can use:

1. Scrum

2. Agile

3. Capability Maturity Model Integration (CMMI)

Let's now take a look at their features and differences.

Scrum, Agile, and CMMI

When you look at the processes, you can see they do not differ very much. The main difference is in the work item types they provide. We look at these processes in the following sections; but, simplified, we can say that Scrum is the most lightweight and CMMI offers support for a more formal process when formal change management is important.

I describe these now so that you can evaluate which model is right for you and your organization. But, before I go into them, let me just say that Microsoft is going to introduce another process we can use. It is called the *Basic process*. Until all details are revealed, I can only say a few words on this. A project that uses the Basic process has three work item types— epics, issues, and tasks—to plan and track work. We recommend you start by adding issues to track your user stories, bugs, or feature items. If you need to group them into a hierarchy, you can define epics. If you want to track additional details of work, you can add tasks to an issue. Within each work item form, you can describe the work to be done, assign work to project contributors, track status, and collaborate with others through the Discussion section. So, this is a simpler model, very much like the standard Jira setup. If you want more information, please check out https://docs. microsoft.com/en-us/azure/devops/boards/get-started/track- issues-tasks?view=azdevops&viewFallbackFrom=vsts.

Scrum

The Scrum process is built on the Scrum framework. Microsoft worked with Scrum.org when it developed the Scrum process for Azure DevOps/VSTS, and this is evident when you look at the terminology used in the process.

In Figure 4-11, you can see that there are work items that work on three different levels. The Scrum process lets you manage work items at the portfolio level as well as the backlog level (work in sprints). There are Epics and Feature work items that help you handle the portfolio backlog level. You can use Azure DevOps/VSTS to implement a program team that manages the overall high-level requirements using these two work item types. For the daily work in sprints, one or more teams can have a subset of the portfolio backlog dedicated to that specific team whereas other teams have their own subsets independent of the other teams. In Chapter 6, we see how we can use the features of Azure DevOps to set up such a scenario.

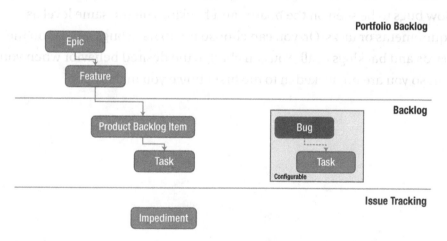

Figure 4-11. *The Scrum process and some of its work items*

Development teams usually work with work items on the backlog level. There you find PBIs and their associated tasks. You can configure bugs and their tasks to be part of this level (Figure 4-12). These work items are followed up only on remaining work, similar to the Agile world.

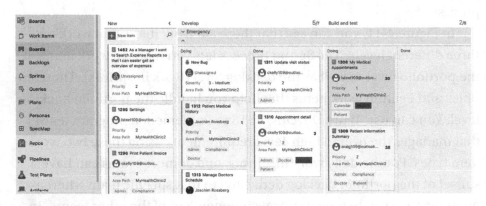

Figure 4-12. *Working with bugs at the backlog level*

How you work with bugs is configurable (Figure 4-13). You can allow bugs to be seen on the boards and backlogs on the same level as requirements or tasks. Or, you can choose not to have bugs appear on the boards and backlogs at all. You can change the desired behavior when you want so you are not locked in to the first choice you make.

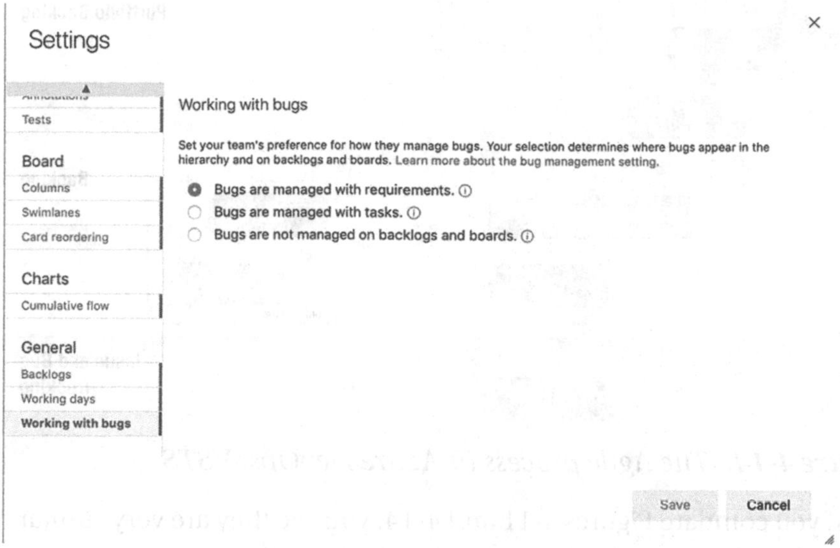

Figure 4-13. *You can change the behavior of how bugs appear in the settings for backlogs and boards*

Agile

The Agile process has been developed in collaboration with the Agile alliance. Originally, it was called the Microsoft Solutions Framework (MSF) for Agile, but now it is only referred to as the Agile process in Azure DevOps/VSTS.

This process is aimed at supporting Agile teams, even those that use Scrum as their process. It tracks development and test activities separately, just like the Scrum process. It also has three levels of work items, as shown in the previous section (Figure 4-14).

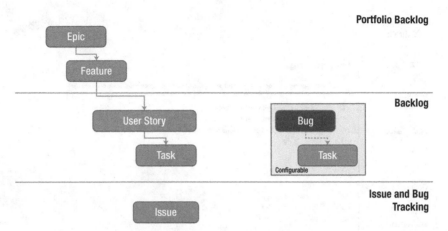

Figure 4-14. *The Agile process in Azure DevOps/VSTS*

If you compare Figures 4-11 and 4-14, you see they are very similar. Only the names are different. For instance, Impediment in Scrum tracking is called Issue in the Agile process, requirements are called User Story in the Agile process and Product Backlog Items in the Scrum process. The difference between the two is more evident if you look at how the requirements are documented (Figures 4-15 and 4-16).

Figure 4-15. *The requirements work item in the Scrum process (PBI)*

Figure 4-16. *The requirements work item in the Agile process (User Story)*

Comparing these two figures, you can see similarities, such as the description and acceptance criteria. But, if you look at the details, you find things that differ. The field for estimating a requirement is called Effort in the Scrum process and Story points in the Agile process.

Another difference is in how you track your progress. In the Agile process, tasks support tracking Original Estimate, Remaining Work, and Completed Work; in the Scrum process, only Remaining Work is tracked. In my view, only the remaining work is important, but I do realize some organizations have a demand for tracking more than this.

Take some time and study the different work item forms in your own environment so that you choose which is best for your organization. Keep in mind that you can always customize the process if you want (see Chapter 5).

CMMI

The last process we discuss is called CMMI. CMMI is a more formal project methodology we can use.

The work item types in CMMI are also on three levels, like Scrum and Agile (Figure 4-17). In CMMI, process requirements are called Requirements, not User Story or PBI.

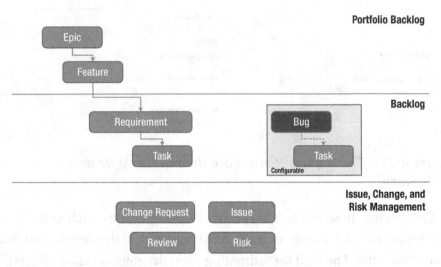

Figure 4-17. *The CMMI process*

Furthermore, you can see that you have more work item types for tracking your projects: Change Request, Issue, Review, and Risk. Using this process you can implement a formal change management process, such as the one found find ITIL.

ITIL, formerly an acronym for Information Technology Infrastructure Library, is a set of practices for IT Service Management (ITSM) that focuses on aligning IT services with the needs of business. In its current form (known as ITIL 2011 edition), ITIL is published as a series of five core volumes, each of which covers a different ITSM life cycle stage. International Organization for Standardization (ISO) develops and publish many international standards. Although ITIL underpins ISO/IEC 20000 (previously BS15000), the International Service Management Standard for IT service management, there are some differences between the ISO 20000 standard and the ITIL framework. ITIL will be updated to version 4 in early 2019.

ITIL describes processes, procedures, tasks, and checklists that are not organization specific, but can be applied by an organization to establish integration with the organization's strategy, to deliver value, and to maintain a minimum level of competency. ITIL allows an organization to establish a baseline from which it can plan, implement, and measure. ITIL is used to demonstrate compliance and to measure improvement.

Figure 4-18 shows differences between how requirements are documented in CMMI compared to the two other requirements types discussed. You can see quickly that more details can be filled out by default. And like the Agile process, CMMI also supports tracking original estimates, remaining work, and completed work at the task level.

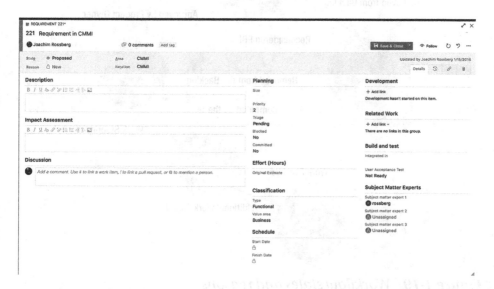

Figure 4-18. *The Requirement work item in the CMMI process*

There are other work item types in these processes that are the same for all processes. We take a look at them shortly, but first a few words on workflow states.

Workflow States

Workflow states support tracking the status of work as it moves from a New state to a Closed or Done state. In Azure DevOps/VSTS, a workflow consists of a set of states, the valid transitions between the states, and the reasons for transitioning the work item to the selected state (Figure 4-19).

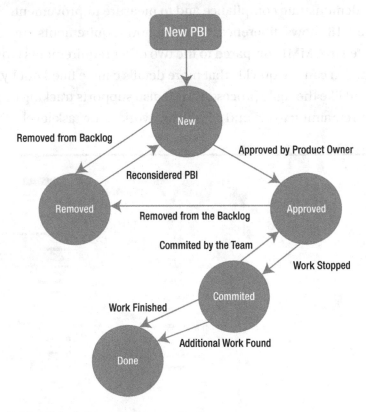

Figure 4-19. *Workflow states and reasons*

Figure 4-19 shows the states for the Scrum process PBI. Table 4-1 shows the differences in states for the three processes and also for Test work items. Keep in mind that this is configurable, as seen in Chapter 5.

Table 4-1. *Workflow States for the Three Processes*

Categories	Agile	Scrum	CMMI	Test WITs
Proposed: Assign to states associated with newly added work items that should appear on the backlog. The first column on the Kanban or taskboard maps to a Proposed state.	New	New Approved To Do (Task)	Proposed	Design (Test Case)
In Progress: Assign to states that represent active work. Work items assigned to states mapped to this category will appear in the backlog (unless you choose to hide them) and make up the middle columns on the Kanban boards.	Active Resolved (Epic, Feature, User Story)	Committed Open (Impediment)	Active Resolved (Epic, Feature, Requirement, Task)	Active (Test Plan) In Planning (Test Suite) In Progress (Test Suite) Ready (Test Case)

(*continued*)

Table 4-1. (*continued*)

Categories	Agile	Scrum	CMMI	Test WITs
Resolved: Assign to states that represent a solution has been implemented, but are not yet verified. Generally these states apply to bug WITs. Work items in a Resolved state appear on the backlog by default. The Agile tools treat the Resolved state category exactly the same as the In Progress state category.	Resolved (Bug)	n/a	Resolved (Bug, Issue, Review, Risk)	n/a
Completed: Assigned to states that represent work has finished. Work items whose state is in this category don't appear on the backlog and do appear in the last column of the Kanban board. Note that you can't modify states in this category nor can you add states to this category.	Closed	Done	Closed	Closed (Test Case) Completed (Test Suite) Inactive (Test Plan)

(*continued*)

Table 4-1. (*continued*)

Categories	Agile	Scrum	CMMI	Test WITs
Removed: Assigned to the Removed state. Work items in a state mapped to the Removed category are hidden from the backlog and board experiences. Note: You should avoid using the Removed state and Removed state category as they are in the process of being deprecated. Instead, you should Delete work items to remove them from the backlog.	Removed	Removed	n/a	n/a

When you change the state of a work item to Removed, Closed, or Done, the system behaves like this:

> *Closed or Done*: Closed or Done work items do not appear on the portfolio backlog and backlog pages. However, they do appear on the sprint backlog pages, Kanban board, and task board. Also, when you change the portfolio backlog view to show backlog items (for example, to view Features to PBIs), items in the Closed and Done states appear.

> *Removed*: Work items in this state do not appear on any backlog or board.

Work items are maintained in a team project as long as the team project is active. Even if you set them to Closed, Done, or Removed, a record is kept in the data store, which means you can use this data to create queries or reports.

If you need to delete a work item permanently, you can use the witadmin destroywi command-line tool. This tool is not discussed in this book.

Most work items that appear on backlogs and boards support any-to-any transitions. This means you can update the status of a work item using a Kanban board or a task board by dragging it to its corresponding state column.

You can also change the workflow so that you can have the states, transitions, and reasons you need in your team or organization. (More on this in the Chapter 5).

Work Item Types for All Processes

There are some work item types that are the same for all three processes. They have three different purposes:

1. Support Microsoft Test Manager (MTM)

2. Support rFeedback Request

3. Support My Work and Code Review

Let's now take a brief look at them.

Work Items That Support MTM

Our testers and test managers often work with these work item types. The goal of this book is not to discuss testing in general, but we will provide a brief example here. Many test efforts are structured like this:

A test plan is created for a sprint using MTM or Azure DevOps. The test plan contains the high-level view of the testing effort. There is a Test Plan work item type included in all processes.

One or more Test Suites (another work item type) are created and included in the test plan. The suites themselves includes one or more Test Cases (work item type). The test cases are used to describe, step by step, how a tester should test the application or functionality being developed. Test cases are often associated with a requirement so that you can see which tests cover a specific requirement.

So, using test plans, test suites, and test cases, you can structure your testing efforts in a way that gives both traceability as well as visibility of your tests (Figure 4-20). You can generate reports and graphs that show the status of these work item types.

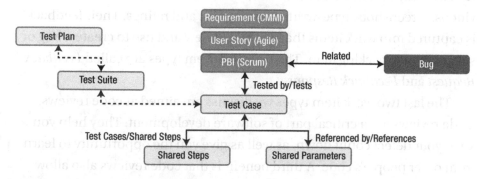

Figure 4-20. *Traceability of test work items*

There are two more work item types for test, as shown in Figure 4-20:

1. *Shared Steps*: This work item type includes test steps that can be reused in many test cases. They help in removing redundant test steps by allowing you to reuse them.

2. *Shared Parameters*: When you write a manual test, you often want to specify that the test should be repeated several times with different test data. For example, if your users can add different quantities of a product to a shopping cart, you might want to check that a quantity of 200 works just as well as a quantity of one. To do this, you insert parameters in your test steps. Along with the test steps, you provide a table of parameter values. These parameters can be used to create shared parameters, which can be reused in other test cases.

When you develop an application, you usually want stakeholders or end users to provide feedback on what you have done. Using the feedback functionality of Azure DevOps/VSTS, you can ask reviewers to provide videos, screenshots, type-written comments, and ratings. Their feedback is captured into work items that you can review and use to create a bug or suggest a new backlog item. The two work item types are called *Feedback Request* and *Feedback Response*.

The last two work item types we discuss are aimed at code reviews. Code reviews are a critical part of software development. They help you keep your defect count down, as well as give you the opportunity to learn from other people's code. A third benefit is that code reviews also allow teams to communicate to their peers changes to the application.

In Azure DevOps, there are two work items types that help with code reviews:

1. *Code Review Request*: This type is a request a developer creates and sends to a peer to ask for a review of some part of the code.

2. *Code Review Response*: A response gets created when the code review request goes out. The reviewer can choose to accept or reject the review.

Summary

This chapter discussed many concepts regarding work items and processes in Azure DevOps and VSTS. You saw how the work item tracking system works and how work items can help you increase both visibility and traceability. Simply put, work items are the core of Azure DevOps/VSTS. Almost everything you do involves work items in one way or the other.

The work items at your disposal are determined by the process you choose for your project, such as Scrum, Agile, and CMMI. These processes have similarities and differences.

If a process is not sufficient for your needs, you learned that you can adjust it and add or remove things as you see fit.

CHAPTER 5

Customizing the Process Template in Azure DevOps

Process Customization

As you have seen so far, it is essential to automate the ALM process to realize the benefits of it fully. TFS 2018 can help quite a lot by letting you have one or more process templates on the TFS server that define the way you work with the ALM process.

In this chapter, we look at how you can modify the TFS process templates in both TFS on-premise and in Azure DevOps.

The whole point of an extensible product such as TFS is that you have the ability to customize it to your needs. One of the biggest advantages of TFS is the capability to customize your process template so that you can realize your ALM process in the tools you use for your projects. Let's take a closer look at how the process template is built and how it can be changed by using the extensible features of TFS.

© Joachim Rossberg 2019
J. Rossberg, *Agile Project Management with Azure DevOps*,
https://doi.org/10.1007/978-1-4842-4483-8_5

Modifying the Process Template in TFS 2018 On-Premise

There are two ways to modify the XML files for the project templates. You can use manual customization or you can use Process Editor, which is a Power Tool from Microsoft.

If you are daring, we can edit the XML files manually. This can be done by exporting the files from the TFS server using the witadmin command-line tool (see `https://docs.microsoft.com/sv-se/azure/devops/ reference/witadmin/witadmin-customize-and-manage-objects-for- tracking-work?view=tfs-2018&viewFallbackFrom=vsts for more information`). Or, you can use the Process Template Manager that comes with the TFS Power Tools.

You can update the work items (or the whole process) of an existing template (Figure 5-1) or, if you are even more daring, you can start from scratch. We suggest you use an already-existing process template and modify that.

Later in the chapter we look at the possibilities of modifying the process template using Azure DevOps.

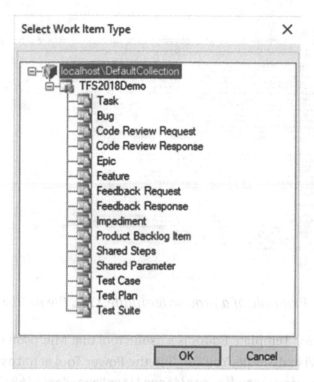

Figure 5-1. *Exporting (download) a work item type from TFS 2018 using the Process Template Manager*

After you have the work item in Visual Studio, you can start modifying all aspects of it. In Figure 5-2, you can see an excerpt of what one of the XML files looks like when seen in Visual Studio. Note the nice user interface you get with the Process Template Editor; you don't have to see the pure XML if you don't want to.

Figure 5-2. *Example of a process template XML file in Visual Studio*

The Process Template Editor is a useful tool that Microsoft provides for TFS and Visual Studio. You can find the Power Tool at `https://marketplace.visualstudio.com/items?itemName=KarthikBalasubramanianMSFT.TFSProcessTemplateEditor`.

The Process Template Editor also provides tools for updating global lists and work item types, as well as for viewing the attributes of work item fields. This tool was formerly provided via TFS 2015 Power Tools (and earlier versions). It is a client extension that needs to be installed by users locally for their own version of Visual Studio.

The Process Template Editor edits TFS process templates inside the Visual Studio IDE (Figure 5-3).

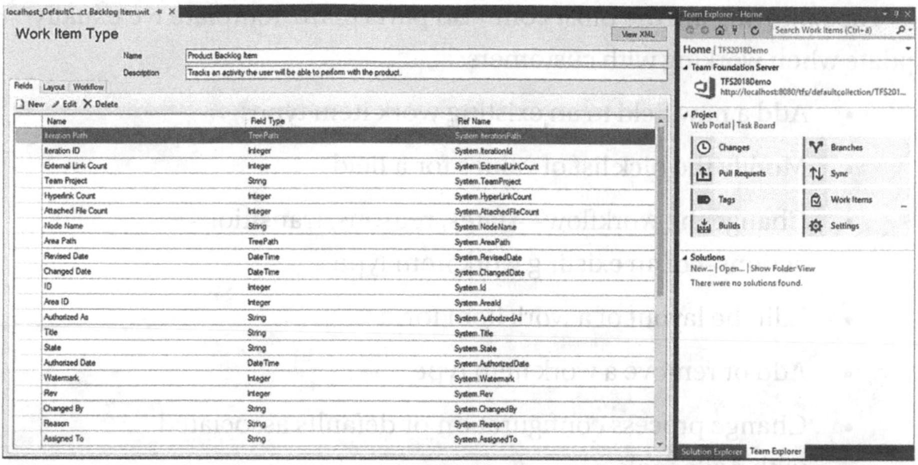

Figure 5-3. *Editing the product backlog work item type from the Scrum process using the Process Template Editor inside Visual Studio*

Common Adaptations of the Process Template

What are the most common things people change in the process template? I would say that this depends on your needs, and I strongly suggest you consider your needs before starting to customize the templates. You should gather information to help point out these needs by doing an ALM assessment or other evaluation. Because the process template is a representation of your ALM process, it makes good sense to understand your way of working. What are your organization's needs? Which information is important in your bugs? How do you handle CRs? How do you handle requirements?

Do an assessment, run some workshops about the results, and talk about what your requirements are for the process templates. Then, select one project to use to pilot the process template and see the results. You will probably need to adjust your template after the pilot, but that is quite all right; that's the purpose of a pilot.

163

The following are the most common parts of the template we usually update when working with customers:

- Add a new field to an existing work item types

- Modify the pick list of values for a field

- Change the workflow—states, reasons, transitions, actions—of an existing work item type

- Edit the layout of a work item form

- Add or remove a work item type

- Change process configuration or defaults associated with Agile tools

Work Item Types

You can use the work item types that Microsoft ships with Azure DevOps in the three templates. But, as mentioned earlier, we think you should really consider your own needs in the organization and make adjustments to the templates based on them. Your organization might need more work items or might need to extend the information required for them. If your PMs use Microsoft Office Project, you might want to change the mapping between fields in TFS against fields in Project. Another thing to consider is the workflow of the work items. How is the process in your organization? Between which states can a bug transition? Microsoft supplies a set of default work item instances when a project is created that represent tasks that need to be done in all projects. Your organization might have different needs for default work items.

Work Item Queries

What information do you need to query about your work items? If you have made many changes to the work items, you might also need to change the queries so they reflect these changes. What queries does your DevOps process need? In Figure 5-4, you can see the queries of the MSF for Agile template.

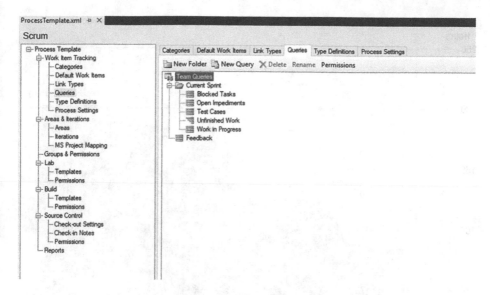

Figure 5-4. *The work item queries in the Scrum process*

Reports

Most of our customers modify their reports. The reports in the processes are very good. Figure 5-5 shows one of them that represents how much work is left in a project. When choosing which reports and information you need, we once again come back to the fact that this is something you need to discuss with your project teams and with stakeholders and managers. What information is important to the various roles in your ALM process? What do the managers need to see? How can you provide great feedback on project status to the team?

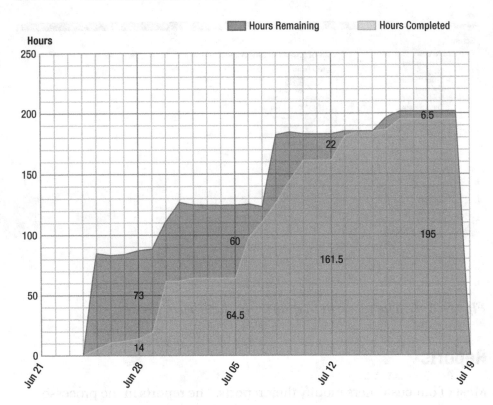

Figure 5-5. *A report showing work remaining on a project*

Areas and Iterations

Areas and iterations are interesting concepts. Iterations are what the term sounds like, basically. You use iterations to name the different versions of your project. You can name them anything you want. We have most often used the names Iteration 1, 2, 3, and so on, but how you name them is up to you. You can nest them and build an iteration hierarchy if you want.

Areas are labels you can attach to just about anything. One customer uses labels named after their Windows or web forms in their projects. Another uses them for each component in their system. Then they can use areas and iterations to describe which areas (forms) belong to a certain iteration.

What we want to say about this is that you can use areas and iterations to label specific parts of your projects. These concepts are flexible, and you have the freedom to use them as you want. All work items can be labeled later with both an area and an iteration. Depending on your DevOps process, you might use this for various reasons. If you run a project using SAFe, you might want to use the iterations by naming them after the ARTs, then you can nest iterations below each train depending on your need. Figure 5-6 shows an example of what this could look like. And if, during the project, you need more iterations in one phase, you can simply add them.

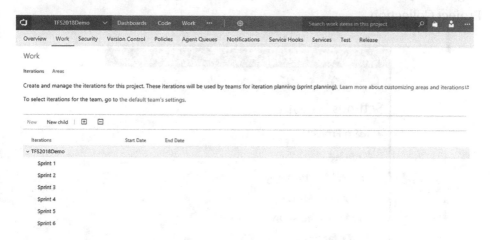

Figure 5-6. *Areas and iterations in the team settings*

You can decide what you want to use labels and areas for. In our opinion, they are very useful. They give you enormous freedom in how you set up your projects, so I suggest you make good use of them.

Modifying Work Items

Microsoft encourages modification of process templates. We've found that work items are worth modifying. Many organizations have needed information in their work items that is not available in the three

Microsoft templates. In these cases, we adjusted the work items to fit the organization better. This strategy has turned out to be very successful in all cases. One thing we changed was the workflow of the work items.

How to Open the Process Template

You can start creating an entire new process template if you want, but it is far easier to start by modifying an existing one. First you need to download the process template from the TFS server. In Team Explorer, go to Settings (Figure 5-7) and choose Process Template Manager, which is below Team Project Collection.

Figure 5-7. *Starting the Process Template Manager from Team Explorer*

Select a process template for download and click Export from the Process tab in the web user interface the Process Template Manager opens (Figure 5-8). Select a location to download the process template. Close the Process Template Manager when you are done.

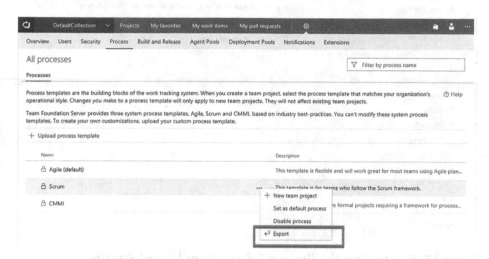

Figure 5-8. *Selecting a process to download*

To modify the process template you just downloaded, go to the Tools menu in Visual Studio and start the Process Editor (Figure 5-9). You are provided with several options for what you can edit. As you can see in Figure 5-9, you can chose to edit the downloaded process template files or select an item from the server. With the latter option, you can edit the current installed process template, changing all future projects created using that template.

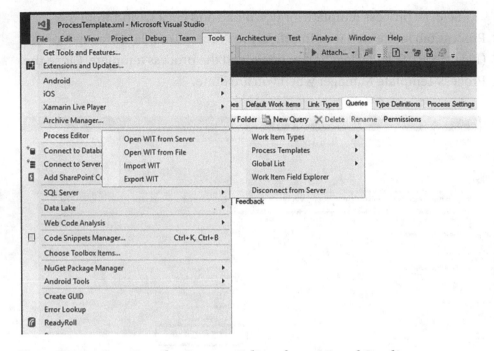

Figure 5-9. *Starting the Process Editor from Visual Studio*

After you finished editing the downloaded process template, you can rename it and upload it to the server as a new process template available for all new team projects.

Work Item Fields

The default work items in TFS include a lot of information in their fields. Sometimes you may need to include more fields or remove fields so the work items better ft your organization. You do this by using the Process Template Editor. In Figure 5-10, you can see the fields from the PBI in the Microsoft Scrum template; you can see their names, their data type, and their ref name.

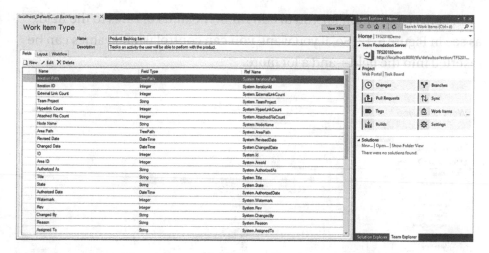

Figure 5-10. *Fields in the PBI work item from the Microsoft Scrum template*

If you double-click a field, you are presented with the Field Definition, as seen in Figure 5-11. In this dialog box you can change all aspects of the field itself.

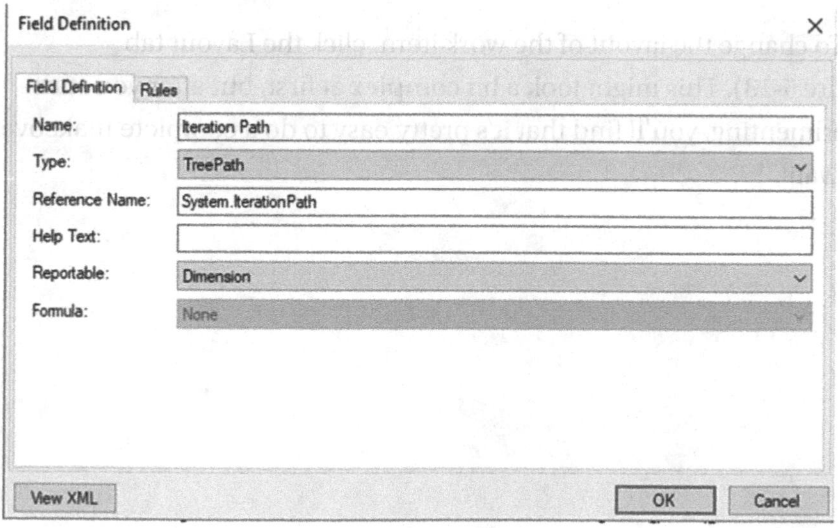

Figure 5-11. *Field Definition dialog box*

There is the option for you to add different kinds of rules to the field, as see in Figure 5-12. So, if you want, you can control which values can be inserted into the field—and a lot more.

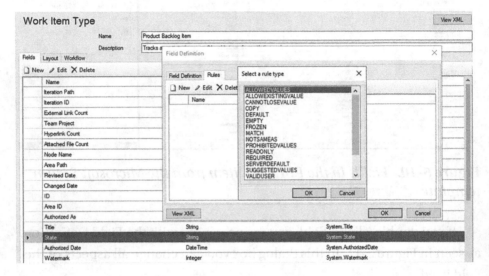

Figure 5-12. *An example of a rule for a PBI work item*

To change the layout of the work item, click the Layout tab (Figure 5-13). This might look a bit complex at first, but after you start experimenting, you'll find that it's pretty easy to do a complete makeover if you want.

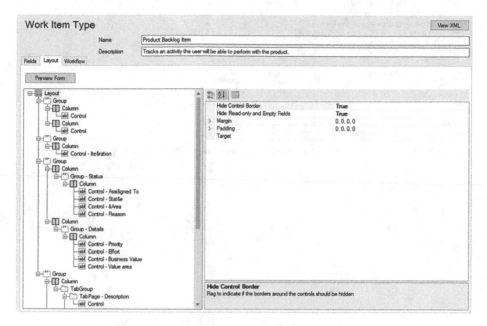

Figure 5-13.   *The Layout editor for work items*

Select Preview Form to see your changes (Figure 5-14).

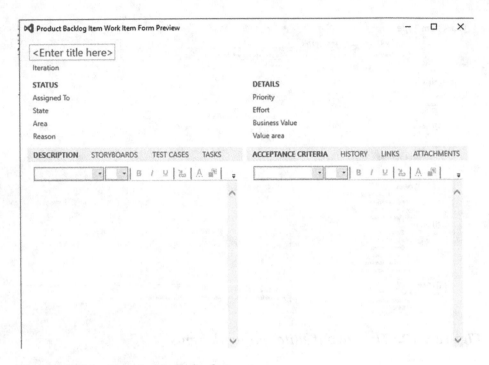

Figure 5-14.   *Previewing the layout*

Work Item Workflow

There is a workflow you can add to the work items. A Bug work item has a State field, for instance, where the state flows through different levels. In this field, you can set the status of the bug, such as active, closed, resolved, and so on. A typical workflow looks like the one shown in Figure 5-15.

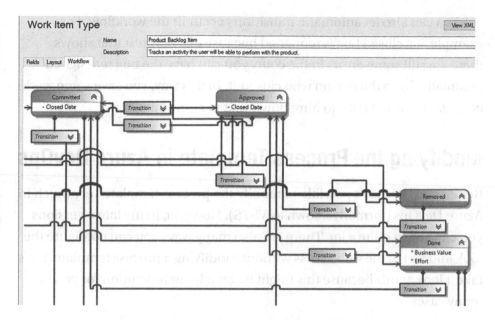

Figure 5-15. *An example of a workflow for a PBI work item*

In this example, you can see the workflow for a PBI work item in Microsoft Scrum. This particular work item can have one of five states: New, Approved, Committed, Done, or Removed. The PBI can transition through these states in the following ways:

- New to Approved

- New to Removed

- Approved to Committed

- Approved to Removed

- Committed to Done

- Removed to New

You can also let automatic transitions occur in the workflow. For example, if a closed bug is reopened because of a new test that shows there are still some errors in the code, you can have the bug reassigned automatically to the person who closed it. In this way, you save some work because you don't have to hunt down that person yourself.

Modifying the Process Template in Azure DevOps

Before now, it wasn't possible to modify the process template very much in Azure DevOps (formerly known as VSTS). However, in the latest versions you can adjust quite a lot. There are also many ways you can configure the look and feel of the web access without modifying a process template. Let's take a look at this because this might be an adequate solution for you in many cases.

Modifications to the Web Access

So what can you modify in the web access? Well, quite a lot associated with what things look like when you work in the web-based GUI. By clicking the Configure team settings icon in the backlog view, you reach the settings for changing the Kanban board (Figure 5-16).

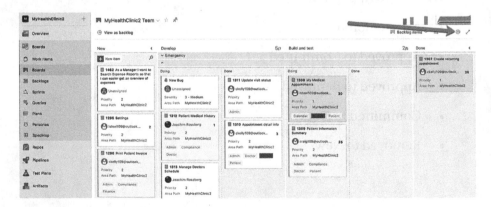

Figure 5-16. *Configuring the Kanban board*

Doing this opens up a new window (Figure 5-17) in which you can modify the following aspects of the GUI:

- Cards

- Board

- Charts

- General

- Cards

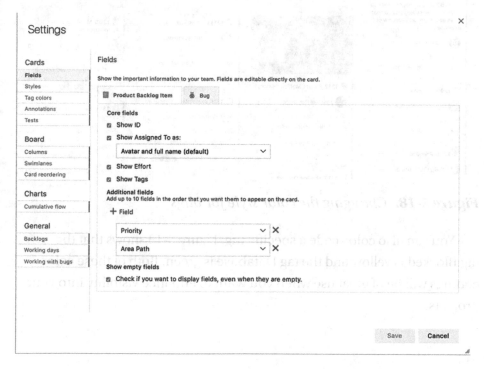

Figure 5-17. *Modifying the GUI*

You can change the fields you presents on your cards. Although Microsoft has limited which fields you can show, you still have a fair collection at your disposal.

You can also create style rules that allow you to color-code a card based on a work item query. In this way, you can, for instance, stipulate that all bugs appear in red on the board (Figure 5-18).

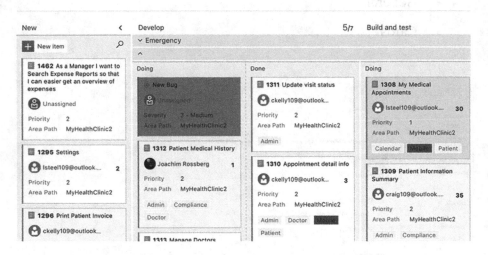

Figure 5-18. *Changing the color style for bugs*

You can also color-code a specific tag. Figure 5-19 shows that the tag Blocked is yellow and the tag Database is green. Both of these color codings will be of great use when you want to enhance visibility into your projects.

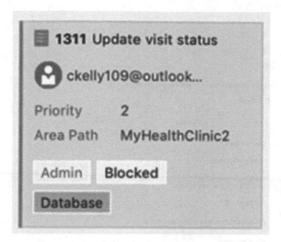

Figure 5-19. *Changing the color code for tags*

When it comes to boards, you can add and arrange your columns on the board (Figure 5-20). If you are configuring the Kanban board, you can add a WIP limit, for instance. There is also an option to split a column into Doing and Done. This creates two columns of one, so you can show more easily that a specific PBI is ready for the next step in the process flow. In Figure 5-18, the Develop columns is split using this method and makes visible to testers that a PBI is ready for testing after developers are done working on the functionality. This is a good way to avoid adding a new column or state.

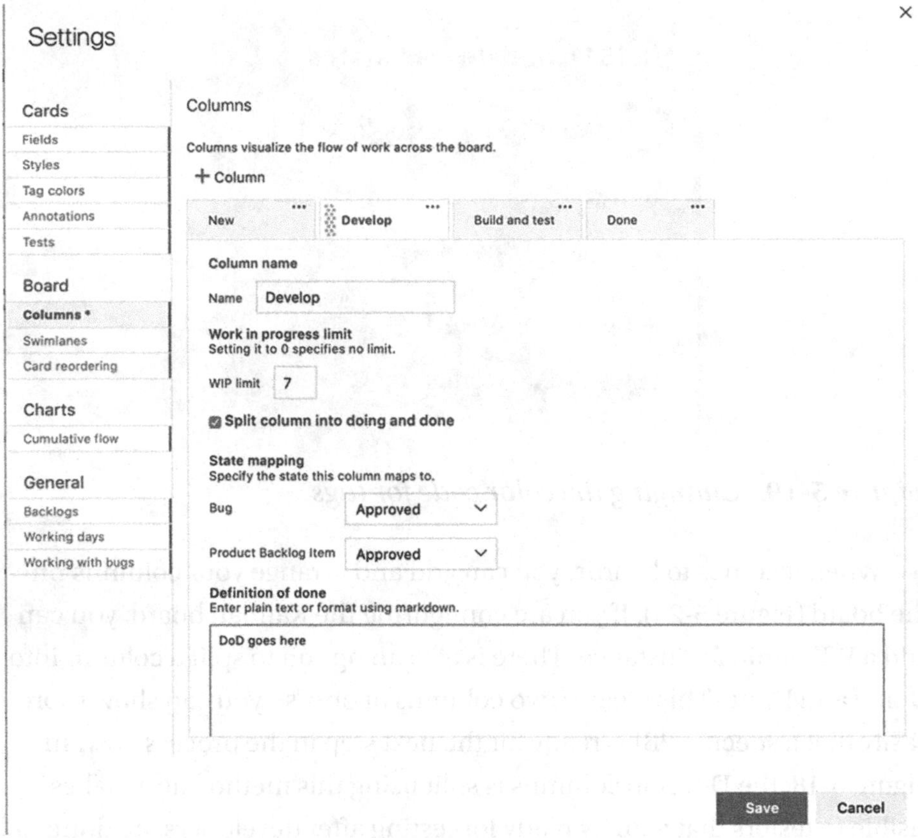

Figure 5-20. Configuring columns on the board

Another thing you can do is add "swim lanes" to your board. For instance, during a project when I worked as a service manager for a large intranet, we used swim lanes to keep track of different issues that came into the support group. Bugs had their own swim lane and CRs had their own as well. In this way, we increased visibility for all in the maintenance team as well as for stakeholders. Swim lanes are basically just rows in a board that can be used for whatever purpose you want—a nice inclusion by Microsoft.

If you need to change the way work items are reordered on a board, there are two choices for doing so:

1. Work items reorder when changing columns, and the backlog reflects the new order.

2. Work items follow the backlog order when changing columns.

The Charts feature does not provide many options. Basically, you can choose the time interval for the cumulative flow diagram. The default is 30 weeks, you can shorten that time span. You can also choose to include the first and last columns of your board.

There is one last section, which is the General section. From here you can select whether you want to show Epics, Features, and Backlog items in the backlog. For example, in Figure 5-16, you can see that Backlog does not include Epics. By selecting the check box for Epics in Figure 5-21, you can tell Azure DevOps to show Epics.

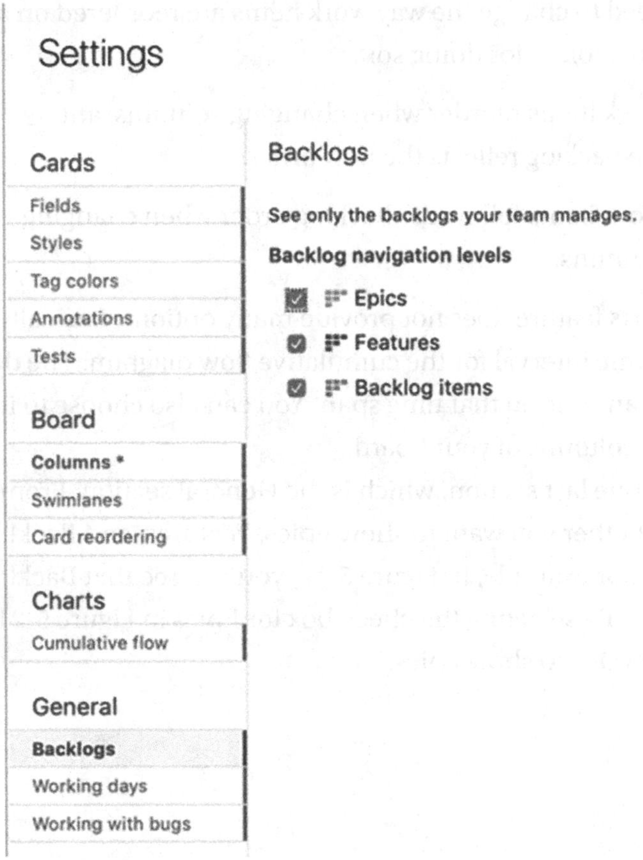

Settings

Cards

Fields

Styles

Tag colors

Annotations

Tests

Board

Columns *

Swimlanes

Card reordering

Charts

Cumulative flow

General

Backlogs

Working days

Working with bugs

Backlogs

See only the backlogs your team manages.

Backlog navigation levels

☑ ░ Epics

☑ ░ Features

☑ ░ Backlog items

Figure 5-21. *Showing Epics in Backlog*

You can also select the working days you will use during your project. Most people will obviously use Monday through Friday, but you can include weekends as well.

The last thing you can change is the way bugs are displayed in the backlogs. There are three options:

1. Bugs appear on the backlogs and boards with requirements

2. Bugs appear on the backlogs and boards with tasks

3.   Bugs do not appear on backlogs and boards

The choice is yours to make. Evaluate which way works best for your team; you can always change it later.

Modifications to the Process Templates in Azure DevOps

In earlier versions of Azure DevOps, it wasn't possible to change many aspects of a process; you had to use what Microsoft chose for you. These days, however, you have many options to customize you process, which is a great step forward for Azure DevOps.

There still are some differences between the ways you can modify templates. Azure DevOps, for instance, uses a different model than TFS for relating projects and processes. In TFS, process templates are used as starting points for projects and, after a project is created, the project is the scope you customize. In Azure DevOps, a process is shared across multiple projects and this is the scope you customize.

Otherwise, the syntax and structure used in defining a process is basically the same. There are only a few minor differences between templates you customize for Azure DevOps and those you upload to support an on-premises TFS.

Let's take a look at how you access the process template in Azure DevOps. In Figure 5-22, you can see that you should point to the configuration wheel in the left corner of the interface for the Azure DevOps instance. This brings us to the Organization settings for Azure DevOps, where you can access the processes (Figure 5-23).

Figure 5-22. *Accessing the organization settings in Azure DevOps*

The changes you make are made on all projects in the collection, not on a single project. In Figure 5-23, you can see the three default processes from Azure DevOps to work with and the two inherited processes.

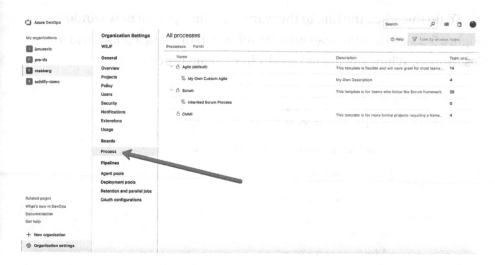

Figure 5-23. *To see the processes in an Azure DevOps instance, make sure you select Organization settings*

To modify a process, you click the process name in the list, but there is one thing you need to consider. You cannot modify any of the three default processes in Azure DevOps. Azure DevOps displays a warning, like the one in Figure 5-24. What you need to do is create a copy (an inherited process) of the process you want to modify.

System processes cannot be customized. To add customization create an inherited process.

All processes > Agile	
Work item types Backlog levels Projects	
Name	Description
🐞 Bug	Describes a divergence between required and actual behavior, and tracks the work done to correct the d...
🏔 Epic	Epics help teams effectively manage and groom their product backlog
🏆 Feature	Tracks a feature that will be released with the product
⚠ Issue	Tracks an obstacle to progress.
📋 Task	Tracks work that needs to be done.
🗂 Test Case	Server-side data for a set of steps to be tested.
🗒 Test Plan	Tracks test activities for a specific milestone or release.

Figure 5-24. *You cannot modify any of the three system processes*

To do this, click the link in the warning. This opens a new window (Figure 5-25), where you can give the inherited process a name and a description. When you are satisfied, click Create process.

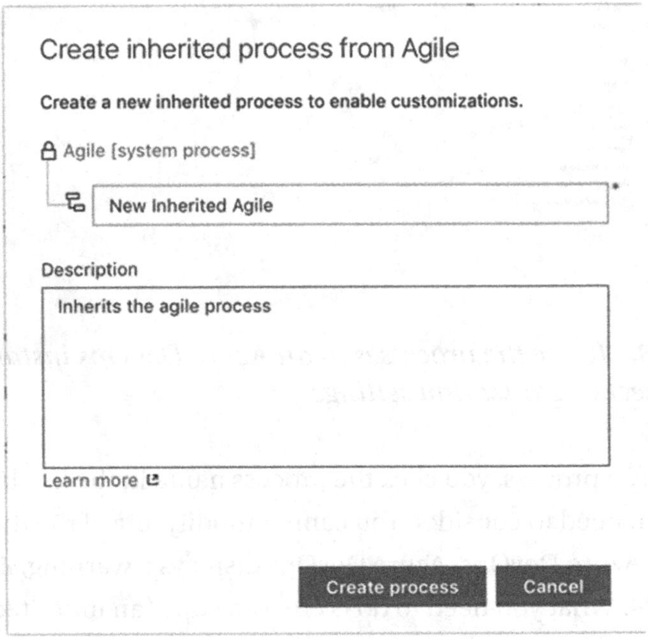

Figure 5-25. *Creating a shared process for editing*

Now you can access the inherited process and start editing. By clicking the three dots (the dots are hidden behind the pop-up in Figure 5-26), you can access the Edit mode.

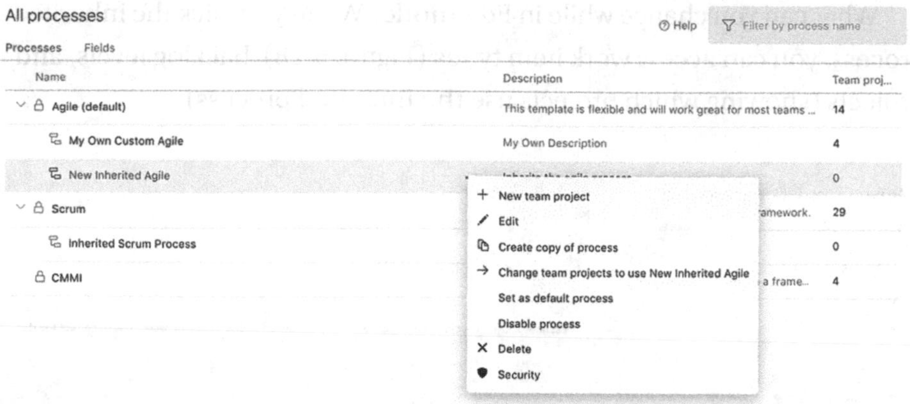

All processes

Processes   Fields

Name	Description	Team proj...
∨ 🔒 Agile (default)	This template is flexible and will work great for most teams ...	14
⬠ My Own Custom Agile	My Own Description	4
⬠ New Inherited Agile	Inherits the agile process	0
∨ 🔒 Scrum		amework. 29
⬠ Inherited Scrum Process		0
🔒 CMMI		a frame... 4

Menu:
- + New team project
- ✎ Edit
- ⧉ Create copy of process
- → Change team projects to use New Inherited Agile
- Set as default process
- Disable process
- ✕ Delete
- ♥ Security

Figure 5-26. *Accessing Edit mode*

Click Edit to bring up the edit menu. The first thing you see when you enter Edit mode is the overview of your new process (called New Inherited Agile in Figure 5-27). You can change the name of the process as well as the description.

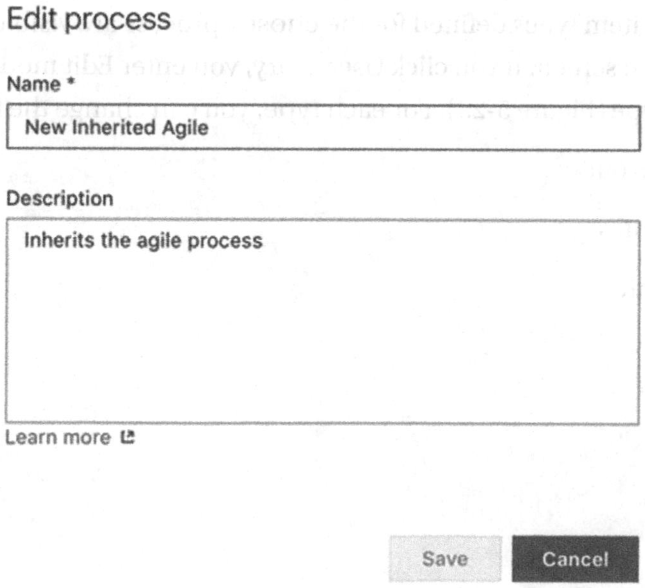

Edit process

Name *

New Inherited Agile

Description

Inherits the agile process

Learn more ⬈

Save   Cancel

Figure 5-27. *Starting to edit the inherited process*

What can you change while in Edit mode? When you click the inherited process, you can access work item types (Figure 5-28), backlog levels, and projects (showing which projects use the inherited process).

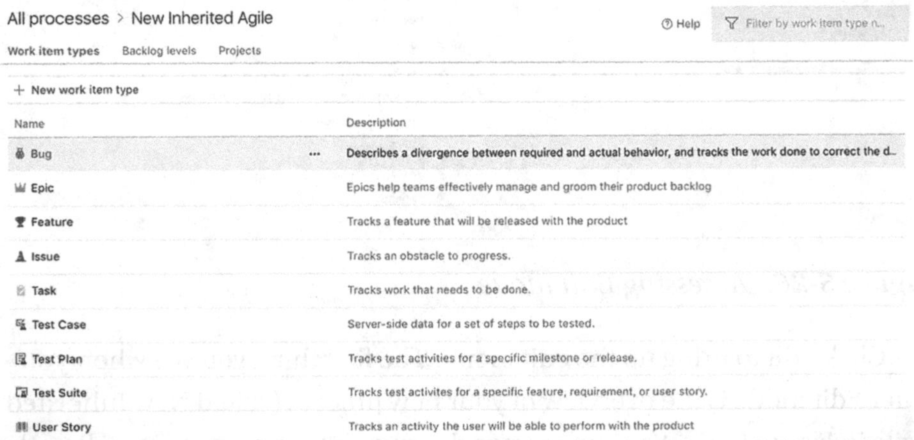

All processes > New Inherited Agile   ⑦ Help   ▽ Filter by work item type n...

Work item types   Backlog levels   Projects

+ New work item type

Name	Description
🐞 Bug	Describes a divergence between required and actual behavior, and tracks the work done to correct the d...
ᴸᵃᵈ Epic	Epics help teams effectively manage and groom their product backlog
🏆 Feature	Tracks a feature that will be released with the product
⚠ Issue	Tracks an obstacle to progress.
🗒 Task	Tracks work that needs to be done.
🖥 Test Case	Server-side data for a set of steps to be tested.
🗒 Test Plan	Tracks test activities for a specific milestone or release.
🖼 Test Suite	Tracks test activites for a specific feature, requirement, or user story.
▦ User Story	Tracks an activity the user will be able to perform with the product

Figure 5-28. *The work item types accessed in the inherited Agile process*

All work item types defined for the chosen process are visible on the left side of the screen. If you click User Story, you enter Edit mode for that work item type (Figure 5-29). For each type, you can change the following:

- Layout

- States

- Rules

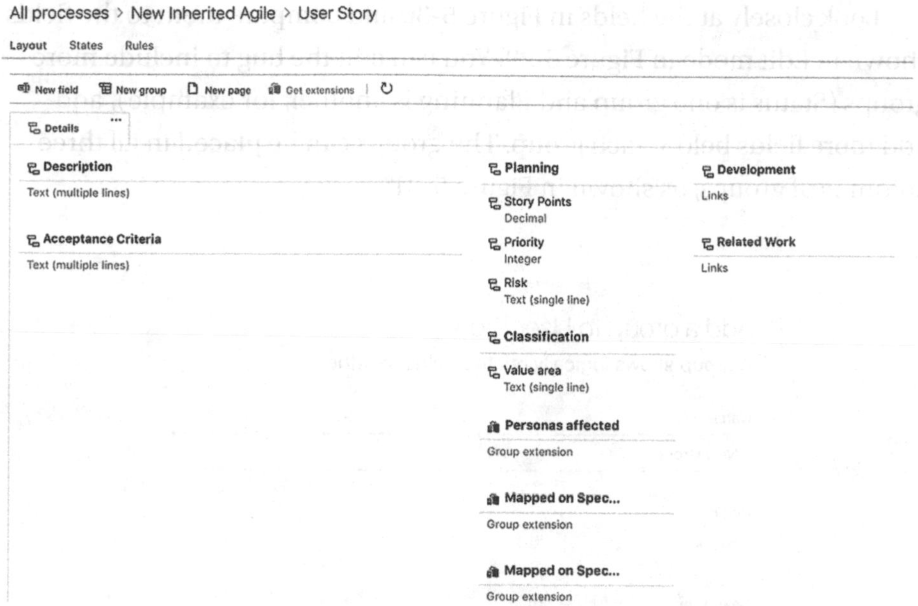

All processes > New Inherited Agile > User Story

Layout   States   Rules

New field   New group   New page   Get extensions

Details

Description
Text (multiple lines)

Acceptance Criteria
Text (multiple lines)

Planning
Story Points
Decimal

Priority
Integer

Risk
Text (single line)

Classification

Value area
Text (single line)

Personas affected
Group extension

Mapped on Spec...
Group extension

Mapped on Spec...
Group extension

Development
Links

Related Work
Links

Figure 5-29. *Changing the User Story work item type*

You can add new fields, new groups, or new pages for the work item type. Figure 5-30 shows what a sample layout of a user story in the Agile process looks like when you create a new story.

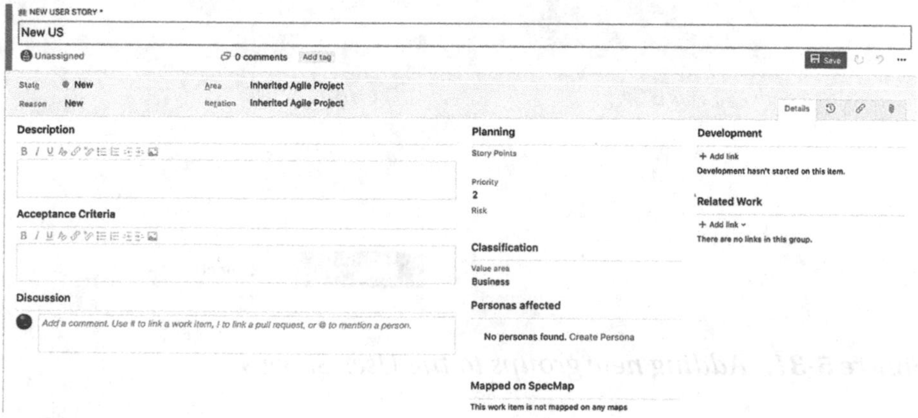

NEW USER STORY *
New US

Unassigned   0 comments   Add tag   Save

State   New   Area   Inherited Agile Project
Reason New   Iteration Inherited Agile Project   Details

Description
B I U ...

Acceptance Criteria
B I U ...

Discussion
Add a comment. Use # to link a work item, ! to link a pull request, or @ to mention a person.

Planning
Story Points

Priority
2
Risk

Classification
Value area
Business

Personas affected
No personas found. Create Persona

Mapped on SpecMap
This work item is not mapped on any maps

Development
+ Add link
Development hasn't started on this item.

Related Work
+ Add link ~
There are no links in this group.

Figure 5-30. *The User Story form in the Agile process*

189

Look closely at the fields in Figure 5-30 and compare them to the fields shown in Edit mode in Figure 5-29. You can edit the bug to include more groups (Status is one group and Planning is another, for example), and add more fields below each group. The groups can be placed in all three columns of groups, as shown in Figure 5-31.

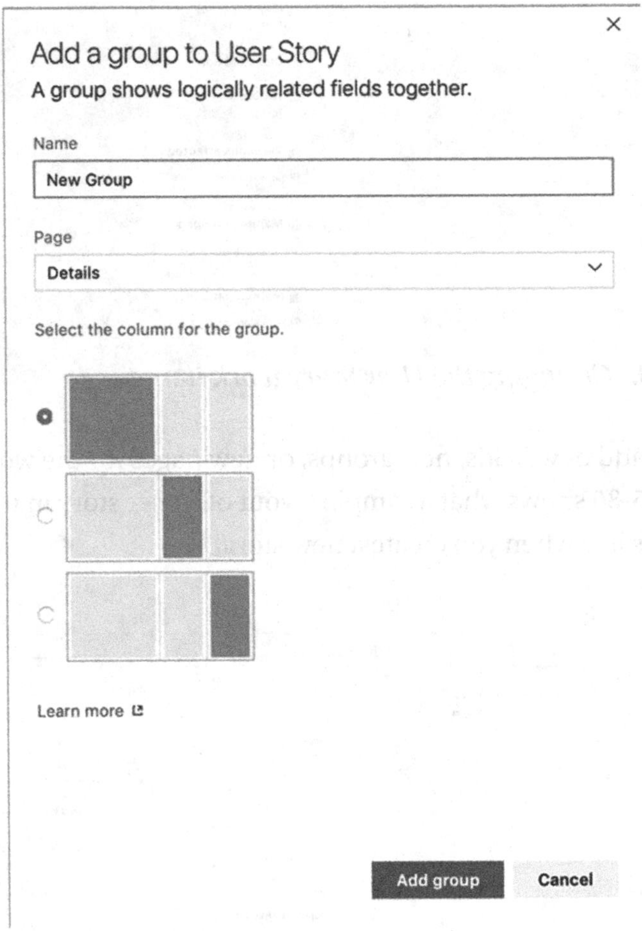

Figure 5-31. *Adding new groups to the User Story*

The result can be seen in Figure 5-32.

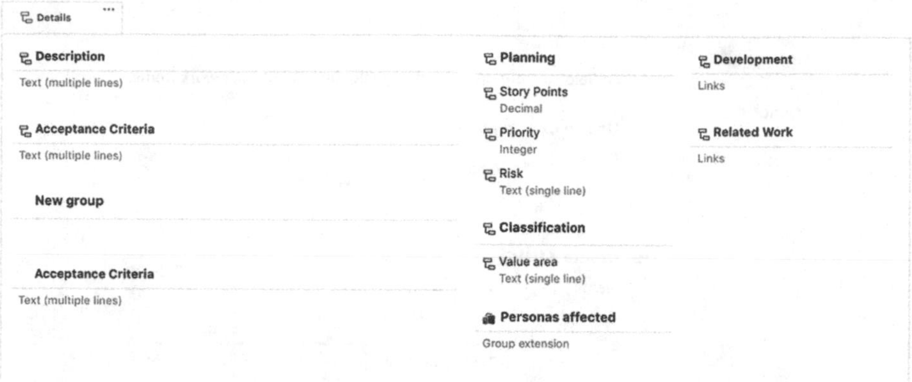

Figure 5-32. *Adding a new group to the User Story*

For each group, you can add, edit, or remove fields, so you can configure the group and enter the information your organization thinks is important for a work item type.

The Fields view lets you add or modify the attributes of a custom field or the attributes of an inherited field (Figure 5-33). Keep in mind that you cannot modify system fields. In the example shown in Figure 5-33, you work only with the fields present in the work item type you are currently editing.

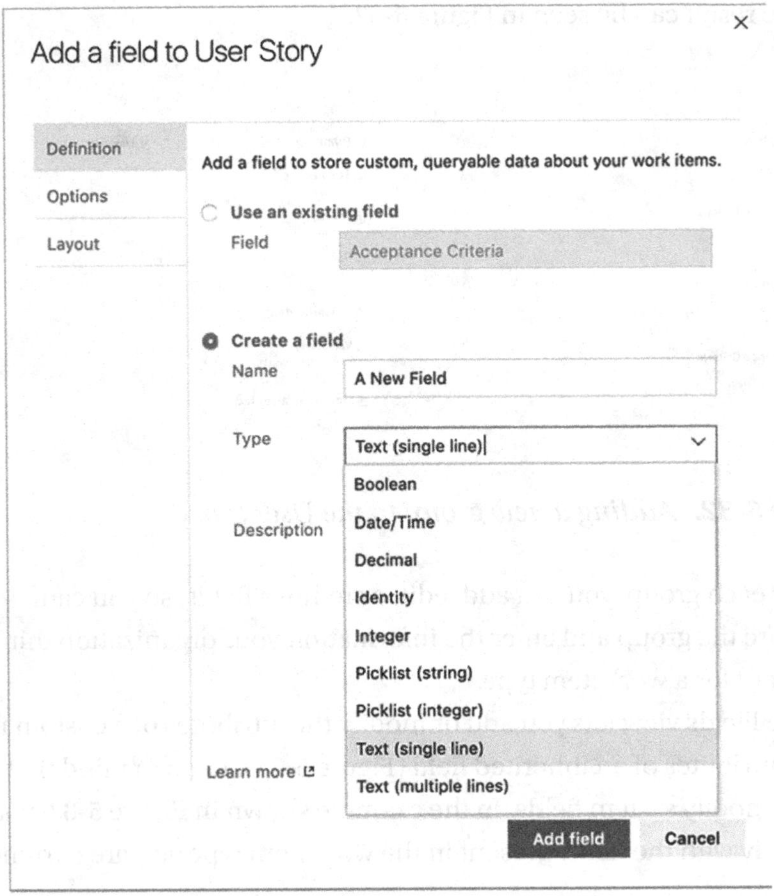

Figure 5-33. *Adding a new field*

For each custom field, you also have options for each field (Figure 5-34).

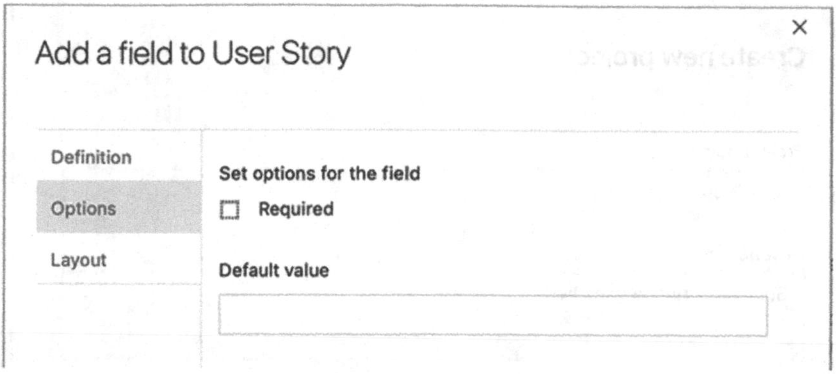

Figure 5-34. *Editing options for a new field*

Figure 5-35 shows that you can also make some adjustments to where a new fields should appear in the layout.

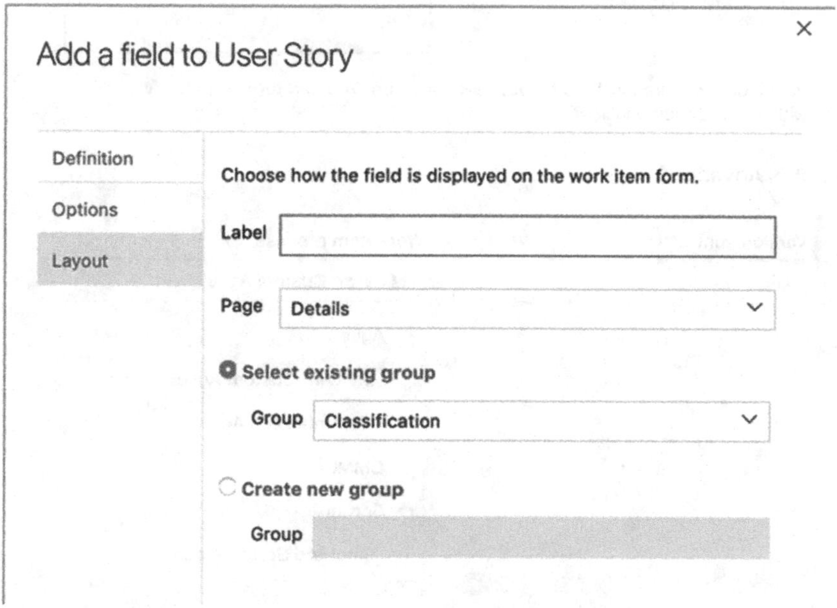

Figure 5-35. *Editing the layout for a new field*

After you are done editing your process, you can access it and create a new Azure DevOps project using your own customized process, as shown in Figure 5-36.

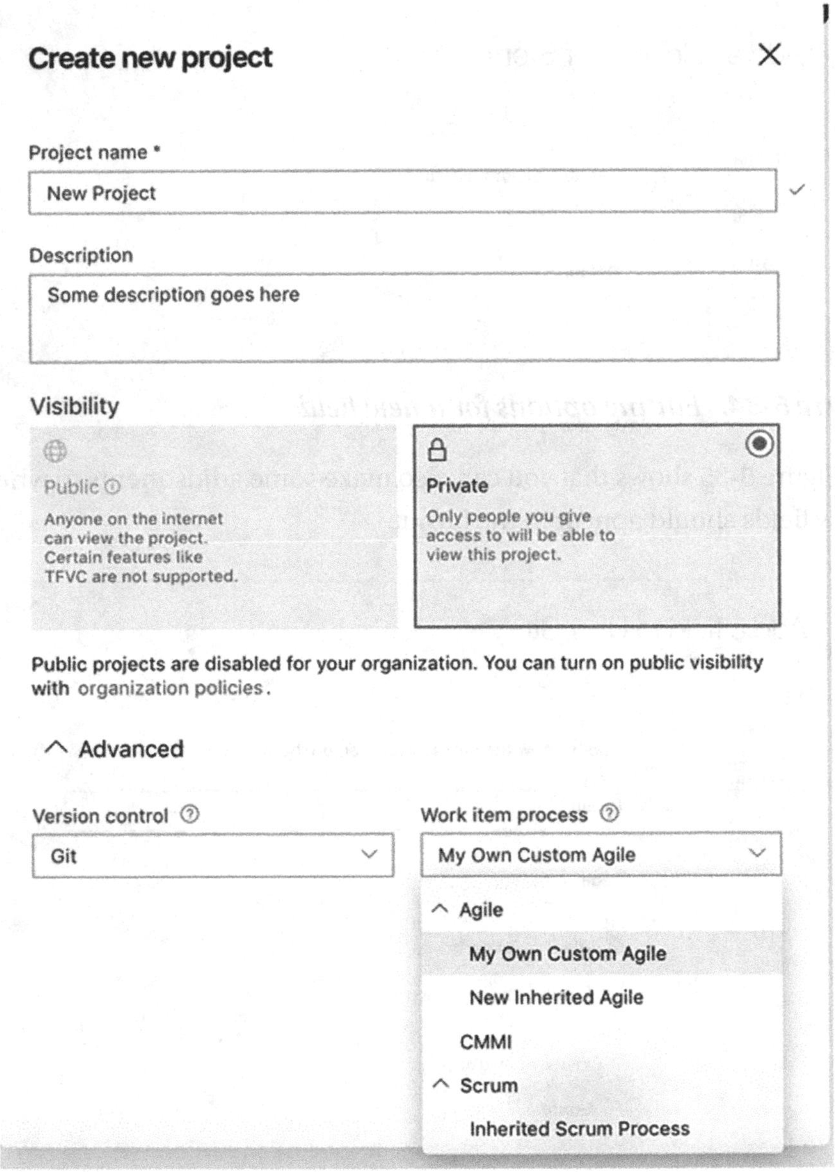

Figure 5-36. *After you create a custom process, you can use it to create new Azure DevOps projects*

Summary

In this chapter you have looked at how you can customize your process in TFS on-premise as well as in Azure DevOps. Most customizations can be done on-premise, but Microsoft has added great support for editing a cloud-based Azure DevOps project as well.

CHAPTER 6

Agile Practices in Azure DevOps and TFS

This chapter focuses on more technical aspects of Agile practices. They might not be linked directly to project management or product management, but they are great ways to enhance the quality of your coding efforts. In Chapter 3, you were given a brief overview of eXtreme Programming, or XP, as it is called. As you may remember, Scrum, for example, does not say how you should work using the Scrum framework. XP is much more practice oriented; it gives you hands-on advice on how you should work.

XP focuses on 12 practices, but some of them (regarding project management) overlap what is covered by Scrum and, in my opinion, Scrum handles them better than XP. If I have a choice, I generally use Scrum as a project management framework and XP for development tasks. Here I focus on the following practices in XP:

- Agile testing

- TDD and automated testing

- CI/CD

- Coding standards

- Refactoring

- Pair programming

© Joachim Rossberg 2019
J. Rossberg, *Agile Project Management with Azure DevOps*,
https://doi.org/10.1007/978-1-4842-4483-8_6

You might be asking yourself: Why is he focusing on these practices only? Well, the answer is: Because they are code-quality enhancing and they are very common for developers to use in Agile projects. So, let's start with Agile testing and move on from there.

Agile Testing

Agile projects can be challenging. If you have the mind-set that change will come and you embrace the changes, working iteratively and delivering incrementally, you have a better chance of delivering what the customer wants "now," not what they thought they wanted several months earlier.

Delivering software incrementally at short intervals means you need to rethink the testing approach you use. Working with incremental development typically means you need to do lots of regression testing to make sure the features you developed and tested continue to work as the product evolves. You need to have an efficient test process or else you will spend lots of time in the life cycle of the project preparing for testing rather than actually running the tests.

Consider Amazon.com. I have read many times that they deploy to production every 11.6 seconds.[1] Without knowing the actual process Amazon.com uses to accomplish this, I can only guess that they have a lot of automated testing in place to make sure that new code does not interfere with old code.

To solve the problems and challenges this deployment implies, you need to design your tests carefully. Maintain only those tests that give value to your product. As the product evolves through increments, so should the tests, and you can choose to add relevant tests only to your regression test suite. To make testing more efficient, automate the tests and include them in your CI/CD workflow to get the most value from the tests.

---

[1] http://joshuaseiden.com/blog/2013/12/amazon-deploys-to-production-every-11-6-seconds/.

Acceptance Criteria

A wise man (my boss and cowriter from time to time), Mathias Olausson, once said:

> *Acceptance criteria are to testing what user stories are to product owners. Acceptance criteria sharpen the definition of a user story or requirement. We can use acceptance criteria to define what needs to be fulfilled for a product owner to approve a user story.*

This is very true indeed.

One way to describe requirements is to use user stories. When writing user stories, you usually write them like this:

- As a service repair person, I want to be able to view ticket details from the dashboard so that the tickets are easy to access when we're with our customers.

This, of course, is not the entire requirement—just a description of it. You can detail a user story in different ways:

- Breaking down the story into several new stories

- Adding acceptance criteria

When discussing the previous user story with the product owner, you might come up with questions such as these:

- How should the service rep view the tickets? Search? Filter?

- In what way will the service rep access the tickets? Via the Web? Phone? Tablet?

- Is the ticket read-only or can the service rep edit it? Assign to someone else?

You then use this information to formulate acceptance criteria. Consider the question: How should the service rep view the tickets? Based on this question, you can formulate acceptance criteria such as the following:

- A service rep should
  - Be able to click the service ticket number in the list on the dashboard and see the details
  - Be able to search by customer, geography, and time
  - Be able to filter the result to get a better overview

Here are three ways we can write these acceptance criteria:

1. *Test That*: Start relevant acceptance criteria with the phrase "Test that . . . ." This gets people into a testing mind-set right off the bat. For each PBI, what will be tested to ensure the item is done?

2. *Demonstrate That*: Start relevant acceptance criteria with the words "Demonstrate that . . . ." This gets people to think about the review and what they want to show the product owner and stakeholders.

3. *Given, When, Then*: Given <a precondition>, when <a user action occurs>, then <the expected result>. This Gherkin syntax serves two purposes: documentation and automated tests. The text can be read by anyone, yet it is can also be parsed by test automation tools.

Hopefully, this discussion leads to more questions for the product owner, which will help to understand better what should be tested. The answers will help to define the product more clearly.

In TFS or Azure DevOps, you can collect all this important information in a PBI (or user story or requirement, depending on the process template you use).

The PBI gives good traceability to follow the requirement to its acceptance criteria. Figure 6-1 shows an example of how the Visual Studio Scrum template in Azure DevOps displays this information.

Figure 6-1. *Documenting acceptance criteria as part of a PBI*

Evolving Tests

In an Agile process, during which development is done in small increments, you also need to make sure the tests follow an iterative way of working. The tests need to sync with the flow of the application development; otherwise, you might run in to a lot of problems down the line.

Early in a project life cycle, little is known about a new feature, and you need to run tests against all acceptance criteria defined for the requirement. When a feature is completed, you should be confident it has been tested according to the test cases and that it works as expected. After that, you only need to run tests to validate changes in the requirement. This means you must have a process for knowing which tests to run.

Running all tests manually is tedious and takes a lot of effort in consideration. Instead, rethink how you design your test cases. You could, for example, think of your test base as a pyramid (Figure 6-2). Figure 6-2 shows how different types of tests can be put in proportion in a specific case.

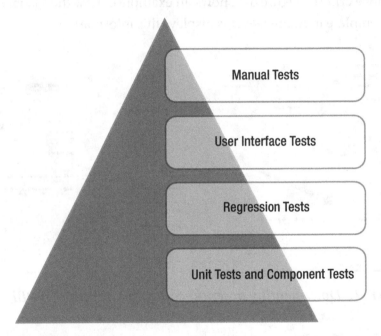

Figure 6-2. *Proportions of types of tests*

At the bottom of the pyramid are the unit and component tests, which are the main part of the testing effort. These tests are relatively cheap to create and maintain; but, to test the system as a whole, you probably need to add regression tests that run end-to-end tests as well.

Some of the regression tests should be implemented as user interface tests to simulate how an end user uses the system. However, user interface tests are more complex to design and maintain, and often it isn't practical to have more than a small set of them. Most of these tests can and should be automated to provide an efficient way of maintaining changes in the product.

With this way of designing tests, you end up with a small number of manual tests at the top of the pyramid. This means manual tests are always necessary to some extent.

Now let's talk a little about how TFS can help us manage our tests.

Clients for Managing Tests

There are two options for managing tests in TFS 2015:

1. Microsoft Test Manager, or MTM, which is a desktop application

2. Microsoft Web Test Case Manager, which is a web-based application inside the Azure DevOps GUI

Microsoft Test Manager

MTM is a stand-alone desktop application and was included in the Visual Studio family when TFS 2010 was released. View it as the Visual Studio for testers—the one-stop shop for the entire test process. A tester can do almost all testing activities within a single application.

At a high level, MTM provides functionality for the following:

- *Exploratory testing*: Records actions while a test is performed without preplanned steps.

- *Planning of manual tests*: Plans tests with the option of creating steps from recorded actions.

- *Running manual tests*: Displays test cases on the side of the screen while tests are running. Records actions, screenshots, and other diagnostic data automatically for inclusion in test results and bug reports.

- *Specifying test platforms*: Creates multiple versions of a test to be performed on different hardware or software configurations.

203

- *Collecting more diagnostic data in manual tests*:
  Collects event logs, IntelliTrace data, video, and other
  diagnostic data while tests are performed.

- *Testing Windows Store apps*: Collects diagnostic data and
  screenshots while tests are performed on a Windows 8
  device or PC, with MTM running on a separate PC.

- *Copying and cloning test suites and test cases*: Copies
  test suites or plans from one project to another.

- *Recording and playing back manual tests*: Records
  keystrokes and gestures while tests are running, then
  repeats the actions rapidly on a later occasion.

- *Planning application tests from a Microsoft Excel or
  Microsoft Word document*: Uses Microsoft Excel to
  edit test plans in bulk and synchronizes with plans
  embedded in Microsoft Word documents.

- *Testing in a lab environment*: Gathers diagnostic data
  from servers while tests are running. Manages the
  assignment of server machines to testers. Sets up fresh
  test configurations quickly by using virtual machines.

- *Tracking software quality*: Monitors the progress of a project
  by tracking the tests that pass or fail; manages bugs.

- *Automating system tests*: Links test methods in code to
  emulate manual tests so they can be repeated regularly.
  Automates deployment of applications and tests to
  a lab environment. Sets up a completely automatic
  build–deploy–test workflow. Adds existing automated
  tests from Visual Studio to a test suite.

MTM will soon be deprecated. Microsoft's goal is to have everybody
switch to the web-based testing tools in Azure DevOps.

Azure Test Plans

The second option for working with test cases is Azure Test, which is found in the Azure DevOps web GUI. Azure Test was introduced with the TFS 2012 Update 2 release. Azure Test Plans is a lightweight solution when you want the integrated testing experience with TFS/Azure DevOps that offers most of MTM functionality. But let's be honest here, most testers I have met just don't think this is the best solution for their testing needs. Most turn to tools like ReqTest and such instead.

As a core part of TFS, the Test Hub enables you to create and run manual tests through an easy-to-use Web-based interface that can be accessed via all major browsers on any platform.

The Test Hub isn't just for manual testers. It's a tool that product owners and business analysts can use to evaluate how their features measure up against acceptance criteria. It can be used to keep track of acceptance criteria for requirements; later, it can be used for sign-off, if you want that functionality. In summary, the Test Hub offers the following:

- Customization of workflows with test plan, test suite, and test case work items

- End-to-end traceability from requirements to test cases and bugs with requirement-based test suites

- Criteria-based test selection with query-based test suites

- Excel-like interface with a grid for easy test case creation

- Reusable test steps and test data, with shared steps and shared parameters

- Sharable test plans, test suites, and test cases for reviewing with stakeholders

- Browser-based test execution on any platform

- Real-time charts for tracking test activity

To use Azure Test, you must have a valid license for MTM.

TDD and Automated Testing
Test-Driven Development

TDD is a practice that originated with Kent Beck, who is credited with having developed or "rediscovered" the technique. TDD is one of the core practices in XP, but has created lots of general interest in its own right. So, even if you do not use XP, you can still use this practice as a way to help developers write better code.

TDD relies on the repetition of a very short development cycle. First, the developer writes an (initially failing) automated test case that defines a desired improvement or new function, then produces the minimum amount of code to pass that test, and then refactors the new code to acceptable standards. Kent Beck stated in 2003 that TDD encourages simple designs and inspires confidence.

Instead of designing a module, then coding it and then testing it, you turn the process around and do the testing first. To put it another way, you don't write a single line of production code until you have a test that fails.

In traditional software development, tests were thought to verify that an existing bit of code was written correctly. When you do TDD, however, your tests are used to define the behavior of a class before you write it.

With TDD, you want your tests to run frequently to get continuous feedback about the written code. A change in code that breaks one or more tests is something that demands immediate notification. You can configure Visual Studio 2015 to run unit tests automatically after build so that as soon as the code is compiled, all tests the tests are run and feedback is generated regarding their results. This means the feedback loop is very short. The loop is the time it takes for (in this case) a developer to make a code change to when that developer gets feedback on whether the change was successful.

Working with Automated Tests

To achieve the goals of automated testing, you need to plan ahead and think about what you really want to get out of your automation efforts. Visual Studio 2015 helps you to set up your test environment and to select which test types to use.

Visual Studio 2015 has support for a number of different test types, ranging from basic unit tests, to automated user interface tests, up to complete load-testing capabilities (Table 6-1). What is really nice with working with tests in Visual Studio is its shared tooling for designing and running tests. This is very convenient because now you can start by learning the type of test with which you want to begin working, then you can leverage the framework and how you design, and last, run and follow-up test runs. As you add additional types of automated tests, you do not have to learn new practices—just add the new ones to the existing platform. Table 6-1 presents the purpose of some test types in Visual Studio.

Table 6-1. *Test Types Supported in Visual Studio 2015*

Test types	Purpose
Basic unit test	An empty unit test
Unit test	A basic unit test with a test context and additional test attributes
Coded user interface test	A coded user interface test
Coded user interface test map	A user interface test map that can be used to split into smaller pieces the user interface definitions in a coded user interface test
Generic test	A test that wraps an existing function into an Azure DevOps Test plans test
Ordered test	A test used to control a set of tests.
Web performance test	A test that records a web test using Internet Explorer
Load test	A test that launches a wizard to generate a load test configuration

The following sections on CI/CD are inspired by my boss, Mathias Olausson. He is an expert in this area, so make sure to check out his recent book about CD with Visual Studio ALM 2015 at http://www.apress. com/9781484212738?gtmf=s. It is a great reference for this topic.

Continuous Integration/Continuous Delivery

Continuous Integration

> *Continuous Integration is a software development practice where members of a team integrate their work frequently; usually each person integrates at least daily – leading to multiple integrations per day.*[2]

CI is a practice in XP that has come to be the defacto standard in Agile projects. Martin Fowler was the person who introduced it to the more general public, but it was first named and proposed by Grady Booch in 1991.[3] CI is a practice that integrates the code base frequently. In combination with running automated unit tests in the developer's local environment and verifying they all pass before committing to the mainline, CI aims to make sure the developer is not checking in code that breaks any other developers' code. Over time, this practice has evolved, and now builds run on build servers that run the unit tests automatically and periodically—or even after every commit—and report the results to the developers. CI has spread outside the Agile community and is now used frequently in other types of projects as well.

In addition to running the unit and integration tests, you can also run static and dynamic tests, measure and profile performance, extract and format documentation from the source code, and facilitate manual quality assurance processes. In this way, you get continuous quality control of your software as well.

---

[2]Martin Fowler. https://martinfowler.com/articles/continuous Integration.html

[3]https://en.wikipedia.org/wiki/Grady_Booch.

An Agile project requires new ways of working and, just like Scrum, aims to be all about common sense. So is CI. But, there are several problems with Agile DevOps from a deployment perspective, including the following:

- *Testing*: Because you develop your software incrementally in short iterations, you need to rethink how you test.

- *Cross-functional teams*: Ideally, the team should be self-organized—meaning, more people should have the ability to deploy software.

- *Shippable product in every iteration*: With short iterations (perhaps a two-week sprint), it is no longer possible to spend a week on installation. Hence, you need to automate tasks that were manual previously.

CI can help resolve these issues. In fact, Scrum has a solution for this; use the retrospective to find ways to improve.

Why Continuous Integration?

How can CI help you? Well, CI does the following:

- Reduces risks

- Reduces manual routines

- Creates shippable software

- Improves confidence in the product

- Identifies deficiencies early

- Reduces time spent on testing

- Improving project visibility

Keep in mind that CI is not free of costs. You need to maintain your CI solution, including the build environment, over time. It can also take quite some effort to introduce it into your organization. And don't forget that CI has costs for setting up the new build and CI infrastructure as well.

To get CI working, teams need to agree on some rules for the process. If the rules are not followed, there is a potential risk that the quality of the result will degrade, and people will lose confidence in the process. Mathias Olausson recommends using at least the following rules as a starting point

- *Check in often*: The CI process needs changes to work. The smaller the changes and the more specific they are, the faster we can react to things that go wrong.

- *Do not check in broken code*: Checking in often is great, but don't overdo it. Don't check in code until it works, and *never* check in broken code. If you need to switch contexts, use the Suspend feature in TFS to put things aside for a while.

- *Fix broken build immediately*: If you break something, it is your responsibility to fix it.

- *Write unit tests*: The system needs to know what works and not. Unit tests and other inspection tools should be used to make sure the code does more than just compile.

- *All tests and inspections must pass*: With inspections in place, you must pay attention to the results. Use feedback mechanisms to make people aware when something is broken.

- *Run private builds*: If you can do a test build before check-in, you can avoid committing things that don't work. TFS can build from a shelve set using a feature called Gated Checkin.

- *Avoid getting broken code*: Last, if the build is broken,
  don't get the latest code. Why go through the hassle of
  working on code that doesn't work? Instead, use the
  version control system and get the latest version that
  worked.

Figure 6-3 shows a process that is a complete CI solution. It should be
what you strive to achieve.

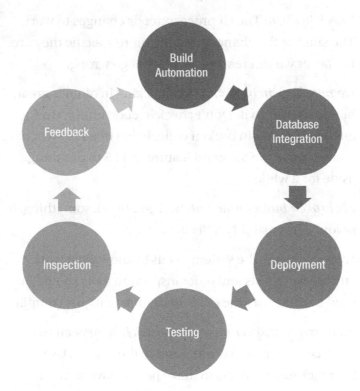

Figure 6-3. *Components in the CI process*

Continuous Delivery

The problem with CI is that it can be a solution to a nonexistent problem. Deployment as part of the CI flow is not just about automating the build, test, and release process. You really need to think about delivery to add value to the deployment process.

CI is great, and it supplies a framework for producing software efficiently in a controlled fashion. But, to get the most out of it, you need to look at how it fits into the overall process of delivering software. In an Agile project, you want to deliver working software in every iteration. Unfortunately, this is easier said than done. It often turns out that, even if you implement CI and get the build process to produce a new installation package in a few minutes, it takes several days to get a new piece of software tested and released into production. So how can you make this process work better?

Let's start by asking the following simple question:

How long does it take to release one changed line of code into production?

Probably, the answer is: Much longer than you would want to. Why is this? First, you must know more about how you release your product. Mathias Olausson says that even in organizations that follow good engineering practices, the release process is often neglected. A common reason why this happens is simply because releasing software needs collaboration across different disciplines in the process. To improve the situation, you need to sit down as a team and document the steps required to go from a code change to the software released into production. Figure 6-4 shows a typical delivery process. In practice, work happens sequentially, just like in the picture.

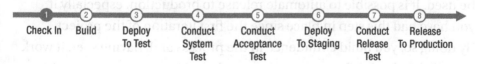

Figure 6-4. A typical delivery process

When you have come this far, you now know a lot more about the delivery process, which means you can start optimizing the process:

1. Look at the steps in the process. Which steps take the most time? What can be done to improve them?

2. Look at the steps in the process? Which steps go wrong most often? What is causing this?

3. Look at the sequence of steps. How should they be run in sequence?

Having looked at the process and answered the previous questions, you should now have a better process, as shown in Figure 6-5.

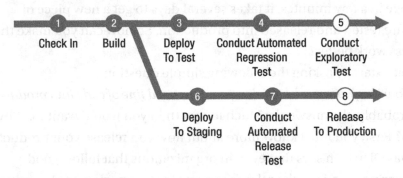

Figure 6-5. *An optimized delivery process*

With this model (Figure 6-5), the process is changed so that most steps are automated by implementing automated tests as well as automated build and deployment. Releasing to production automatically is not for the faint-hearted, so this would be done manually, but the same automated scripts as the automated deploy to test and staging environments should be used. It is possible to automate release to production, especially if you have had this step in place since the first iteration of the project. By doing so, you build confidence in the process and, having seen it work throughout the development cycle, you should trust the process at this critical stage. Also, in the model, parallelization the acceptance test and preparation of the production environment has occurred. By doing these steps in parallel, you can push the release to production as soon as the acceptance tests are green, instead of the traditional stage to production first after the acceptance tests have passed.

CD is a great practice to produce updates in a controlled and effective manner. But, without an intentional release management discipline, you can lose much of its value. What you need to add to the picture is how the release planning ties into the deployment process and then ensure you know which features you want to deploy where and when. This is not covered in the scope of this book, but please refer to Mathias Olausson's book mentioned earlier for more details and best practices.

Azure Pipelines

With Azure DevOps, you can use the service Azure Pipelines to automate your CI/CD flow. You can build, test, and deploy Node.js, Python, Java, PHP, Ruby, C/C++, .NET, Android, and iOS apps. And, you can run in parallel on Linux, macOS, and Windows.

You can also build and push images to various container registries such as the Azure Container Registry or Docker Hub. Or, you can deploy your containers to individual hosts or Kubernetes, which is an open-source system for automating deployment, scaling, and management of "containerized" applications.

You can further use Azure Pipelines to implement your CD of software to any cloud, including Azure, Amazon Web Services (AWS), and Google Cloud Platform (GCP). Using Azure DevOps, you can visualize deployment to any number of interdependent stages as well.

Coding Standards

Coding standard is an agreed-on set of rules that the entire development team agrees to adhere to throughout the project. The standard specifies a consistent style and format for source code within the chosen programming language, as well as various programming constructs and patterns that should be avoided to reduce the probability of defects. The coding standard may be a standard convention specified by the language vendor (e.g., the code conventions for the Java Programming Language, recommended by Sun) or a custom defined by the development team.

XP backers advocate code that is self-documenting to the furthest degree possible, which reduces the need for code comments, which can get out of sync with the code itself. This can be especially useful if you have a new developer coming in to write code or if you use many consultants in the development. It will be easier to make sure that all developers adhere to the same coding standards so that the code is maintainable over time.

In Visual Studio, you can require that code analysis be run on all code projects in a team project by using the code analysis check-in policy. Requiring code analysis improves the quality of the code that is checked into the code base. The feedback loop is very short before developers find code that does not follow the standard.

Code analysis check-in policies are set in the team project settings and apply to each code project in the team project. Code analysis runs are configured for code projects in the project file for the code project. Code analysis runs are performed on a local computer. When you enable a code analysis check-in policy, files in a code project that are to be checked in must be compiled after their last edit, and a code analysis run that contains, at a minimum, the rules in the team project settings must be performed on the computer where the changes were made.

For managed code, you set the check-in policy by specifying a rule set that contains a subset of the code analysis rules. After you specify a check-in policy for managed code, team members can synchronize their code analysis settings for code projects to the team project policy settings.

For C/C++ code, the check-in policy requires that all code analysis rules be run. You can add preprocessor directives to disable specific rules for the individual code projects in your team project.

Refactoring

Code refactoring is the process of restructuring existing computer code—changing the factoring—without changing its external behavior. Refactoring improves nonfunctional attributes of the software. Advantages include improved code readability and reduced complexity, which can improve source code maintainability and create a more expressive internal architecture or object model to improve extensibility.

Typically, refactoring applies a series of standardized, basic smaller refactorings, each of which is (usually) a tiny change in a computer program's source code that either preserves the behavior of the software or at least does not modify its conformance to functional requirements. Many development environments provide automated support for performing the mechanical aspects of these basic refactorings. If done extremely well, code refactoring may also resolve hidden, dormant, or undiscovered computer bugs or vulnerabilities in the system by simplifying the underlying logic and eliminating unnecessary levels of complexity. If done poorly, it may fail the requirement that external functionality not be changed and/or may introduce new bugs.

Why do we use refactoring? Well, we want the developers to think constantly about they can keep the code simpler and more easily maintained. Often, there is no need for gold plating on code. Product owners are more interested in the value to the organization the code adds, not how cool or complicated it is.

Pair Programming

Pair programming means that all code is produced by two people programming on one task on one computer. One programmer has control over the workstation (the driver) and thinks mostly about the coding in detail. The other programmer is more focused on the big picture and reviews the code continually that is being produced by the first programmer. Programmers switch roles after a while so both are in the driver's seat at one time or another.

The pairs might not be fixed either. In many projects, programmers switch partners frequently so that everyone knows what everyone is doing. This practice also lets everybody remain familiar with the whole system, even the parts outside their skill set. Doing this improves communication and cross-functionality of the team.

Why is this a good practice? In my experience, pair programming reduces bugs with somewhere 15% to 50%. Reducing bugs by these numbers lowers the amount of time and effort spent chasing bugs in production.

Another benefit is that there are two pairs of eyes that go over the implementation of the requirement. The idea is that any misconceptions of the requirement on which the pair is working can be found quickly because two people are writing the code collaboratively. If there had been only a single developer writing the code, it would be harder to find such misconceptions. In addition, if using one developer, that developer might also write the unit tests included in the CD model, and they would run successfully because the tests were written by the same developer who wrote the code. In this scenario, we also would not see the misconceptions in the tests unless another set of eyes reviewed the code.

Are there any drawbacks to pair programming? Of course there are. One of the most discussed is that two programmers working at the same time cost twice as much as if only one developer did the job. This is true. But here you need to consider the cost reduction of finding defects early during the development process, not during production when the cost associated with fixing the defect is great. Our general advice is to use pair programming on complicated features, important features, or high-risk features for which there are greater quality standards than for some other code. Use pair programming wisely; don't be afraid to use it.

Another way to enhance code quality is to have a peer review of important code. In this instance one developer writes the code then sends a code review request to a peer for a review. This is an effective way of working and does not require two developers full time.

SAFe in Azure DevOps

Because organizations are applying an Agile way of working more and more, many are asking themselves how they can get agility to work at scale. There are several frameworks available for scaling Agile such as LeSS and Nexus, but many organizations turn to SAFe. There is no process that supports SAFe out of the box in Azure DevOps, so you need to work with the ones you have got unless you want to create a custom process.

Let's take a look at SAFe in Figure 6-6. This is the largest SAFe configuration, called the Full SAFe. There are four levels—Portfolio, Large Solution, Program, and Essential SAFe—that cover most organizational needs. Microsoft has four work item types that can be used to support this setup: Epics, Features, User Stories, and Tasks. There is a hierarchy to these work item types (Figure 6-7). The hierarchy originates from the Agile process, but works the same for Scrum and CMMI. So, if you're interested in using SAFe, you can configure projects created with the Scrum, Agile, or CMMI processes to track SAFe criteria.

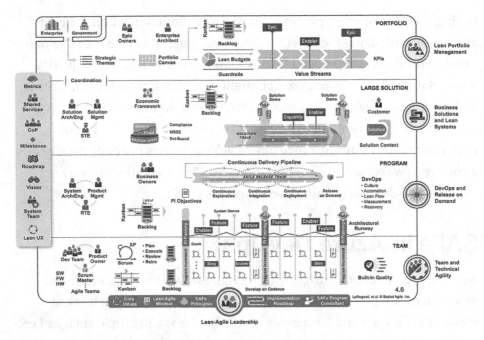

Figure 6-6. Full SAFe implementation

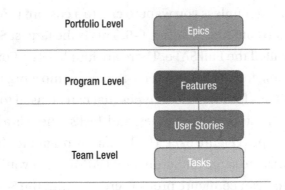

Figure 6-7. The relationship between SAFe levels and work items in Azure DevOps

Figure 6-7 shows at what SAFe level these workt item types would be used. Epics support the Portfolio level; Features, the Program level; and User Stories and Tasks support the Team level. To support SAFe in Azure DevOps further, you need to work with your areas and iterations in Project Settings. Figure 6-8 shows one way of implementing SAFe in the iterations view.

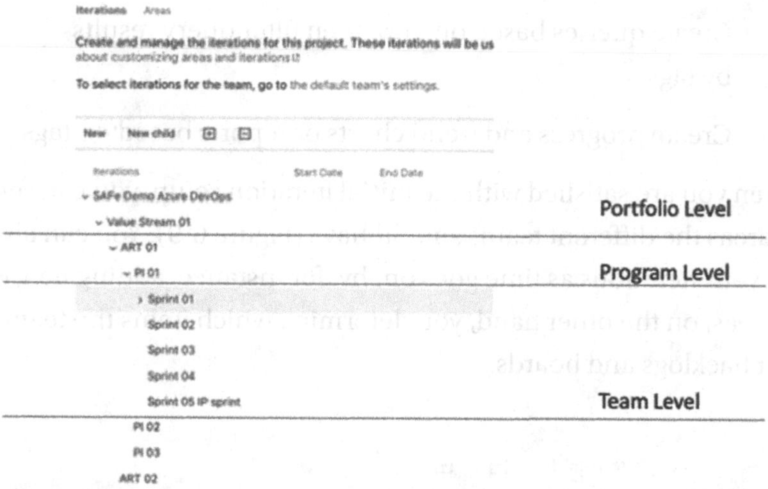

Figure 6-8. *Configurating iterations for SAFe in Azure DevOps*

You can see the overall Portfolio level (SAFe Demo Azure DevOps) with one value stream present (Value Stream 01). The value stream includes the ARTs (the Program Level)—in this case, ART 01 and ART 02—which lead to three program increments (PI 01, PI 02, and PI03), followed by the configured the sprints for each PI.

Because epics can span several release trains, the portfolio team probably wouldn't be associated with any specific iterations. Program teams, on the other hand, track their features, which ship with a PI. The feature teams work in sprints to complete the stories chosen for the PI. Each team in turn chooses which iterations support them in tracking their deliverables.

Because you are free to configure iterations any way you want, this is only one way you can use iteration configuration. You need to discuss what your setup should look like before you implement it in Azure DevOps. One way to simplify the iteration setup is to use tags for value streams. With tags added to work items, you can do the following:

- Filter any backlog or Kanban board

- Create queries based on tags, then filter query results by tags

- Create progress and trend charts or reports based on tags

When you are satisfied with the initial iteration setup, you can select which areas the different teams should have (Figure 6-9). You can always modify your iterations as time goes on, by, for instance, adding new PIs. Using areas, on the other hand, you determine which items the teams see on their backlogs and boards.

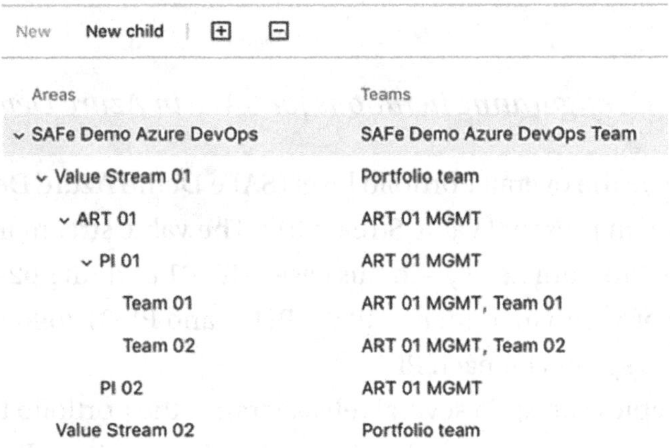

New New child ⊞ ⊟	
Areas	Teams
⌄ SAFe Demo Azure DevOps	SAFe Demo Azure DevOps Team
⌄ Value Stream 01	Portfolio team
⌄ ART 01	ART 01 MGMT
⌄ PI 01	ART 01 MGMT
Team 01	ART 01 MGMT, Team 01
Team 02	ART 01 MGMT, Team 02
PI 02	ART 01 MGMT
Value Stream 02	Portfolio team

Figure 6-9. *Configurating areas for SAFe in Azure DevOps*

As you can see in Figure 6-9, the Portfolio team will track epics in each value stream and thus will keep track of higher level efforts. The team can also use a Kanban board (Figure 6-10).

Figure 6-10. *Working with areas enables different teams to see their individual Kanban boards*

The ARTs are tracked by the ART management teams (ART 01 MGMT). These teams can also follow everything that happens in each PI at the ART, PI, and team levels. Figure 6-11 shows the ART team tracking features on the Kanban board.

Order	Work Item Type	Title		State	Effort	Busin...	Value Area	Tags
1	Feature	> 🏆 Feature 02	...	● New			Business	
2	Feature	> 🏆 Feature 01		● New			Business	
3	Feature	> 🏆 Feature 03		● New			Business	

Figure 6-11. *The ART 01 MGMT team follows progress on its backlog (or Kanban board)*

The individual teams (Team 01 and Team 02) will work with things on their own backlogs (subsets of the program backlog), so they can focus on their work. As seen in Figure 6-12, Team 01 can follow its PBIs on separate backlogs or Kanban boards.

Order	Work Item Type	Title	State	Effort	Value Area	Iteration Path	Tags
1	Product Backlog Item ···	User Story 01	● New		Business	SAFe Demo Azure DevOps\Va...	
2	Product Backlog Item	User Story 02	● New		Business	SAFe Demo Azure DevOps\Va...	
3	Product Backlog Item	User Story 03	● New		Business	SAFe Demo Azure DevOps\Va...	

Figure 6-12. *The Backlog for Team 01*

This is one way of using Azure DevOps to support SAFe. Keep in mind that the flexibility of Azure DevOps and Azure DevOps Server makes it possible for to customize implementations. Before we leave this chapter, I want to say a few words about Nexus and Scaled Professional Scrum from Scrum.org.

Nexus in Azure DevOps

This section is written in part by one of my excellent coworkers—Jesper Fernström—who works for Solidify in Stockholm. Solidify is a certified Scrum.org training organization that is has considerable expertise with Azure DevOps. Let's take another look at the Nexus framework (Figure 6-13).

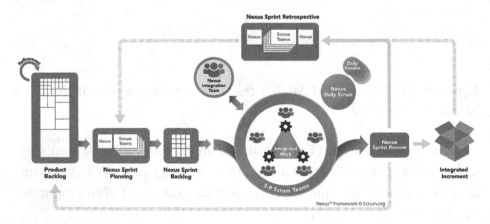

Figure 6-13. *The Nexus framework revisited*

If you know Scrum, Figure 6-13 should look very familiar to you. Unlike some other frameworks, when you scale Scrum using Nexus, Scrum is still Scrum. What you get with the Nexus framework are a few additions to Scrum to handle cross-team dependencies and issues, and improvement opportunities to ensure teams can deliver an integrated increment at the end of every sprint. Without going deeper into the Nexus framework, Figure 6-14 shows what is added to the mix.

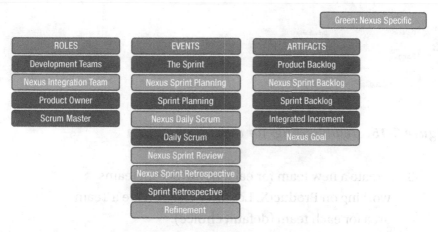

Figure 6-14. *Differences between Scrum and Nexus*

The neat thing with Nexus is that it requires *no change* to your process template in Azure DevOps because you are still doing Scrum! The new role, events, and the Nexus goal do not need to be modeled into your process template. The Nexus sprint backlog is just an aggregated view of all the individual team sprint backlogs. So, the only thing you need to do is set up your teams so they have one common aggregated "view of everything" and their own filtered team views, which is basically what everyone wants for any multiteam effort—and is supported out of the box by Azure DevOps.

225

In a scenario in which there is one team working on ProductX in Azure DevOps, you need to do the following to scale to multiple teams working in Nexus:

1. Go into Project settings and rename your existing team "Nexus."

2. Select the Area Path root as Default area for this team and set "sub-areas are included" (Figure 6-15).

Figure 6-15.   *Team settings for default area path*

3. Create a new team for each of the Scrum teams working on ProductX. Let the wizard create a Team area for each team (default choice).

4. For each new team, go to Team configuration and select the same iterations as for the Nexus team.

And you are done!

For "anything Nexus," such as Nexus sprint planning and Nexus sprint backlog, use the view of Nexus team. For team-specific stuff, use the individual team views, just as you did when there was only one team.

Why Not a Dedicated Team for the Nexus Integration Team?

This is what the *Nexus Guide (https://www.scrum.org/resources/nexus-guide)* says about the Nexus integration team:

> *The Nexus Integration Team is accountable for ensuring that a "Done" Integrated Increment (the combined work completed by a Nexus) is produced at least once every Sprint. The Scrum Teams are responsible for delivering "Done" Increments of potentially releasable products, as prescribed in Scrum. . . . Members of the Nexus Integration Team are often also members of the individual Scrum Teams in that Nexus. . . . Common activities the Nexus Integration Team might perform include coaching, consulting, and highlighting awareness of dependencies and cross-team issues. It might also perform work from the Product Backlog.*

So, when trying to scale Scrum using Nexus, the Nexus integration team is a sort of semivirtual team with a "servant–leader" flavor. Although the last sentence of the quote says the team might perform work from the backlog, this should be rare and more of an emergency action than anything else. All in all, you are much better served by an aggregated "Nexus view" from which you can get an overview of the current situation.

Further Improvements

There are a lot of things you can do to make your life just a little bit easier on a day-to-day basis while trying to scale Scrum using Nexus. Here is some advice:

- Use the predecessor/successor work item links to indicate dependencies.

- Check out various Azure DevOps extensions that might help you, such as the following:

- Work Item Visualization for visualizing dependencies

- Feature timeline and Epic Roadmap for visualizing dependencies

- Dependency Tracker for tracking cross-team dependencies

- Definition of Done to ensure all teams adhere to a common definition of done

And with these words, we end this chapter and thank Jesper for his input.

Summary

This chapter focused on some of the most common Agile practices. Many of them stem from XP and are great quality enhancers for development projects. Visual Studio and TFS has good support for implementing these practices. Keep in mind that these practices can be used in more "traditional" projects to increase quality.

In the next chapter, we discuss some key metrics that can be used to monitor the status of Agile projects.

CHAPTER 7

Metrics in Agile Projects

A key performance indicator (KPI) is a performance measurement used in most organizations to evaluate an organization's success or the success of a particular activity within the organization. Often, KPIs are used to measure the effects of a change project—for instance, implementing a good DevOps process—or to evaluate the progress of a development project.

You can use the score from a DevOps online assessment as a KPI and compare the assessment scores before and after the implementation of a DevOps process improvement. In this way, you get an indication of whether you have improved as a result of implementing a new process.

During projects, you should also be able to use the reports from your DevOps toolset to determine whether you're constantly improving your work. Continuous improvement, in my opinion, is something to strive for. When it comes to project management, you can, for instance, look at the team's velocity (how fast the team is able to work) and determine whether it's increasing or decreasing. By using reports and metrics from your DevOps tools, you can choose the KPIs you want and learn how to evaluate them.

© Joachim Rossberg 2019
J. Rossberg, *Agile Project Management with Azure DevOps*,
https://doi.org/10.1007/978-1-4842-4483-8_7

This chapter looks at metrics for five topics that cover most aspects of software development. Keep in mind they are not only for Agile projects, but can be used in many other projects as well:

- Project management

- Architecture, analysis, and design

- Developer practices

- Software testing

- Release management

Keep one thing in mind while you read about some of the reports. Reports are not available in Azure DevOps—only in TFS 2018. For Azure DevOps, I encourage you to use charts instead to get the information you need. Charts are described later in this chapter.

Some reports require that the team project collection that contains your team project was provisioned with SQL Server Reporting Services. The report is not available if Reports does not appear when you open Team Explorer and expand your team project node.

Metrics for Project Management

To get good metrics about the status of your projects, it's important to measure your progress. You can do this in several ways. If you're using Agile as a methodology, many of these metrics and reports should be familiar. To others, they may be new. Keep in mind that not all of these reports are available in Azure DevOps, but only in TFS on-prem.

Agile Metrics

Let's look at some important reports that are commonly used in Agile practices:

- Backlog overview

- Sprint burndown

- Velocity report

- Release burndown

- Remaining work

- Unplanned work

The *backlog overview report* lists all user stories, filtered by tags and iteration, and order of importance. Basically, this is a list of user stories filtered by the criteria you need. Many people use Excel (or another spreadsheet application) to create this report, but many DevOps tools have built-in support for producing it. Figure 7-1 shows what it looks like in Azure DevOps.

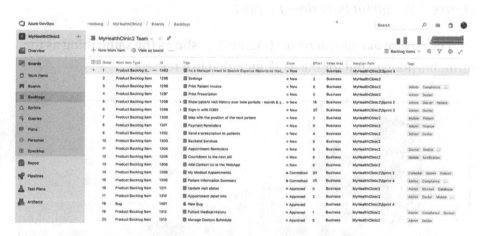

Figure 7-1. *The backlog overview in Azure DevOps*

I've mentioned the *sprint burndown report* before (Figure 7-2). This report shows how much work there is left to do in a sprint. Using it, you can predict when the team will finish the work assigned to this sprint, either during the sprint or after the sprint is finished. Based on this information, the team and the product owner can take actions to make sure they deliver what they have committed to deliver.

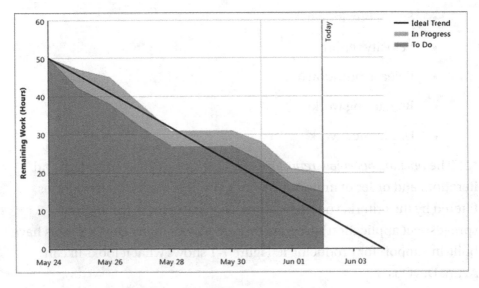

Figure 7-2. *Sprint burndown report*

The *release burndown report* (Figure 7-3) shows the same thing as the sprint burndown, but for the work included in a release.

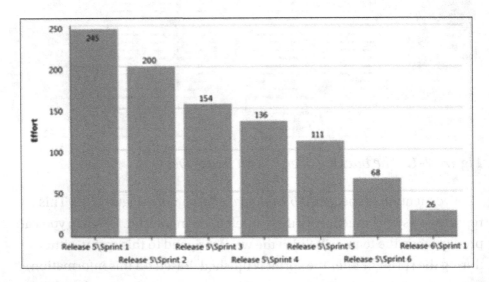

Figure 7-3. *Release burndown report*

A *burndown and burn rate report* (Figure 7-4) is another way to show a project's burndown. No surprises here: This is the same information shown in Figure 7-1. The burn rate provides summaries for the completed and required rate of work for a specified time period. In some tools, you can also see the information for team members. You can sometimes choose to see the report based on hours worked or number of work items.

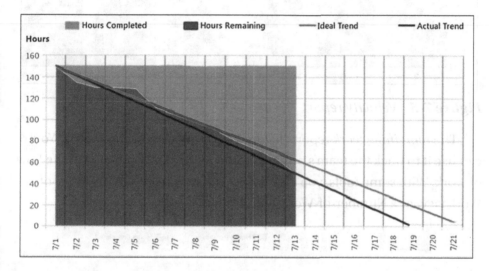

Figure 7-4. *Burndown and burn rate report*

Velocity (how much work a team can take on in a sprint) is important, especially for a product owner planning how much work can be accomplished in coming sprints. Velocity is usually a measure of the effect per story point that the team can accomplish.

Before any work is started, the product owner calculates a theoretical velocity to begin planning. As time goes by, it's updated with the team's real velocity based on how much work it delivers in each sprint. This helps the product owner estimate how much work the team can take on in coming sprints. The *velocity report* (Figure 7-5) can help you retrieve this information easily. Here you see how much effort the team has delivered for each sprint.

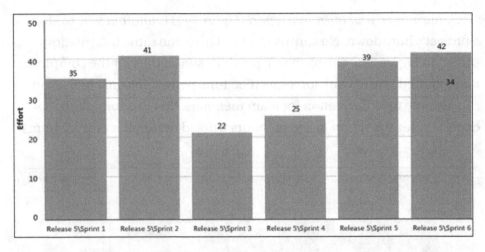

Figure 7-5. *Velocity report*

The *remaining work* report (Figure 7-6) is another useful metric. You can use it to track the team's progress and identify any problems in the flow of work. With some tools, you can view this report in either an Hours-of-Work view or a Number-of-Work-Items view.

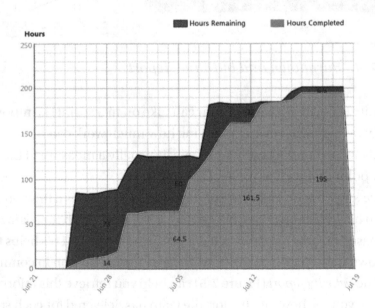

Figure 7-6. *Remaining work report*

The *unplanned work report* (Figure 7-7) is useful when the team plans an iteration by identifying all work items it intends to resolve or close during the course of the iteration. Work items assigned to the iteration by the plan completion date of the report are considered planned work. All work items added to the iteration after that date are identified as unplanned work.

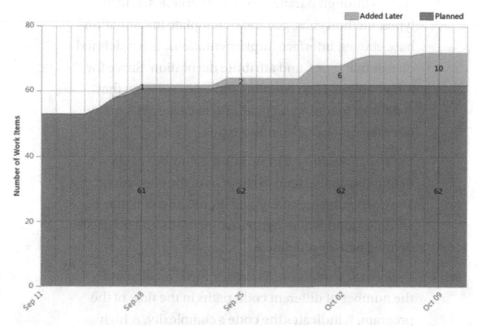

Figure 7-7. Unplanned work report

Metrics for Architecture, Analysis, and Design

DevOps tools don't include many metrics you can use for KPI assessment for architecture, but you can use some taken from the development area. Using code metrics, you can get information about how your architecture and design are working, including the following:

- *Lines of code:* Presents an approximate number based on Intermediate Language (IL) code. A high count may indicate that a type or method is doing too much work and should be split up. This may also be a warning that code will be hard to maintain.

- *Class coupling:* Measures the coupling to unique classes through parameters, local variables, return types, method calls, generic or template instantiations, base classes, interface implementations, fields defined on external types, and attribute decoration. Strive for low coupling. High coupling indicates a design that is difficult to reuse and maintain because of its many interdependencies on other types.

- *Depth of inheritance:* Indicates the number of class definitions that extend to the root of the class hierarchy. The deeper the hierarchy, the more difficult it may be to understand where particular methods and fields are defined and/or redefined.

- *Cyclomatic complexity:* Is determined by calculating the number of different code paths in the flow of the program. It indicates the code's complexity. A high complexity makes maintainability suffer, and it can also be hard to get good code coverage.

- *Maintainability index:* Is an index value between 0 and 100 that represents the relative ease of maintaining the code. The higher the better; a rating of more than 60 is good. Less than that, maintainability suffers.

Some DevOps tools can generate dependency graphs. These graphs are used to visualize code and its relationships. Running analyzers on these graphs can give you useful information as well:

- *Circular references* are nodes that have circular dependencies on one another.

- *Hubs* are nodes that are in the top 25% of highly connected nodes.

- *Unreferenced nodes* have no references from any other nodes.

Using these analyzers, you can determine whether you have loops or circular dependencies so that you can simplify them or break the cycles. You also can determine whether you have too many dependencies, which could be a sign that they're performing too many functions. To make the code easier to maintain, test, change, and perhaps reuse, you need to look into whether you should refactor these code areas to make them more defined. You may also be able to find code that performs similar functionality and merge with it. If the code has no dependencies, you should reconsider keeping it.

Metrics for Developer Practices

Metrics for developer practices are KPIs that can help you understand if you're working successfully to improve your code. These measures are useful from both the architectural and design viewpoints as well as from a developer viewpoint. Using them helps you improve how you design your application or system.

Several important metrics are available automatically in many tools and can help you get a good understanding of the quality of your development work:

- Code coverage
- Code metrics
- Compiler warnings
- Code analysis warnings

Code Coverage

Code coverage shows you how much of the code has been covered by automated unit tests. You get the value as a percentage of the entire code base. The difficulty often is deciding what percentage is enough. Should you always strive for 100%? Or is 80% enough? This is something the team has to discuss with the product owner when using Scrum or a similar decision maker when using other processes. This value is input as the definition of done.

Code Metrics

You can look at several different code metrics. Lines of code, class coupling, depth of inheritance, cyclomatic complexity, and the maintainability index—as described in the earlier section "Metrics for Architecture, Analysis, and Design"—also apply to code metrics.

Compiler Warnings

Errors and warnings should be avoided in a project. Allowing more than zero errors or warnings tends to result in the team accepting lower quality in the code base, which over time causes the code to lose maintainability.

Track this metric to make sure the number of errors is zero. Ideally, this should be enforced by automatic build policies.

Code Analysis Warnings

Code analysis in development tools performs static analysis on code, which helps developers identify potential design, globalization, interoperability, performance, and security problems, to name a few. Much of this functionality is currently available only for .NET development; if you're using Java, things may be different.

Code analysis tools provide warnings that indicate rule violations in managed code libraries. The warnings are organized into rule areas such as design, localization, performance, and security. Each warning signifies a violation of a code analysis rule.

Code analysis can be used to enforce company policies on the code developers write. Many DevOps tools offer good support for code analysis, and usually include a set of rules. Often, you can extend the functionality by writing your own rule set or by suppressing the rules you don't want. Definitely discuss this analysis with your development team and the product owner, because the warnings have an impact on the effort required before the definition of done is fulfilled.

Metrics for Software Testing

Software testing is an important area. Testing should be a constant part of any development effort, not just a phase at the end of a project. There are good metrics you can use during your projects to make sure you have high-quality testing in place. The following are a number of metrics you can use as KPIs for software testing:

- *Number of bugs per state*: This metric tells you how many bugs are active, resolved, or closed; whether the number of active bugs is increasing and whether the number of resolved and closed bugs is constant. If the numbers stay constant, you need to look into how you perform your testing.

- *Number of bugs sent back from testers for more information (aka "reactivated bugs")*: A large number of reactivated bus may indicate that communication between developers and testers must improve.

- *Code coverage*: This metric shows how much of the code has been covered by automated unit tests. You get the value as a percentage of the entire code base.

- *Test run results*: This metric indicates how your tests performing, and whether you have many failed tests. If you do, you need to look at what can be done to improve the tests.

- *Percentage of requirements covered by test cases*: As the title implies, this metric indicates the percentage of requirements covered by test cases.

- *Percentage of requirements covered by testing*: Do you actually verify the requirements with the test cases you have? If this figure is low and the figure for percentage of requirements covered by test cases is high, you may have an issue you need to deal with.

Example Reports

The metrics you get in your reports concerning testing can be very helpful to your projects. The reports described here are found in many tools:

- Bug status reports

- Reactivations reports

- Bug trend reports

Bug Status Report

The *bug status report* gives you information about the cumulative bug count based on bug state, priority, to whom the but is assigned, and bug severity. The document shows you the number of bugs and the number of resolved bugs (see Figures 7-8 and 7-9).

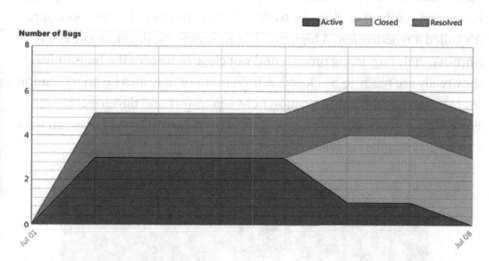

Figure 7-8. *Bug status report*

Figure 7-8 shows the number of bugs over time. You can see how the numbers of active, closed, and resolved bugs change. In this case, the number of active bugs is decreasing and the number of closed and resolved bugs is increasing, leading to a point where the number of active bugs is zero.

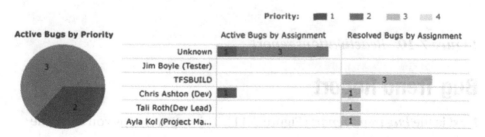

Figure 7-9. *Bug status report*

Figure 7-9 shows a report that displays how many bugs are assigned to an individual user. You can also see the priority of each bug as well as how many bugs have been resolved by the users.

Reactivations Report

The *reactivations report* (Figure 7-10) is used to determine how many bugs have been resolved or closed too early. If a bug needs to be opened again, it's called a *reactivation*. A high number indicates the developers need to improve their bug-fixing process and not close or resolve the bugs unless they really are ready to be closed. A high number may also be an indication that you have bad communication between testers and developers. For instance, incomplete test reports and poorly written test cases can lead to a greater number of reactivations.

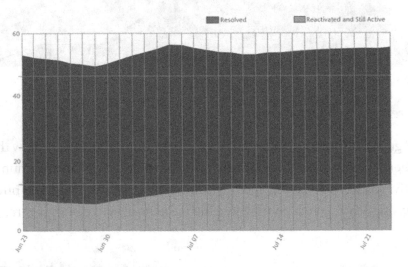

Figure 7-10. *Reactivations report*

Bug Trend Report

Next is the *bug trend report* (Figure 7-11). This report helps you track the rate at which your team is finding, resolving, and closing bugs.

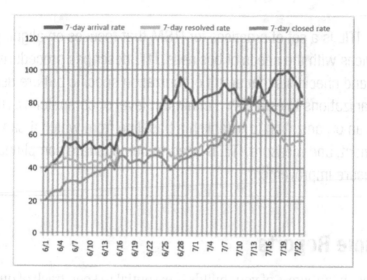

Figure 7-11. *Bug trend report*

Metrics for Release Management

A quick look at the ITIL (www.itilnews.com/ITIL_v3_Suggested_
Release_and_Deployment_KPIs.html) will give you some other KPIs you
can use. If you want to use them, you may need to create your own reports
to automate the retrieval of this information. ITIL mentions these KPIs,
among others:

- Number of software defects in production [the number
  of bugs or software defects of applications (versions)
  that are in production]

- Percentage of successful software upgrades (excludes
  full installations)

- Number of untested releases (not tested and signed off)

- Number of urgent releases

- Average costs of release, for which costs are most likely
  based on man-hours spent

243

Note   ITIL is a set of practices for ITSM that focuses on aligning IT services with the needs of business. ITIL describes procedures, tasks, and checklists that aren't organization specific but are used by organizations to establish a minimum level of competency. ITIL allows an organization to establish a baseline from which it can plan, implement, and measure. ITIL is used to demonstrate compliance and to measure improvement.

Example Reports

Following the progress of your builds is essential to keep track of quality. These build reports differ from DevOps platform to platform, but let's look at some examples. Use them as inspiration for what you can look for in your platform:

- Build quality indicators
- Build success over time
- Build summary report

The *build quality indicators report* (Figure 7-12) shows a summary of some important values for your builds. Using these data, you can determine whether you're close to releasing a build. Some of the other information this report contains includes the following:

- *Active bugs*: The number of active bugs that exist at the time of the build

- *Code churn*: The number of lines of code that have been added, removed, and changed in the check-ins before the build

- *Code coverage*: The percentage of code covered by tests

- *Inconclusive tests*: The number of tests that didn't succeed or were paused. If the build didn't succeed, the tests are either not counted or counted as inconclusive.

- *Failed tests*: The number of tests that failed during the build

- *Passed tests*: The number of tests that passed during the build

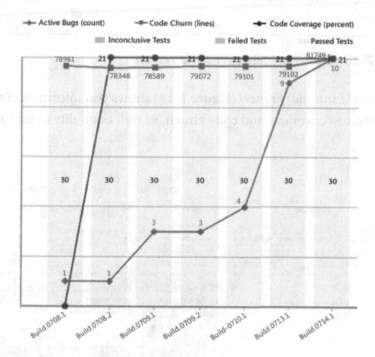

Figure 7-12. *Build quality indicators report*

The *build success over time report* (Figure 7-13) shows you the status of the last build for each build category (a combination of build definition, platform, and configuration) run each day. You can use this report to keep track of the quality of the code you check in. Furthermore, for any day on which a build ran, you can view the build summary for that specific day.

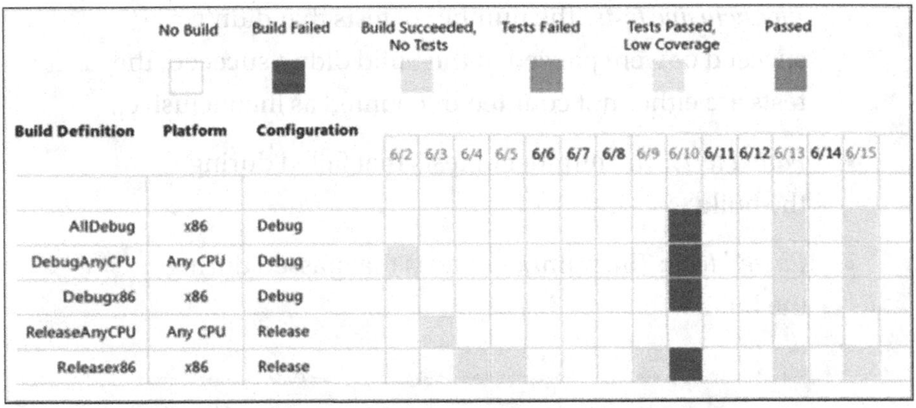

Build Definition	Platform	Configuration	6/2	6/3	6/4	6/5	6/6	6/7	6/8	6/9	6/10	6/11	6/12	6/13	6/14	6/15
AllDebug	x86	Debug														
DebugAnyCPU	Any CPU	Debug														
Debugx86	x86	Debug														
ReleaseAnyCPU	Any CPU	Release														
Releasex86	x86	Release														

Legend: No Build, Build Failed, Build Succeeded No Tests, Tests Failed, Tests Passed Low Coverage, Passed

Figure 7-13. *Build success over time report*

The *build summary report* (Figure 7-14) shows you information about test results, test coverage, and code churn, as well as quality notes for each build.

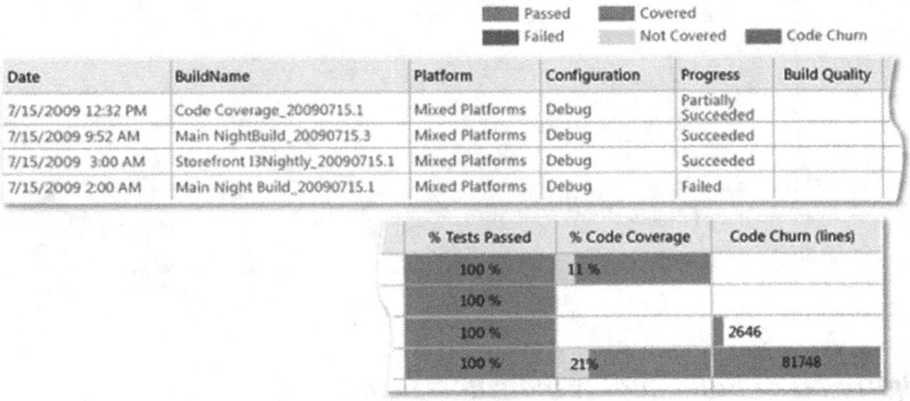

Legend: Passed, Failed, Covered, Not Covered, Code Churn

Date	BuildName	Platform	Configuration	Progress	Build Quality
7/15/2009 12:32 PM	Code Coverage_20090715.1	Mixed Platforms	Debug	Partially Succeeded	
7/15/2009 9:52 AM	Main NightBuild_20090715.3	Mixed Platforms	Debug	Succeeded	
7/15/2009 3:00 AM	Storefront 13Nightly_20090715.1	Mixed Platforms	Debug	Succeeded	
7/15/2009 2:00 AM	Main Night Build_20090715.1	Mixed Platforms	Debug	Failed	

% Tests Passed	% Code Coverage	Code Churn (lines)
100 %	11 %	
100 %		
100 %		2646
100 %	21%	81748

Figure 7-14. *Build summary report*

These metrics are suggestions that you can use as a base for following up on progress and quality in your projects. Different DevOps tools offer different possibilities for reporting and collecting information. Thus, it's important that you think through what you want for your organization when choosing an DevOps platform.

Using Charts to Monitor Metrics

In TFS and Azure DevOps, you can also add charts as a way of displaying information about your projects. Figure 7-15 shows how charts can be created if you navigate to Queries and then select Charts.

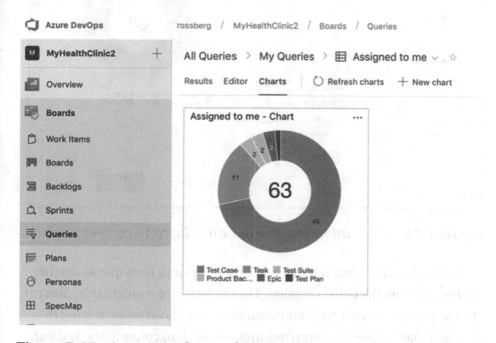

Figure 7-15. *Accessing Charts editing*

You can create charts from many of the queries you create using the query editor. We can choose to create many types of charts (Figure 7-16) including pie, bar, column, stacked bar, and so on, so you can display your results as you want. If you created a chart useful to the entire team, you can add that chart to your dashboard so that it shows up when you open the dashboard. For this functionality to work, you must create your original query as a shared query.

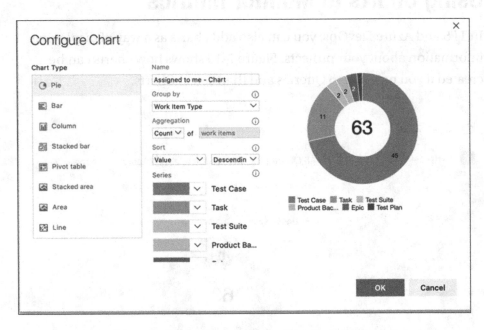

Figure 7-16. *Chart information can be displayed in various ways*

With Azure DevOps, you can add charts for work item queries to the dashboard from the widget catalog. These charts are configurable. You can choose a query, a chart type, and visualization options while staying in the dashboard context. Chart types include pie, bar, column, stacked bar, line, area, and stacked area. You can also display data in a pivot table. And, you can still add charts from the Charts tab in the work hub and configure them just like you've always done.

Summary

Metrics and KPIs are valuable for any organization if it wants to evaluate progress and quality. This chapter showed some examples of metrics used with Agile projects, but they are not limited to these projects. Metrics help you run your projects more efficiently, with greater application quality as an end result.

Keep in mind that different organizations find different metrics valuable. This chapter gave examples of metrics that are commonly used, but there may be others that are better suited for you.

The next chapter walks you through a scenario in which you implement Agile processes on different levels in a software development project.

CHAPTER 8

Agile Project Management in Azure DevOps and TFS

In this chapter, you follow the startup of an Agile project using Azure DevOps. Many of the concepts covered earlier in the book are exemplified in this chapter, so you can see how to move from planning to implementation. We also look at how Azure DevOps can support the Agile project management process during sprints. Keep in mind that although Azure DevOps is used as an example, you can do most of the things I show you (and then some) in an on-premise TFS.

For this purpose, I use a fictitious company in the examples. In this way, there is a common denominator to things presented so you can understand more easily the process and how Azure DevOps supports development organizations.

The main part of this chapter is written from the perspective of the product owner, whom is introduced shortly. There is a personal touch to some parts of the text. The reason for this is because part of a project focuses so much on collaboration and interaction among people.

© Joachim Rossberg 2019
J. Rossberg, *Agile Project Management with Azure DevOps*,
https://doi.org/10.1007/978-1-4842-4483-8_8

Case Study

Let's start with the company used in the example. Any similarities to real companies are totally unintentional.

Company Background

MyHealthClinic provides health care and related services to the United States. It is a rapidly growing company that has embraced Windows Azure to scale the customer-facing web site directly to end users to allow them to create self-service tickets and track technicians. The company also uses an on-premises ASP.NET Model–View–Controller application for its customer service representatives to administer customer orders.

MyHealthClinic development manager Anna Heinz has decided to implement a pilot project using the DevOps features of Azure DevOps to bridge the gap between what they have today and what they can benefit from in Azure DevOps. If the pilot is successful, MyHealthClinic will migrate all its development to the Azure DevOps platform.

Anna and Bob Peak (the IT manager) have decided to use Scrum as the preferred project management method, and the developers agree on using XP practices to enhance the quality of the software and therefore increase business value to the company.

The Pilot Project

The project MyHealthClinic has decided to use as a pilot for the DevOps implementation is an expense-reporting application (MyHealthClinic Expense Reporting). In the early days, expenses were handled easily by the administrative staff, but because the company has grown quickly and salespeople are located and traveling all over the United States, things have become a bit more complicated. The admin staff members want an application that will make their jobs easier and at the same time make sure employees get reimbursed for expenses quickly. The requirements for this application are covered in the section "Requirements" later in this chapter.

Because this project will be using Scrum as a project management process, Anna and Bob have appointed Fiona Gallos as product owner for the application. Fiona has only been working for MyHealthClinic for six months. She is experienced as a product owner for this pilot study because her previous employer used Scrum extensively. Fiona also has product owner certification from both Scrum Alliance and Scrum.org.

Important stakeholders for the project are Bob Peak, Anna Heinz, and Karen Jones. Karen is manager for the admin department and will represent the end users as well as the admin organization. Because the project aims to be a pilot program for a DevOps implementation, Dave Applemust from the infrastructure side and Harry Bryan from the development organization are also considered important stakeholders:

The People

- Alice Miller, CEO

- Bob Peak, IT manager

- Anna Heinz, development manager

- Fiona Gallos, product owner

- Karen Jones, admin manager

- Dave Applemust, infrastructure specialist

- Eric Parrot, business analyst

- Guillio Peters, Scrum master

- Harry Bryan, senior developer

- Mikael Swansson, developer

- Petter Ivarsson, user experience

- Ingrid Svensson, senior tester

Project Startup Phase

This section follows the product owner, Fiona Gallos, during the startup phase of the project. We will see how Azure DevOps is used to insert the information Fiona collects during this phase.

Starting Work

The idea for this project started when MyHealthClinic noticed that bug fixes in the epense reporting system created new bugs and that the new bugs sometimes appeared in parts of the system considered not to be affected by the original bug fix. MyHealthClinic soon realized it lacked traceability and had no way of knowing where a bug fix might have its impact in addition to the actual code change.

Fiona has just attended a conference and has added to her already-considerable knowledge of DevOps, Agile concepts, and Azure DevOps. She comes up with the idea of getting a better grip on the DevOps process and, at the same time, start using Agile practices at MyHealthClinic. Both of these efforts would greatly improve things at MyHealthClinic.

At the same time, Fiona sees that collaboration between two developer teams could improve if they to use Azure DevOps. Fiona writes a business case and presents it to the management team. After a few discussions, they agree to a pilot project. Because the expense-reporting project is in the pipeline, upper management decides to use it for the pilot. At this point, it's hard to calculate ROI, but anything to improve customer perception is worth going for.

Building the Initial Team

Fiona knows that it is recommended that product owners start with a small team during initial planning of the project. Therefore, she selects Anna Heinz, Harry Bryan, and Eric Parrot as initial team members because they are experienced within the company and they have experience as senior team members when they worked for other companies as well. In addition, they are available for the entire pilot project, which is an important aspect for Fiona. She knows the importance of having consistency among the team members during a project. She also selects Guillio Peters as Scrum master for the entire project. She'll pick the rest of the team a bit later in the project.

Fiona creates the project in Azure DevOps (Figure 8-1) from the web portal using the Scrum template. She names it MyHealthClinic Pilot, then she chooses Scrum and Git Version Control. As the initial team, they had discussed which version control to use, Git or TFVC, and they decided to go for the former.

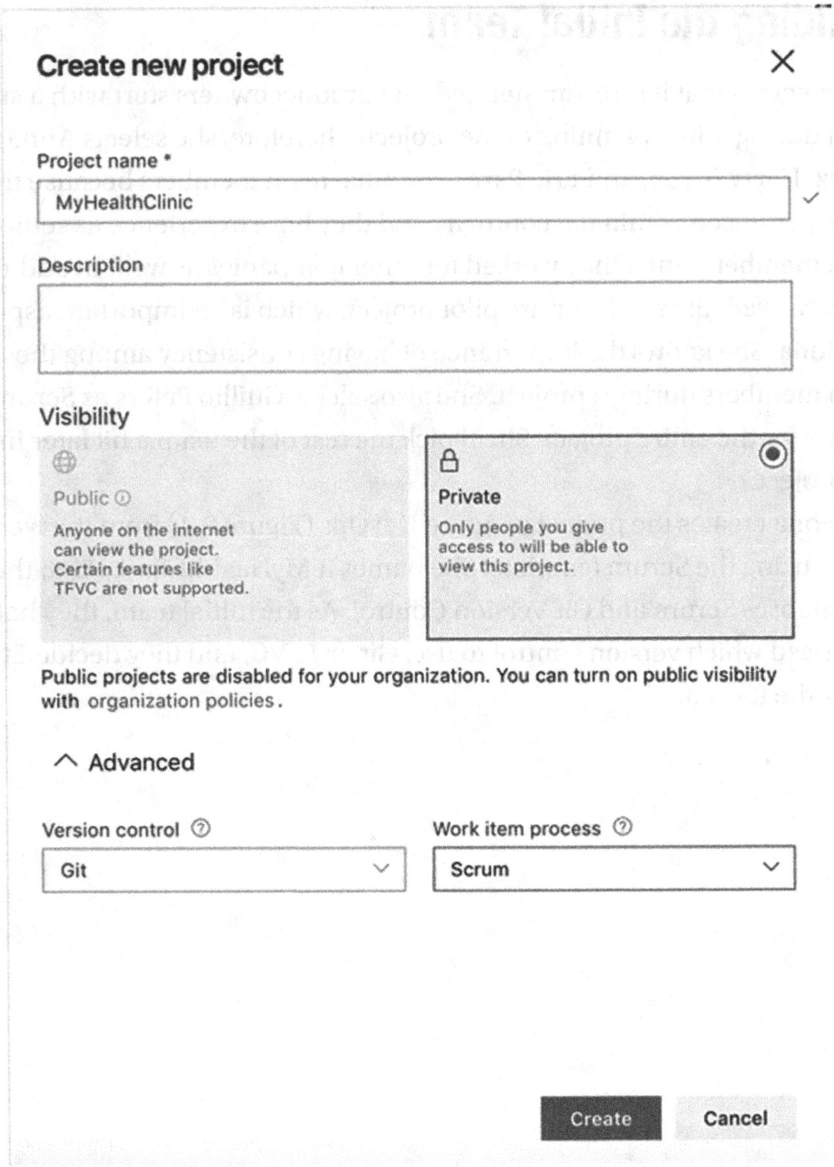

Figure 8-1. *Creating the MyHealthClinic pilot project in Azure DevOps*

Fiona then starts creating the teams necessary for the project.

Creating New Teams

In Azure DevOps, a team is simply a way of recognizing the team or teams you have, whether that is one team working on a project, or several teams. One person can be a member of several teams. Using area paths, you can indicate the development work that belongs to a specific team. You can visualize quickly which work items belong to which team. If a work item is assigned to an area path that is assigned to a team, that work item is placed into the backlog for the team.

A team is a concept used by Microsoft, but it might not necessarily match something in your organization. A team can be anything; it can also represent your product. It can be easier for the user to think about products instead of teams, and then just using the team concept to staff the product development. One thing you should not do is mimic the organizational structure of a company in these teams. Because a company is organized by different criteria (department, broken down into subject teams), a development team for a product may cross these borders. This means that the teams to consider here are based on the products you are building.

There are several ways you can use teams. Some let a specific team work on a specific part of a solution while another team works on other parts, all with separate backlogs. In large Scrum projects or when using SAFe, you might also need several teams working in parallel on the same backlog, but you need to distinguish between the teams and the work they do. The best way is to try one team setup in a project and see what works best for you.

The default team has an area path and an iteration path configured for it automatically when you create a new team project. As soon as you choose areas and iterations for a team, a backlog is also generated for it automatically. If your project uses more than one team, you can add new teams easily by selecting Project settings from the left menu (Figure 8-2).

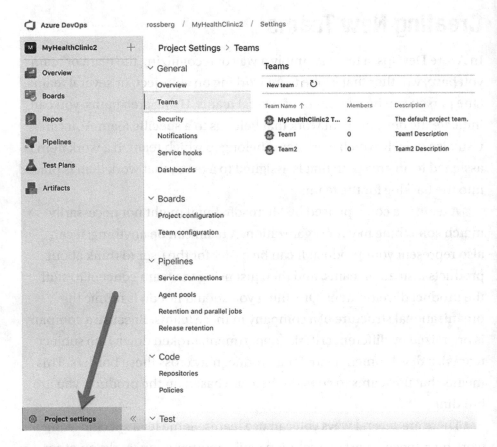

Figure 8-2. *Opening Project settings*

In the Teams view (Figure 8-3), you create a new team by clicking the New team option.

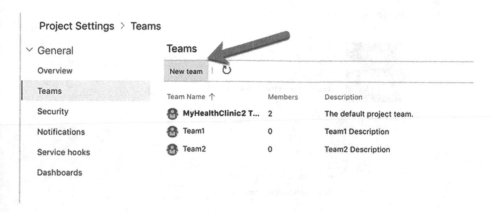

Figure 8-3. *Creating a new team from the Project profile page*

Fill in all information about the team (Figure 8-4). In this screen you can also select permissions for the team by adding it to an existing security group (more about this in a later section). You can also create a team area at this time as well. If you don't, you can associate it with an area later. When you are done, click Create team and, in a few seconds, the new team is created and you can start adding users to it.

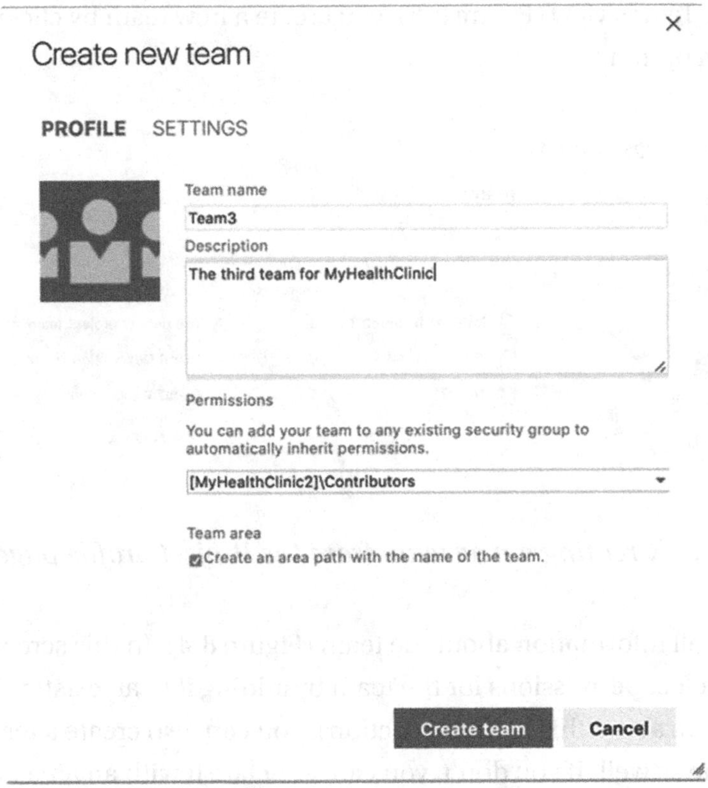

Figure 8-4. Entering values for the new team

Creating the Backlog and Team Structure for the MyHealthClinic Pilot

Fiona decides to have two development teams working on the project. They will both work from a common backlog managed by the MyHealthClinic program team. However, each team does not have to see the others' PBIs. Fiona wants a subset of the program backlog in the teams' backlog. Figure 8-5 shows an overview of this structure.

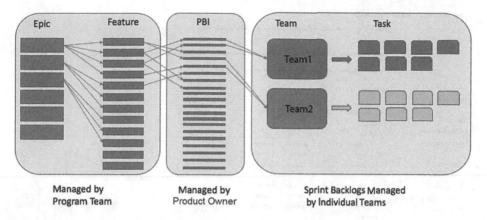

Figure 8-5. *The backlog structure*

To build the structure, Fiona first creates three teams:

- MyHealthClinic Program Team

- MyHealthClinic Team1

- MyHealthClinic Team2

She then configures areas and iterations to accommodate this structure of the backlog. Fiona then creates three areas that do not differ from the team structure, and each team is associated with its respective area in Azure DevOps:

- MyHealthClinic Program Team

- MyHealthClinic Team1

- MyHealthClinic Team2

She then continues to configure the initial sprint structure. She does this within Project settings/Project configuration. So far, Fiona has no estimates and cannot complete the entire release and sprint structure. But, she knows there will be several releases and that each release will have its own sprints. Fiona knows she can change this structure, so for now, she creates the iteration structure shown in Figure 8-6.

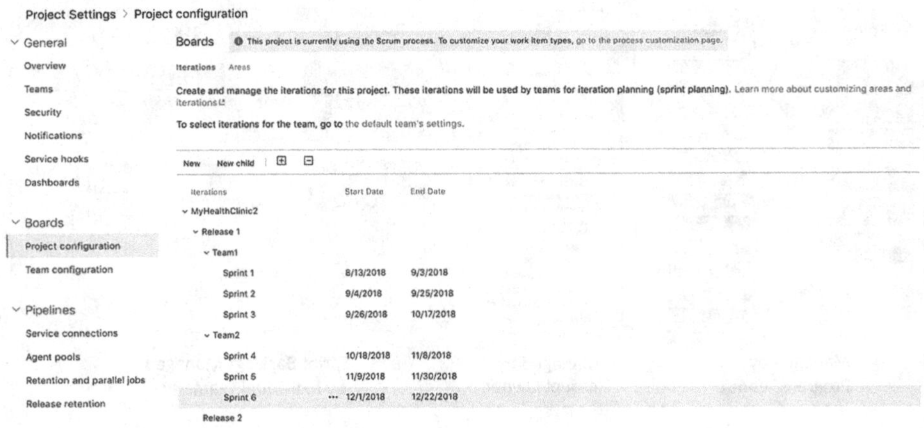

Figure 8-6. *Fiona' starting iteration structure*

For each team, Fiona selects the appropriate iterations they will see in their backlog. By using areas and iterations in this way, she is able to implement the structure she wants.

Building the Teams

Now the team is close to getting started. Fiona has Anna Heinz, Harry Bryan, Eric Parrot, and Guillio Peters as team members thus far. She talks with them about the project and they decide they need three more people to enhance the development and testing competences. They also discuss how they need a skilled user experience person onboard. With these decisions made, Fiona selects the following people to join Team1:

- Mikael Swansson, developer

- Ingrid Svensson, senior tester

- Petter Ivarsson, user experience

She also selects four people to work on Team2. Fiona contacts their managers and makes sure these people are available to work on the project. Luckily, they all are, and when she approaches the potential team members and explains the project, they are happy to come aboard.

Fiona decides to go for two-week sprints because this has always been a good time box, based on her experience. She once had a team that complained that it could not finish the PBIs during the three-week sprints they used. That team always seemed to be late or failed to deliver everything to which they had committed, complaining that the team members needed more time in the sprints. Fiona then told them, "Okay, then we'll use two-week sprints instead of three." The team was very confused, because Fiona had decreased the number of days in the sprints, not increased them. After they started working in two-week sprints, however, they soon found they delivered more in two weeks than they had in three weeks. The team was more focused and did not postpone anything until the end of the sprint; hence, they were more effective.

One part of the responsibilities of the product owner is to staff the project, at least initially. After an initial team is created, it is up to the team members to inform the product owner about which competences they need to fulfill the project vision.

Adding Team Members

Now that Fiona has created the project, she navigates to the web access front page. One team is created by default, so she can start adding team members right away. Fiona clicks Team Members, as shown in Figure 8-7 (see the orange arrow).

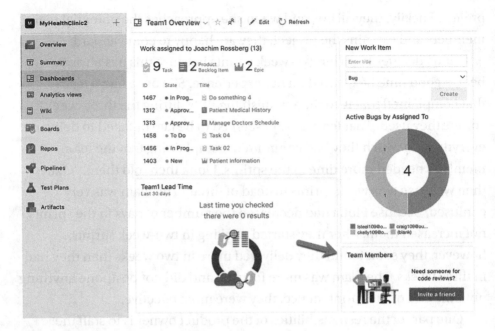

Figure 8-7. *Adding team members*

A dialog box (Figure 8-8) opens and Fiona adds the team members. Fiona then navigates to Project Settings, then Teams (Figure 8-9) to manage the team members for all teams.

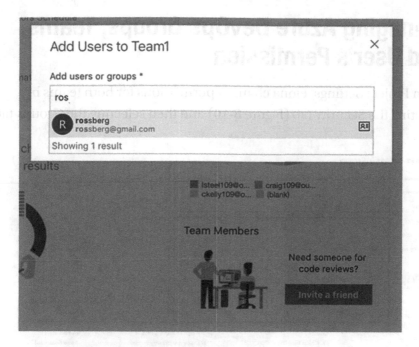

Figure 8-8. *Adding team members*

Figure 8-9. *Managing all team members within Project Settings*

Managing Azure DevOps Groups, Teams, and User's Permission

From Project Settings, Fiona changes permissions for both teams by selecting the Security tab (Figure 8-10) and then selecting the Groups tab.

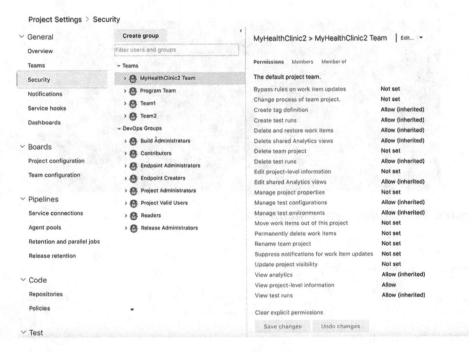

Figure 8-10. *Viewing permissions for DevOps groups and teams in Project Settings*

As you can see in Figure 8-10, there are eight different Azure DevOps groups by default:

- *Build administrators*: Members of this group have build permissions for the project. Members can manage test environments, create test runs, and manage builds.

- *Contributors*: Members of this group can contribute to the project. This means they can add, modify, and delete code; and create and modify work items. By default, the team group created when you create a team project is added to this group. Therefore, any user you add to the team will be a member of this group.

- *Endpoint administrators*

- *Endpoint creators*

- *Project administrators*: Members of this group can administer the team project. However, they cannot create projects.

- *Project valid users*. Members of this group have access to Azure DevOps. This group automatically contains all users and groups that have been added anywhere within Azure DevOps. You cannot modify the membership of this group

- *Readers*: Members of this group can view the project. They may not modify it.

- *Release administrators*: Members of this group can perform all operations on release management.

There are various permissions you can set for the groups and team members.

Note that, by default, most permissions are inherited. You can break the inheritance and define custom permissions here. One common scenario is when you bring in external people who are only allowed to see parts of the work item structure. Very quickly, it can become hard to keep track of these specialized permissions, so use this feature with care.

Managing Notifications

Many activities that occur in Azure DevOps are exposed as Notifications. For example, every time a build completes, or a changeset is checked in, Azure DevOps notifies all interested parties that an event has occurred. As a user, I might be interested in getting notifications when something specific happens that pertains to me. I can get these notices by configuring Notifications in Azure DevOps.

To configure the notifications, you use the Notifications tab in Project Settings in the web portal.

First of all, the Notifications editor (Figure 8-11) lets you select quickly from a list of predefined basic alerts that are common, such as "Build completes."

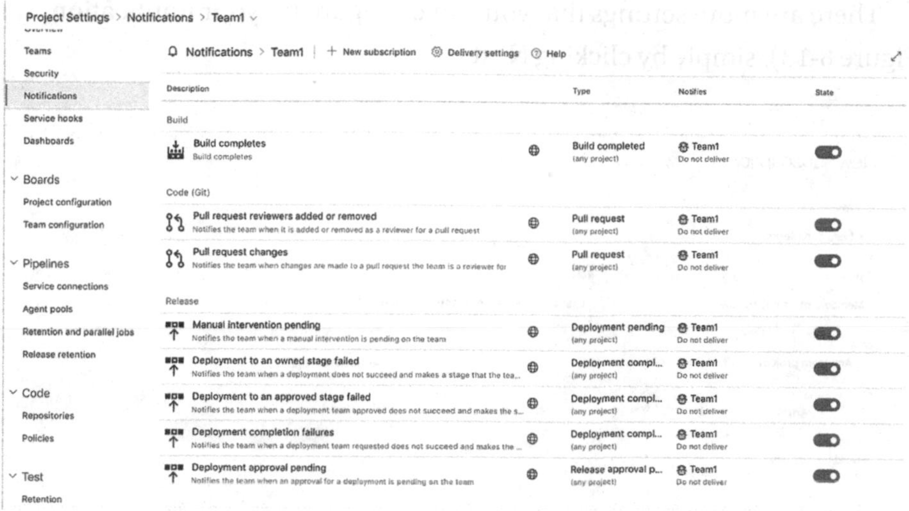

Figure 8-11. *Selecting a notification in Project settings*

Select New subscription to create a notification (Figure 8-12). This tab lets you select from a list of templates when creating a new notification.

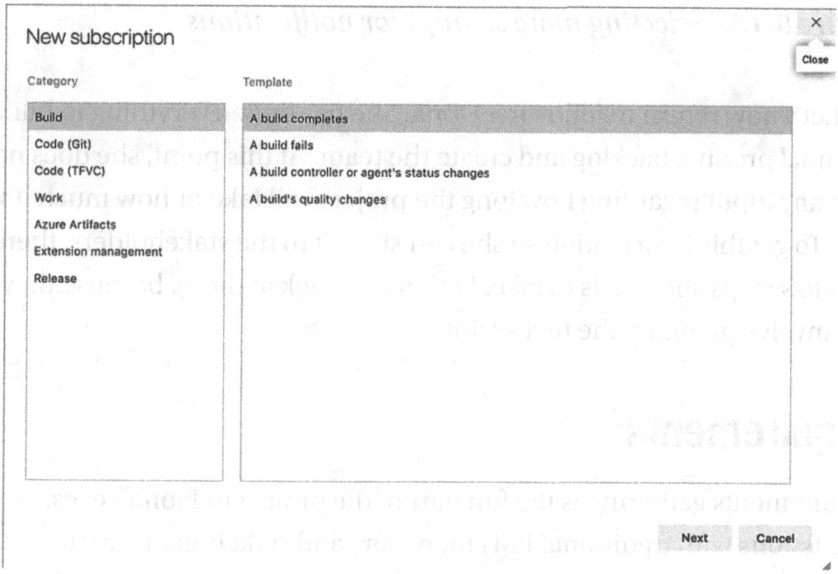

Figure 8-12. *Selecting a custom notification in Project Settings*

There are more settings that you can configure for your notification (Figure 8-13), simply by clicking Next.

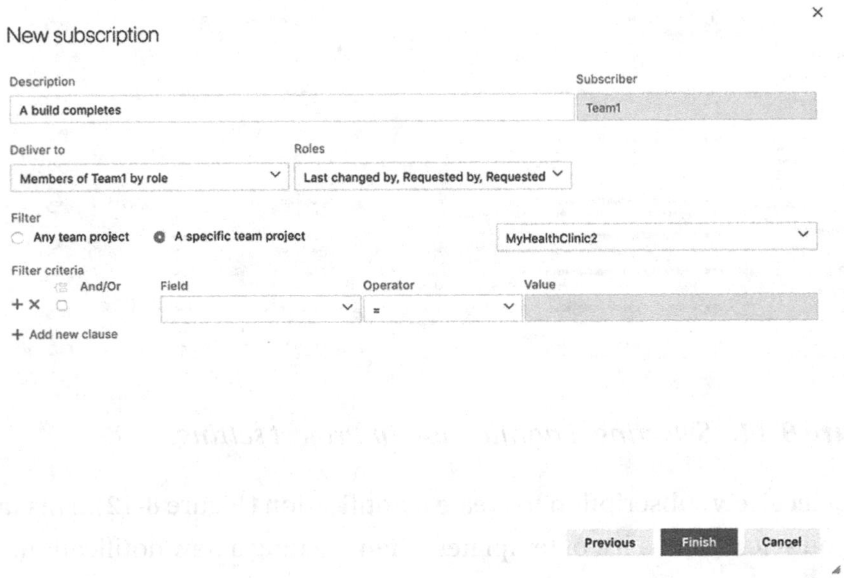

Figure 8-13. *Selecting more settings for notifications*

Let's now return to following Fiona. She has done everything to build an initial product backlog and create the team. At this point, she does not have any input regarding how long the project will take or how much it will cost. To get this information so she can show it to the stakeholders, there are a few steps she needs to take. Let's take a look at these, because they also involve planning the first sprint.

Requirements

Requirements gathering is the fun part of the project in Fiona's eyes. Discussions with traditional PMs managers and stakeholders about requirements are coming up and she enjoys them. Traditionally, all requirements had to be determined at the beginning of the project, and it was hard for many to accept that it is okay to start a project even without specifying everything. The fact that so many of these requirements were wrong or unnecessary in the end didn't seem to bother traditionalists. They still went head-first into projects that often failed or were flawed.

Fiona has run so many successful Agile projects, she knows that catching higher level requirements at the beginning is okay. They can start without all the details because they will be clarified at upcoming retrospectives and sprint planning meetings, and also during the sprints.

Fiona calls the initial team together for a requirements workshop. She adds Karen Jones to the workshop because she is one of the main stakeholders from the business side. Because Guillio (Scrum master) is not present, Fiona explains what they are going to do. She stresses they should look for higher level requirements in the sense that they do not need to detail them yet. There are to be no discussions about solutions or technicalities at this point. These topics will be the responsibility of the development teams to decide when the sprints start.

To avoid any confusion, Fiona explains the concept of a user story for the requirements team. She wants all requirements in the form

> As a <type of user>, I want <some goal> so that
> <some reason>.

Fiona believes the meeting will take three hours, so she books a room with a large whiteboard. She also supplies participants with sticky notes and pens.

Fiona starts by brainstorming user stories. Participants are a bit slow in catching on to the premise, but the meeting takes off when Harry Bryan comes up with two user stories:

1. As a sales person, I want to manage expense reports over the Internet so I can be more efficient.

2. As a manager, I want to search expense reports so I can get an overview of expenses more easily.

Suddenly all the team members start writing. After a little more than an hour, the pace drops, so they move on and spend another hour going over the user stories they created, clarifying them if needed. Fiona feels they've done a great job so far and now have a good foundation for the work ahead of them.

Building the Backlog

After the meeting, Fiona goes to her desk and types the stories into Azure DevOps. Fiona then starts to order the list by dragging and dropping the PBIs in the backlog view. She creates an initial prioritization based on some assumptions:

- Prioritization is based on weighted shorted job first (WSJF).

- After initial sprint planning and estimation, the list will be updated.

WSJF is a prioritization model used to sequence jobs (such as Features, User Stories, and Epics) to produce maximum economic benefit. Don Reinertsen[1] describes a comprehensive model, called *weighted shortest job first* for prioritizing jobs based on the economics of product development flow.

WSJF is estimated as the cost of delay divided by job size (or duration). Jobs with a high WSJF are prioritized over jobs with a lower WSJF. This tool is helpful for product owners working on their backlog prioritization and takes economics into account when working with the order. Table 8-1 shows that feature A has the highest WSJF (10), hence the feature should have the highest priority. WSJF has become very popular as SAFe has emerged in many organizations.

---

[1]Don Reinertsen, *Principles of Product Development Flow: Second Generation Lean Product Development* (Celeritas Publishing, 2009).

Table 8-1. *Working with WSJF*

Feature	Job Size	CoD	WSJF
A	1	10	10
B	3	3	1
C	10	1	0,1

CoD, cost of delay; WSJF, weighted shorted job first.

It takes Fiona roughly an hour to complete the initial sorting. Now she really had something to work with.

Adding Backlog Items in Azure DevOps

Fiona opens the project in Azure DevOps and feels a little bit of excitement when she sees the empty project that she will soon fill with activities. Fiona has lots of input for the backlog. She takes a long look at the results of the initial story-writing workshop and starts by going to the Backlogs tab on the web page (Figure 8-14).

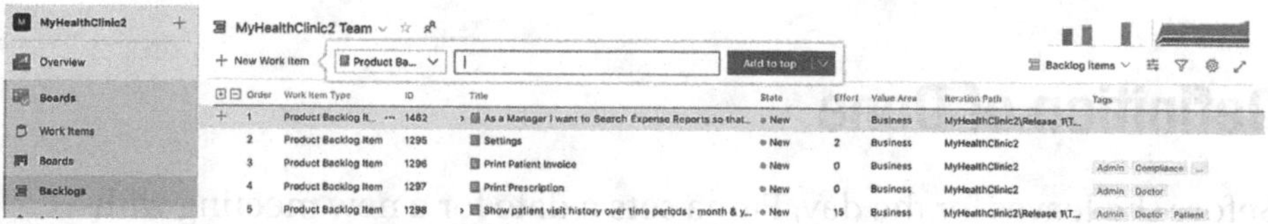

Figure 8-14. *The Backlogs tab*

In New Work Item, she quickly creates the first backlog item. She then opens the form shown in Figure 8-15 by double-clicking the created PBI. She then uses the PBI in her backlog to start filling in the fields. She leaves a lot as it is for now and fills in only the PBI name and description. Area is the MyHealthClinic Program Team and Iteration is the default.

273

Figure 8-15. The first PBI

Fiona then continues recording the rest of the higher level use cases until they are all logged in Azure DevOps. She often finds stories that are Epic size and they have to be broken down into Features and then PBIs. She makes sure that applicable PBIs are associated with their Epic or Feature.

Definition of Done

Before she leaves for the day, Fiona sets a date for a new meeting with the team to establish the definition of done. She includes infrastructure specialist Dave Applemust in this meeting because there are constraints from the infrastructure team when building and deploying new projects that must be considered.

She wants to discuss the definition of done with the team so that all participants have a common view before starting the actual coding. Many times she experienced problems when a definition of done was not in place for a project, so she knows this meeting and its result is important.

Two days later, they meet to determine the definition of done. Fiona explains the importance of this concept and talks about issues she encountered when a project did not have a definition of done. She notices of recognition among the participants as she speaks.

Fiona then asks all participants to write down the things they want to see in the definition of done. After some discussion, they agree on the following list for an approved user story:

- *Environments are prepared for release*: No unintegrated WIP has been left in any development or staging environment. The CI framework has been verified and works, including regression tests and automated code reviews. The build engine is configured to schedule a build on check-in; it triggers hourly or nightly builds. All test data used to validate the features in the release have been validated.

- *Handoff to support is complete* (Note: This may be elided in a DevOps context or when the development team follows the product through to support.): All design models and specifications, including user stories and tests, have been accepted by the support personnel who will maintain the increment moving forward. The support personnel are satisfied they are in control of the supporting environment.

- *Preparation for review is complete*. All sprint metrics are available, including burndown or burnup charts. Any user stories that have not been completed have been reestimated and returned to the product backlog.

- *Code is complete*: Any and all to-do annotations have been resolved. The source code has been commented to the satisfaction of the development team. When

275

necessary, the source code has been refactored to make it understandable, maintainable, and better able to support future changes. (Note that the Red–Green–Refactor pattern found in TDD is helpful here.)

Unit test cases have been designed for all features in development and requirements can be traced to the code implementation (such as by using clear feature-relevant naming conventions). The degree of code coverage is known and meets or exceeds the standard required. Unit test cases have been executed and the increment has been proved to work as expected. Peer reviews are complete. (Note that if pair programming is used, a separate peer review session might not be required.) Source code has been checked in to the configuration management system, with appropriate peer-reviewed comments added (when applicable). The source code has been merged with the main branch and automatic deployment into elevated environments has been verified.

- *Testing is complete*: Functional testing has been completed, including automated testing and manual exploratory testing, and a test report has been generated. All outstanding defects (or incidents such as build issues) have been elicited and resolved or accepted by the team as not being contraindicative to release. Regression testing has been completed, and the functionality provided in previous iterations has been shown to work. Performance, security, and user acceptance testing have been completed, and the product has been shown to work on all required platforms.

Estimation

After establishing the definition of done, the team now has a basis to begin an initial estimation of the work required for the project. Fiona needs to come up with a rough budget to show the stakeholders and an initial release plan. She decides to use "planning poker" to do this. She's used it before and was happy with the results.

Poker Planning/Story Points

Fiona calls another meeting and all participants meet in the same conference room where all the other meetings have been held. This time, the entire team is present, not just the initial team. Fiona has purchased planning poker decks for everybody and she starts the meeting by reading the first user story, then she explains the rules. Fiona reads a story, the team asks any questions for clarifications and then decides on their value.

After a short time, participants select a card from their poker deck but don't show it to the others. After everyone has selected a card, Fiona asks them to turn their cards face up. Anna and Harry are the farthest apart, so Fiona asks them to explain their thoughts on the user story. After that discussion, the team plays again. This time, the participants are closer to each other's points (only one step apart) and the greater value is selected for the story. The team continues to play for all user stories until all story points are determined.

Updating the PBI

After the meeting, Fiona goes back to her desk and starts to update the PBIs. She can now insert the story points for each PBI into the work items in the Effort field. During sprint planning, the PBIs will be broken down into more manageable pieces, and each task will get a time estimate instead of story points (Figure 8-16).

Order	Work Item Type	ID	Title	State	Effort	Value Area	Iteration Path	Tags
1	Product Backlog Item	1470	First PBI	● New	3	Business	MyHealthClinic2\Release 1\T...	
2	Product Backlog Item	1462	As a Manager I want to Search Expense Reports so that...	● New	8	Business	MyHealthClinic2\Release 1\T...	
3	Product Backlog Item	1295	Settings	● New	2	Business	MyHealthClinic2	
4	Product Backlog Item	1296	Print Patient Invoice	● New	8	Business	MyHealthClinic2	Admin Compliance
5	Product Backlog It...	1297	Print Prescription	● New	3	Business	MyHealthClinic2	Admin Doctor
6	Product Backlog Item	1298	Show patient visit history over time periods - month & y...	● New	15	Business	MyHealthClinic2\Release 1\T...	Admin Doctor Patient
7	Product Backlog Item	1299	Sign-in with O365	● New	5	Business	MyHealthClinic2\Release 1\T...	Admin Doctor
8	Product Backlog Item	1300	Map with the position of the next patient	● New	2	Business	MyHealthClinic2	Mobile Patient
9	Product Backlog Item	1301	Payment Reminders	● New	0	Business	MyHealthClinic2	Admin Finance
10	Product Backlog Item	1302	Send e-prescription to patients	● New	4	Business	MyHealthClinic2	Admin Doctor

Figure 8-16. *Story points (effort) in the backlog*

Now that the story points are entered, Fiona wants to do an initial risk assessment before moving on to sprint planning and time estimates.

Risk Assessment

Risk assessment is part of all estimations in Agile projects and should be done throughout the whole project. If any PBI is considered very risky, it might need to be prioritized higher in the backlog. It is always better to address high-risk items as early as possible to avoid surprises later. Fiona knows surprises can crop up at any time.

There are different ways of performing risk assessments. We suggest you choose the one with which you are most familiar. Fiona chooses to do a traditional risk assessment by using the following parameters:

- Severity (scale of 1–5 where 1 is the most severe and 5 the least severe)

- Probability (scale of 1–5 where 1 is most probable and 5 the least probable)

- Risk

- Risk assessment score (Severity × Probability)

- Mitigations

- Probability after mitigation

- Risk assessment score after mitigation (Severity ×
  Probability after mitigation)

Fiona calls another meeting and the team and Fiona conduct a risk assessment for each user story in the backlog. Fiona creates an Excel spreadsheet, which looks like the one in Figure 8-17, that show the results of the risk analysis. Fiona then checks the risk mitigation document into source control for versioning so everyone has access to it.

User Story	Risk	Severity	Probability	Score	Mitigation	Probability after Mitigation	Score after Mitigation
As a Sales person I want to manage expense reports so that I can be more efficient	Expense reports cannot be created	5	3	15	Some Mitigation	1	5
As a Manager I want to Search Expense Reports so that I can							

Figure 8-17. Risk mitigation

Updating the Backlog Order

The team didn't find any extreme risks during the initial risk assessment, so Fiona leaves the backlog almost untouched. She moves two stories a little higher in the list because the developers recommended these particular features be developed a little earlier than previously thought.

Refining the Backlog

Throughout sprints, product owners need to refine the backlog. They do not do this work alone; the team participates as well as any relevant stakeholder or expert. Refining the backlog is an excellent opportunity to get the team's views on upcoming features, and for members to provide feedback and suggest new ideas. Fiona decides to estimate about 10% of the team's time for backlog refinement. This estimate has worked well for her in the past.

Refining the backlog also means product owners have to order (prioritize) it. Using Azure DevOps, they can order the backlog easily by dragging a PBI up and down in the backlog view, thus changing the order of that PBI.

Note   Azure DevOps has a feature that allows you to tag your PBIs. By doing this, you can get much finer granularity into how you've organized your PBIs. You can use the tags any way you want. For example, work items that are going to be included in a specific release can be tagged for the release.

Initial Velocity

Fiona needs a few more pieces of knowledge before she can deduce the time estimates for the project. She needs to know the initial velocity of the team, which is the speed of the team—the number of user stories the team can complete in a given sprint. She also needs to know how many hours are slotted for work during a sprint.

Available Time

To calculate the available time for the team, Fiona uses the following method:

- *How long is a sprint?* Fiona assigns two weeks for each sprint.

- *How many working days are available in the sprint?* Fiona allows for ten working days per sprint.

- *How many days does each team member work during a sprint?* Fiona needs to know team members' planned vacation (or other days off), planned meetings, and so on. She looks at each team member's schedule and assigns the number of days in Azure DevOps.

Fiona deducts the time for sprint planning, review, and retrospective meetings, which are be eight hours per person for a sprint. Azure DevOps calculates the result and Fiona sees the team's capacity before drag. *Drag* is wasted time or unknown activities. Because the team is new and she has not worked a lot with any of the members, she assigns the standard 25% drag because she knows this is a good benchmark. Included in this value is the 10% percent for backlog refinement. Therefore, team capacity is six hours per day. Now Fiona has the number of hours to allot to each 2 week sprint.

Capacity Planning in Azure DevOps

Azure DevOps is excellent to use for capacity planning. For a sprint, click Backlog, then click the Capacity tab (Figure 8-18). You can set capacity, activities, and days out of the office for vacations and holidays. As you set capacity, activities, and days off, graphical information about hours and capacity is generated automatically in the pane at the right of the screen.

Figure 8-18. Entering capacity into Azure DevOps

Figure 8-19 shows the current sprint (sprint 4). The capacity is also shown in the Work details tab at the far right. Work details can be toggled on or off.

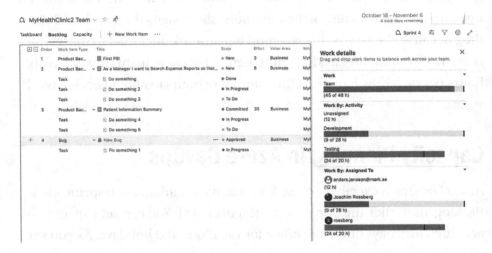

Figure 8-19. *Viewing team capacity in sprint planning*

The sprint planning features in Azure DevOps offer three ways for the product owner to determine whether there is enough capacity to complete the project: by person, by activity, or at whole-team level. These values are displayed in the right panel of Figure 8-19. At the top is the collective work hours for the team. Below that is Work By: Activity, which shows the work that has been done so far for the Development and Testing activities. You can also see Work By: Assigned To, which shows how much of each team member's capacity is assigned to tasks.

Initial Sprint Planning

To calculate the initial velocity of the team, Fiona usually conducts an initial sprint planning meeting. This is exactly the same as any sprint planning except it is performed before the actual sprint starts. Fiona has used this approach with previous projects and found it to be extremely helpful in acquiring the data she needs to come up with the team's capacity.

During this meeting, Fiona and the team estimate the tasks in hours so they can plan the sprint. This value is important in determining how many user stories the team can take on during a sprint. Here is how Fiona and the MyHealthClinic team calculate their velocity:

- Estimate the first user story in detail.

- Break down what the team needs to do to deliver the story.

- Estimate the hours for each activity and summarize.

- Deduct the summary from the available time the team has in the sprint.

- Is there still time left?

  - Take a new user story and repeat the process until no available time is left.

- Summarize the number of story points from the stories that included in the sprint.

Now Fiona has a theoretical velocity.

The first (highest prioritized) user story on the backlog is:

As a sales person, I want to manage expense reports so I can be more efficient.

The number of story points for this story is five (as determined during the planning poker meeting). The story is broken down into smaller tasks:

- Create expense report.

- Delete expense report.

- Modify expense report.

- Send expense report for approval.

- Log on to expense report system.

Together with the team, Fiona prioritizes these items so they have a beginning for the sprint backlog. The sprint backlog looks like the following after prioritization:

- Create expense report.

- Send expense report for approval.

- Modify expense report.

- Delete expense report.

- Log on to expense report system.

The team continues to break down each of these tasks into smaller pieces and estimate them in hours. To create the expense report, they come up with the following tasks:

- Create the GUI.

- Create business logic.

- Fulfill definition of done requirement.

- Write user manual.

The estimated number of hours for this user story is 137. With an available time of 290 hours, they still have 153 hours left in the sprint. This means they have room for more work, so they continue with the next user story on the backlog:

> As a controller, I want to be able to manage the users
> in the system so I have full control over the users.

This user story was worth points. After breaking it down, they have 95.5 hours left, so they continue with another user story worth two story points. When this planning was done there remained 23.5 hours of available time.

Fiona and the team choose not to take on anything more in that sprint. The team is new and if there are problems, the team might need space to handle issues while it flexes its wings. It's better to finish the tasks than to reach the end of a sprint and not be able to finish some of the tasks. If the team has time left in the sprint, it can take on more tasks.

The total amount of story points for the sprint is now ten, which is the team's initial velocity. The sprint backlog now looks like this:

- Create expense report.

- Send expense report for approval.

- Modify expense report.

- Delete expense report.

- Log on to expense report system.

- Create user.

- Modify user.

- Delete user.

- Create customer.

- Modify customer.

- Delete customer.

Each of these PBIs have tasks associated with them that are part of the complete sprint backlog.

Updating Backlog and PBI

Throughout sprint planning, Fiona has been updating the sprint backlog and inserting new tasks into Azure DevOps. She associates them with the first sprint for each team using the Planning field at the right of the screen (Figure 8-20). She also adds the date of the first sprint under Project settings so that Azure DevOps is updated with this information.

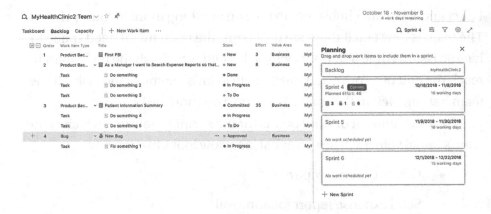

Figure 8-20. *Associating tasks with the sprint*

One thing worth considering here is what to do with the Epic user stories in the backlog after they have been broken down. Are they still valid in the backlog at this point? In my opinion, you can remove these backlog items safely (by setting the status to Removed) as long as you are certain the content is covered in the broken-down tasks. But this choice is a matter of how you want to work. Some people want to keep the Epics; some don't. Microsoft says the Removed state is used "when the team will not implement the backlog item because product requirements or other work conditions have changed." But, as mentioned earlier, this is a matter of how you want to work.

Fiona kept the Epics for reference and gets fine granularity of the backlog items at the top of the backlog and larger epics the farther down the list she moves. At this point, Fiona has a refined backlog as well as a first sprint backlog.

Note   An *Epic* is a large user story that is so big it is impossible to estimate how much effort it would take to develop it. It can also be a user story that is too large to fit into a single sprint, so it needs to be broken down. You can compare an Epic to this user story:

As a human, I would like to have world peace so that we humans do not kill one another anymore.

Although this example is farfetched, so are many Epic user stories—at least until they are broken down into smaller, more manageable user stories.

Forecast in Azure DevOps

There is a nice feature in Azure DevOps that lets you create a forecast on how much work you can have in each sprint. It requires you to fill in the effort estimate on each work item. In the example in Figure 8-21, you see story points estimated in the Effort column. Forecasting is based on the velocity of five story points (in this screen), and Azure DevOps draws automatically the sprints and the work items that will fit into each sprint. The forecast can be switched off if you do not want to see it. Simply toggle on or off, as seen in Figure 8-21.

Figure 8-21. *Forecast in Azure DevOps*

You can use the Velocity report in the upper right corner of the product backlog to look at the historical velocity numbers and, based on them, figure out a good velocity forecast number (Figure 8-22).

287

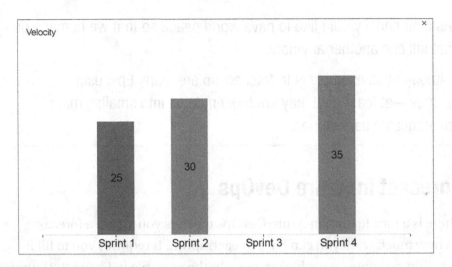

Figure 8-22. *Velocity report in Azure DevOps*

You can also base a forecast on hours instead of story points—just change the values as you want.

Release Planning

Based on the information she now knows, Fiona can start planning the releases of the project. She is aware that management wants to know how many releases are planned, and she wants to give them this information as soon as she can. The first thing she does is look for Epics (in the user stories) so she can come up with a release plan.

Epics

Fiona looks at the backlog and comes up with several Epics:

- Expense report management

- Search functionality

- User management

- Customer management

- Project management

- Smartphone availability

She sees quickly that three Epics are going to be part of the first sprint. According to the initial sprint planning, expense report management, user management, and customer management are all part of the first sprint. Considering the fact that there are many chores in the first sprint, Fiona knows it's not possible to finish all three at the same time. She aims from getting the expense report management Epic only done during the first sprint. The other Epics will have to wait to be addressed during the following sprints.

Fiona also knows the team's initial theoretical velocity—ten story points—which she uses as an input for how much work she can expect in each sprint. With 44 story points total, the project will take 4.4 sprints to complete. Fiona rounds this value up to five sprints.

Note   A *chore* is just something a team needs to do. It could be setting up a build server, fixing the team room, fixing whiteboards, installing necessary software, and so on. Chores are never estimated. In the beginning, the first sprints are probably filled with chores just to get started. This means the velocity in the first sprints will be lower than in upcoming sprints, when most chores are complete. There is just not as much room left for estimated work in the first sprints.

The following is a rough overview of the release plan for the functionality:

- Expense report management will be delivered in sprint 1.

- User management, customer management will be delivered in sprint 2.

- Project management, search management will be delivered in sprint 3.

- Smartphone availability will be delivered in sprints 4 and 5, depending on smartphone type.

Estimated Time Plan

Fiona then uses Excel to create a simple time plan for the project. She knows this is temporary and will most likely change, depending on what happens during the project, so she shows it to the stakeholders only and does not let them keep a copy of it.

Estimated Project Cost

After this is completed, Fiona can come up with an initial estimate of the project cost. She knows how many weeks the project will take based on the initial estimation, which is ten weeks. With the help of the administrative department personnel, she calculates the weekly cost of each of team member. Fiona then multiplies the weekly cost by the number of weeks and comes up with a cost estimate. In addition, she adds hardware, software, and other costs she knows will crop up. She arrives at an estimated project cost, which she uses as input for the management meeting, where she will present the time plan and project budget. Luckily, the management team approves the project and she's good to go.

Fiona is now ready to start the project. She begins by looking at the startup dates, confirming them again with all managers on the team, and then sends out the invitation for the sprint planning meeting to kick off sprint 1. During the sprint planning meeting of sprint 1, the team uses the initial sprint planning to determine whether anything has changed. If there are changes, they will have to break down new user stories or change other aspects of the sprint. Hopefully, the initial sprint planning remains the same as the actual sprint 1 planning. The team finds no substantive changes and is ready to jump in to the first sprint.

We now leave Fiona and the team, and talk more in general terms about how you can use Azure DevOps during your sprints, based on the Scrum process template.

Before we take a look at how Azure DevOps can help you run your sprints, let's take a brief look at the different meetings that take place during a sprint, as a refresher of the material covered in Chapter 2. This chapter uses the Microsoft Scrum template for all of the examples. If you use any other process template, you will see some differences.

Scrum Meetings during a Sprint

During the sprint several meetings are included in the Scrum process:

- *Sprint planning meeting*: At this meeting the development team, together with the product owner, selects user stories from the top of the backlog, breaks them down into tasks, and then estimates the tasks in hours.

- *Daily standup*: During the daily standup, which takes place at the same time—and in the same place—every working day, the team members report what they have done since the last meeting, what they plan to do until the next meeting, and whether they have encountered or foresee any impediments.

- *Sprint review*: During the sprint review, the team demonstrates the software built for the stakeholders and product owner. The results of the feedback from the meeting participants may lead to new user stories, changes to user stories, or perhaps removal of user stories.

- *Sprint retrospective*: During the sprint retrospective, the team discusses what it did well during the sprint, what was not so good, and what they can do to improve the process.

- *Backlog refinement*: Although not an official Scrum meeting, backlog refinement is important. During this session, the product owner and the team look at user stories for coming sprints (usually one or two sprints ahead) and estimate the stories in story points. The estimation occurs after the product owner has explained what each story contains.

Azure DevOps helps support these meetings in various ways during the sprint. Let's start by looking at the sprint planning meeting.

Sprint Planning

Most of the work at the sprint planning meeting is to break down user stories into tasks and estimate the time for each task. The team starts with the top story from the product backlog, breaks it down, and places it on the sprint backlog. They continue doing this until the amount of available time for the sprint is full.

In Azure DevOps, you can add tasks to a user story in a couple of different ways. From inside a PBI, you can go to the Links tab and click the Add link work item icon, as shown in Figure 8-23.

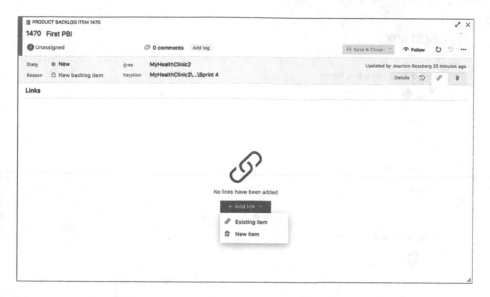

Figure 8-23. *Adding a new task from inside a user story*

This action opens the form shown in Figure 8-24. When the form is open, you can add basic information, such as a title and comments. When you are done, click OK to create the task.

Figure 8-24. *Form for adding a new task*

Note that you cannot add any other work item this way. To link a user story (or other work item) to another work item type, you need to follow another workflow, which we is explained in a bit. Clicking OK opens the task for more detailed editing, as shown in Figure 8-25.

Figure 8-25. *Filling in additional information about a task*

During sprint planning, you can choose to assign the tasks right away or you can wait until all tasks for the sprint have been estimated. This depends entirely on how you want to work.

You can also fill in the description of what the task means, which is something you should not forget to do. We have seen many tasks without a good description, and they often cause confusion after work starts on the task. A good suggestion is to let the team decide on the information included in the task.

One thing that we would say is mandatory to complete is the field Remaining Work, which you is found in the Details section. It is important to register remaining work on a project, and our useful suggestion is to update this field at the end of every working day. This field is the only field you can use in the process template for following up and estimating hours on a task. The burndown chart (Figure 8-26) uses this information to display how much total work time there is left for all tasks in the sprint.

295

This provides you with an immediate visual of when you can expect to be done with all tasks. You have to list all the team members' capacity for the sprint for the total remaining work time to be correct. There isn't a rule that states you should work this way, but it has become a good Agile practice.

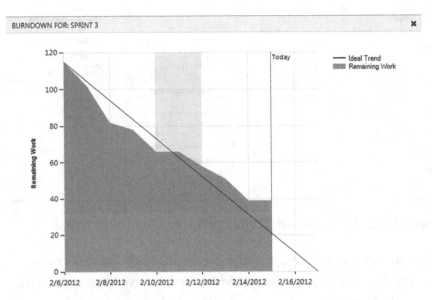

Figure 8-26. *A burndown chart uses the Remaining Work field to calculate when the tasks in a sprint will be done*

You can also add information about to which activity the task is connected. You can define these activities yourself from the Control Panel, which can be tailored to your own needs. The same goes for the Field area. *Activity* is often the field used for defining the part of the process to which a task belongs, and the *Area* is the field often used for functional or component breakdown, but you can use them as you see fit. This gives flexibility in how you can search and find tasks and other work items when you need to.

A new feature added in Visual Studio 2012 update 1 is tagging, which lets you tag a work item with one or more tags and then later filter the backlog using these tags. A *tag* is just short text, and you can define as many as you want.

Figure 8-27 shows that tag has been created on a backlog item that indicates that the work being done is related to integration.

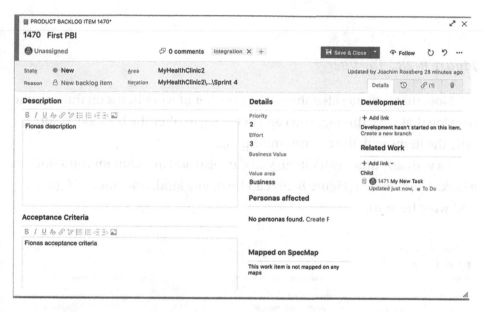

Figure 8-27. *Adding tags to a work item*

Now you can use tags on the product backlog to find only those items related to integration. Click the little filter icon at the very right of the product backlog to see the list of available tags for this backlog, as shown in Figure 8-28.

Figure 8-28. *Tag filter*

Note that each tag also shows the number of work items on the current backlog that have this tag. You can click a tag to filter the backlog to show only the items with the corresponding tag.

As with any other work item, you can also add attachments and links to a task. Attachments (Figure 8-29) can be of any kind: documents, figures, and what have you.

Figure 8-29. *Adding attachments to a work item*

If you want to use the board to create a task, you can do so by clicking the plus sign (Figure 8-30) at the top left corner of a user story column. You are then directed to the same workflow described earlier.

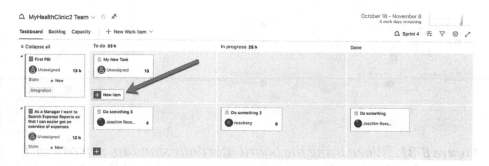

Figure 8-30. *Creating a new task from the Board view*

All these possibilities to break down backlog items into tasks, link to attachments, other work items in conjunction with the tags field, area, activity, remaining work, and so on are essential to have during sprint planning. During this meeting, you can find new user stories that need to be added or impediments you need to create.

Because test cases are included in the things you can create and link to tasks and user stories, testers can also benefit from the Azure DevOps features during sprint planning. Depending on how testers want to work, they can create test cases and link them directly to a PBI. In one recent project, our tester used the acceptance criteria in the PBI to create test cases, linking them directly to our PBI.

Daily Standup

During the daily standup, the team reports what they have done since the last standup and what they will do until the next. During this meeting, it is common to use the sprint board and group it by team members or PBIs (Figure 8-31).

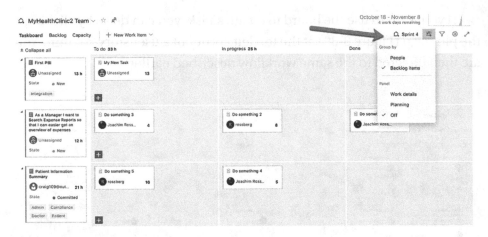

Figure 8-31. *When using the board at a daily standup, you can sort the board on backlog items or on team members, and then team members can discuss their current work*

Team members can the discuss the things on which they are working and update the status of each task. You can update the remaining work by clicking the number at the lower left of the task. The team can also choose to display the board based on backlog items. This view allows the team to see more easily any stories that have been selected for the sprint but still do not have any tasks assigned to them.

Using drag and drop, the team can move a task between the different columns and, for instance, move a task to Done when it is ready as defined in the definition of done. This feature also allows you to move a task between team members quickly; you do not have to open the task and select a new assignee—really useful in our opinion!

Note   The board is based on tasks only. You do not show user stories in the columns. If you want a board for user stories, you can use the Kanban board.

At the daily standup the team also discusses any impediments it might have. Using the linking features described earlier, you can create and link an impediment (Figure 8-32) to a task or user story and assign the impediment to the correct person. You can also select a priority (between 1 and 4) if you want.

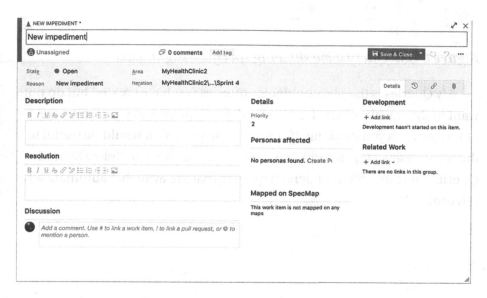

Figure 8-32. *Impediments work item type form*

Retrieving Data from Azure DevOps

When you navigate to the Work items tab on the team web portal, you have options of getting information from Azure DevOps that can be useful during sprints.

The Query tab, by default, shows all work items that have been assigned to an individual (Figure 8-33). If you take a look at the left menu, you see queries that give more information about the status of your projects. You can add queries to My favorites, which is useful if you want to find a specific query quickly. You can also add queries to Team favorites that are accessible by the entire team.

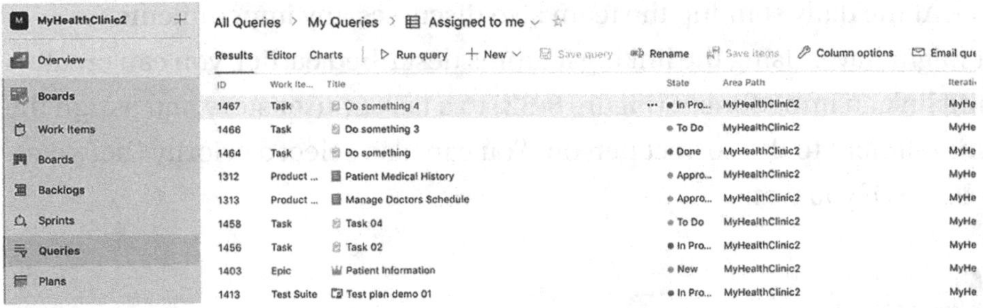

Figure 8-33. *Query view showing specific assignments*

My Queries is the placeholder for queries you have created but do not want to share with others. There is no default query, but you can create new queries as you go along. If you create a query that would be useful to the whole team, you can add it to the Shared Queries list. Below Shared Queries there are different default queries that are available automatically (Figure 8-34).

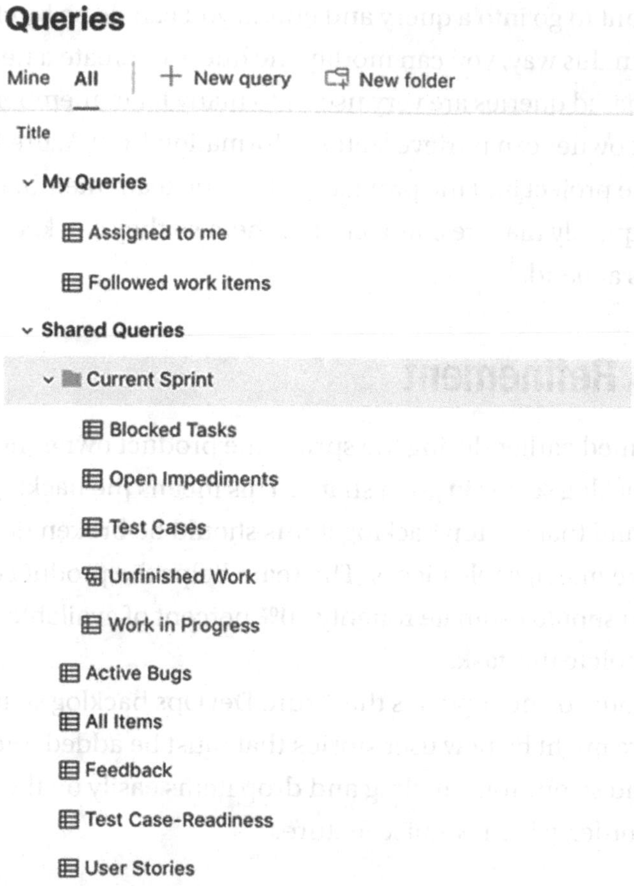

Queries

Mine   All | + New query   ⊐ New folder

Title

∨ **My Queries**

⊞ Assigned to me

⊞ Followed work items

∨ **Shared Queries**

∨ ■ Current Sprint

⊞ Blocked Tasks

⊞ Open Impediments

⊞ Test Cases

⊞ Unfinished Work

⊞ Work in Progress

⊞ Active Bugs

⊞ All Items

⊞ Feedback

⊞ Test Case-Readiness

⊞ User Stories

Figure 8-34. *My Queries and Shared Queries*

Running a query results in a list with the work items affected by the query. Figure 8-35 shows the results from the Open Impediments query.

All Queries > Shared Queries > Current Sprint > ⊞ Open Impediments ∨ ☆   2 work items
                                                                                                                         1 selected

Results   Editor   Charts | ▷ Run query   + New ∨   🖺 Save query   ⇥ Rename   🗒 Save items   ⌀ Column options   ✉ Email query   ···   1 of 2   ↑   ↓   ▽   Off ∨   ↙

ID ↑	Work Ite...	Title	Assigned To	State	Priori...	Created Date ↑
1472	Impedim...	⚠ New Impediment	···	● Open	2	11/5/2018 11:41 ...
1473	Impedim...	⚠ New Impediment		● Open	2	11/5/2018 11:48 ...

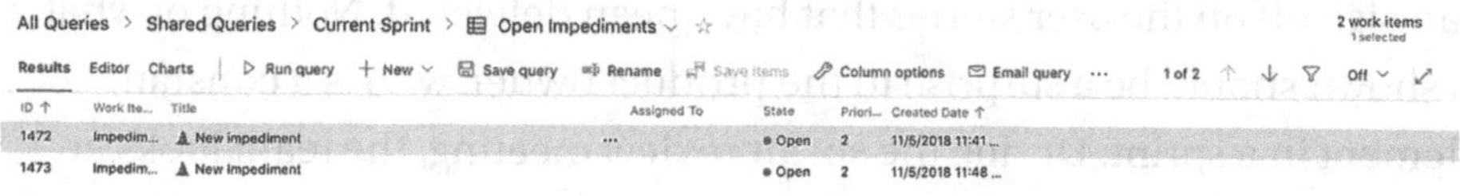

Figure 8-35. *Query result from the Open Impediments query*

If you want to go into a query and edit it, you can do so by clicking the Editor link. In this way, you can modify the query or create a new one.

These shared queries are very useful to many team members. The product owner can retrieve status information from Azure DevOps regarding the project and the project health. The team members can find work items quickly that are connected to them so they can keep track of what work is at hand.

Backlog Refinement

As we explained earlier during the sprint, the product owner needs to refine the backlog so it is in good shape. This means the backlog should be ordered and that the top backlog items should be broken down into smaller, more manageable pieces. The team helps the product owner with this, and you should estimate roughly 10% percent of available time for the team to complete this task.

The product owner updates the Azure DevOps backlog so it reflects reality. There might be new user stories that must be added, modifications to others, and so on. You can drag and drop items easily on the backlog to change the order, which is a nice feature.

Sprint Review

The sprint review is the meeting during which the team shows the product owner and any other stakeholders what it has built during the sprint. Any working software should be demonstrated so that the product owner can sign off on the user stories that have been delivered. Nothing of what is shown should be a surprise to the product owner, who is a constant element in a sprint. During the sprint review meeting, the team looks at the sprint backlog to verify that all backlog items that were worked on and marked as complete are covered during the review.

Sprint Retrospective

During the retrospective, you look at what was good and what was bad during the sprint. This is by far the most important meeting in Scrum. Why? Because this is where you can learn how to improve. Constant retrospection and adaptation are essential for the team if it is to deliver quality software and business value.

This meeting helps you discover what needs to change in the way you run your meetings, for example. You can also determine whether there is a problem with communication with the product owner or another part of the organization. This input is valuable so that you can change the way your teams work to achieve even better results for the next sprint.

We usually execute the sprint retrospective by using a white piece of paper and dividing it with a marker. The left side is what was good (marked by a +) and the right side is what was not good (marked by a -). The team then calls out their opinions and the Scrum master records them on the paper. Sometimes some very hands-on issues, such as writing better comments during check, in are listed, but there can also be softer issues such as "improve communications within the team."

Another way to run this meeting is to answer three questions:

1. What should we stop doing?

2. What should we start doing?

3. What should we continue doing?

The answers to these questions will give great input to your continuous improvement process. Based on the answers and the results of the retrospective, the Scrum master and the team select a few issues from the bad side and commit to improving them. Issues that need to be taken care of are documented as tasks or impediments in Azure DevOps so that you can follow up on them and assign them to the correct person.

Summary

This chapter followed Fiona as she starts the MyHealthClinic project. We saw how she initiated the project and started to use Azure DevOps to run it after it a Go decision was made. Fiona used Azure DevOps, but she could also have been using on-premise TFS as well.

You have now seen how you can use various aspect of the Azure DevOps product to manage an Agile project. This concludes this book. I hope you have enjoyed it.

Index

A, B

© Joachim Rossberg 2019
J. Rossberg, *Agile Project Management with Azure DevOps*,
https://doi.org/10.1007/978-1-4842-4483-8

C

Printed in the United States
By Bookmasters